Y0-AAF-578

THE PLURALISTIC SOCIETY

THE PLURALISTIC SOCIETY

A Community Mental Health Perspective

Edited by

Stanley Sue, Ph.D.

University of California
Los Angeles, California

and

Thom Moore, Ph.D.

University of Illinois
Champaign, Illinois

Community Psychology Series
Volume IX
American Psychological Association
Division of Community Psychology
Series Editor: Bernard Bloom, Ph.D.

HUMAN SCIENCES PRESS, INC.
72 Fifth Avenue
NEW YORK, NY 10011

Copyright © 1984 by Human Sciences Press, Inc.
72 Fifth Avenue, New York, New York 10011

Printed in the United States of America
987654321

Library of Congress Cataloging in Publication Data

Main entry under title:

The Pluralistic society.

    (Community psychology series; v. 9)
    Includes index.
    1. Community mental health services—United States.
2. Minorities—Mental health services—United States.
I. Sue, Stanley. II. Moore, Thom. III. Series.
RA790.6.P58   362.2'0973   82-3131
ISBN 0-89885-055-X   AACR2

THE COMMUNITY PSYCHOLOGY SERIES

Sponsored by

The Division of Community Psychology

of the American Psychological Association

The Community Psychology Series has as its central purpose the building of philosophic, theoretical, scientific, and empirical foundations for action research in the community and in its sub-systems, and for education and training for such action research.

As a publication of the Division of Community Psychology, the series is particularly concerned with the development of community psychology as a sub-area of psychology. In general, it emphasizes the application and integration of theories and findings from other areas of psychology, and in particular the development of community psychology methods, theories, and principles, as these stem from actual community research and practice.

CONTENTS

9

004699

CONTRIBUTORS

DANIEL ADELSON, the First General Editor of the Community Psychology Series, is now on the faculty of the California School of Professional Psychology and a Senior Research Associate at the Wright Institute, Berkeley, California. His interest in social and community psychology and cultural pluralism dates from his work with displaced persons in Europe, first with the U.S. Army and subsequently with the United Nations Relief and Rehabilitation Administration and International Refugee Organization. He is now developing a primary prevention project in Richmond, California and completing a volume entitled *Community Psychology as the Individual's Encounter with History* for Holt, Rinehart, Winston.

CAROLYN L. ATTNEAVE is Professor of Psychology and Adjunct Professor of Psychiatry and Behavioral Sciences, University of Washington. A member of the Delaware Tribe, she is an active consultant to tribes and to agencies working with American Indians and Alaska Natives in the broad field of mental health. She is a founding member and President of the Society of American Indian Psychologists and has served the American Psychological Association as the Chair of its Committee on Equal Opportunity and as a member of its Ad hoc Committee on Minority Affairs.

W. CURTIS BANKS obtained his Ph.D. in psychology from Stanford University. He then served on the Department of Psychology faculty at Princeton University and was appointed to the Task Panel on Black Americans for the President's Commission on Mental Health. Banks is now Senior Research Scientist and Director of the Social Learning Laboratory at the Educational Testing Service. His work currently centers on reinforcement processes in black behavior and research methods in black psychology.

13

EVALINA W. BESTMAN, Ph.D. is Director of the University of Miami-Jackson Memorial Community Mental Health Center, a Senior Staff member of the Mental Health Services Division, Jackson Memorial Hospital, and Research Assistant Professor, Department of Psychiatry, University of Miami School of Medicine. She received her Ph.D. in Educational Psychology from the University of Texas at Austin in 1972. In addition to Miami, she has taught at the University of Pittsburgh and Florida International University and has lectured widely, including the University of Liberia. Recipient of numerous honors and awards, Dr. Bestman served on the Task Force on Black American Mental Health, President's Commission on Mental Health, and is a Consultant in Minority Mental Health for DHEW. A founder of Miami's Center for Family and Child Enrichment, Dr. Bestman also helped establish and is chair of the Miami chapter of the National Association of Black Psychologists. She is currently co-authoring two works dealing with the mental health of black women.

ROBERT CHIN is Professor of Psychology at Boston University. Active in the governance structure of psychology, he has served as President of APA Division 9, President of the Asian American Psychological Association, and a member of the APA Committee on Equal Opportunity in Psychology and the APA Ad Hoc Committee on Ethnic Minority Affairs. Chin has written or edited several books including *Psychological Research in Communist China* (with Ai-li Chin) and *The Planning of Change* (with Warren Bennis and Kenneth Benne). A social psychologist, Chin received his Ph.D. from Columbia University and has served as the Editor of the *Journal of Social Issues*.

IRA ISCOE is Director of the Community Psychology Training Program, The University of Texas at Austin. He played a lead in the Austin Conference on Training in Community Psychology, 1975, and is co-editor with Charles D. Spielberger and Bernard Bloom on *Community Psychology in Transition: A Report of the Austin Conference*. He formerly was Director of the Counseling-Psychological Services Center (1968-1978) University of Texas at Austin, and is presently Director of the Institute of Human Development and Family Studies, in addition to being Professor of Psychology and Director of the Community Psychology Training Program.

SUSAN E. KEEFE received her Ph.D. in anthropology from the University of California, Santa Barbara, in 1974. She was coordinator of a research project concerning mental health service utilization by Mexican Americans in 1974-78 and is currently an Assistant Professor in Anthropology at

Appalachian State University. She is co-editor of *Family and Mental Health in the Mexican American Community* and has published articles on Mexican Americans, family, and mental health in *Human Organization, American Ethnologist,* and the *American Journal of Community Psychology.* Recently she received funding from the National Institute of Mental Health for work on a monograph entitled "The Mexican American Family."

BERNARD M. KRAMER is currently Professor of Psychology at the University of Massachusetts at Boston. He is the author of *Day Hospital: A Study of Partical Hospitalization in Psychiatry.* He co-edited *Social Psychology and Mental Health* (with Henry Wechsler and Leonard Solomon), *Racism and Mental Health* (with Charles V. Willie and Bertram S. Brown) and *Neighborhood Health Centers* (with Robert M. Hollister and Seymour S. Bellin). He is the author of *Dimensions of Prejudice* and the co-author of *Some Roots of Prejudice* (with Gordon W. Allport). He was an undergraduate at Brooklyn College and earned the doctorate in Social Psychology at Harvard in 1950.

MORTON KRAMER is Professor, Department of Mental Hygiene with a joint appointment in the Department of Biostatistics, School of Hygiene and Public Health of The Johns Hopkins University. He received a Doctor of Science in Hygiene (Biostatistics) from The Johns Hopkins University School of Hygiene and Public Health in 1939. In 1949 he served as Chief of the then Biometrics Branch, now the NIMH Division of Biometry and Epidemiology. Dr. Kramer is a member of the Expert Panel on Health Statistics of the World Health Organization and serves as a Consultant to the Division of Mental Health of WHO. He is a Fellow of the American Public Health Association, American Orthopsychiatric Association, and American Statistical Association, and an Honorary Fellow of the American Psychiatric Association. In 1977 he was appointed to a Task Panel of the President's Commission on Mental Health. Dr. Kramer has written extensively on the application of biostatistical and epidemiological methods. He was awarded the DHEW Superior Service Award and the Distinguished Service Award and from the American Public Health Association the Rema Lapouse Award.

HARRIET P. LEFLEY, Ph.D. is Associate Professor, Department of Psychiatry, University of Miami School of Medicine, and Director of Research and Evaluation, University of Miami-Jackson Memorial Community Mental Health Center. She received her Ph.D. in Personality-Social Psychology from the University of Miami in 1973. Specializing in cross-cultural and ethno-psychology, she has conducted research in the Caribbean, where she was Resident Research Director and later Primary

Consultant in Social Research to the Ministry of Labor & Welfare, Government of the Bahamas. Her many publications have also included extensive research in child-rearing, self-concept, and socio-cultural change among the Miccosukee and Seminole Indians of Florida—much of it at the specific invitation of the tribes; ongoing studies of mental health patterns in the major ethnic groups in Miami; and contributions on social and cultural aspects of mental illness and mental health care. Dr. Lefley is a co-director of the University of Miami's Cross-Cultural Training Institute for Mental Health Professionals, newly funded by NIMH.

THOM MOORE is in the Counseling Center at the University of Illinois in Champaign-Urbana. For the last four years he has been Co-Chair of the Division 27 Minority Task Force. His major interest is the study of social system impact on human behavior and the development of social interventions.

DONNA NAGATA is currently an Assistant Professor of Psychology at Smith College. Dr. Nagata's special interest is in understanding the impact of culture on human behavior and the use of cultural styles in social interventions. She is a member of the Asian American Psychological Association and was an A.P.A. Minority Fellow.

AMADO M. PADILLA received his Ph.D. in Experimental Psychology from the University of New Mexico. He has taught at UC Santa Barbara and is currently on the faculty at UCLA where he is a Professor of Psychology. He has conducted research on child bilingualism, the utilization of mental health services by Hispanics, and on acculturation. He is the co-author of *Crossing-Cultures in Therapy* (Brooks/Cole, 1980) and the editor of *Acculturation: Theory, Models and Some New Findings* (Westview Press, 1980).

ELIGIO PADILLA is a native of Alameda, New Mexico. He obtained his undergraduate degree from the University of New Mexico and his Ph.D. in clinical psychology from the University of Washington. Following an internship at the Department of Psychiatry, UCLA School of Medicine, he accepted an Assistant Professorship in the same department. He is now Assistant Professor of Psychology and Psychiatry at the University of New Mexico. Funded research projects focus on issues of the assessment of psychopathology among Chicanos, the psychological evaluation of Indian children, and the study of violent death, i.e., suicide, homicide, and accidental death.

LONNIE SNOWDEN is Assistant Professor in the School of Social Welfare, University of California, Berkeley. A Clinical Psychologist by training, Snowden is currently interested in several problems in the field of community psychology: Evaluation of drug and alcohol programs, assessment of psychosocial competence, cultural issues in minority mental health. Snowden has published articles in each of these areas, and has served as consultant to the National Institute on Alcohol Abuse and Alcoholism, and as committee member, Psychology Education Review Committee, National Institute of Mental Health.

STANLEY SUE is Professor of Psychology at the University of California, Los Angeles. He was previously a faculty member at the University of Washington and Director of Clinical and Community Psychology Training at the National Asian American Psychology Training Center in San Francisco. He has served on the Board of Social and Ethical Responsibility in Psychology of the American Psychological Association and on the Editorial Boards of the *American Psychologist* and the *American Journal of Community Psychology*. Sue received his Ph.D. from the University of California, Los Angeles and his B.S. from the University of Oregon. His research interests are in the areas of ethnicity and mental health, social support systems, and community psychology.

RENEE WHATLEY, a graduate student at the University of Illinois in Clinical Community Psychology, has had considerable experience with social programs across cultural groups. More recently she has been interested in community organization strategies for grassroots groups.

CHARLES V. WILLIE is Professor of Education and Urban Studies, Harvard Graduate School of Education. He was a member of the President's Commission on Mental Health, former President of the Eastern Sociological Society, and has been a visiting lecturer in the Laboratory of Community Psychiatry of the Harvard Medical School. He is co-editor of *Racism and Mental Health* with Bernard Kramer and Bertram Brown.

NOLAN W. S. ZANE received his Bachelor of Science degree in psychology from Stanford University. Initially entering the graduate program in social psychology, Zane decided to enroll in the clinical psychology program at the University of Washington where he could pursue his clinical and community psychology interests. He has served on the Student Editorial Board of the *American Journal of Community Psychology* and has co-authored several publications on Asian American mental health and on the application of learned helplessness theory to community settings.

FOREWORD

With the publication of this volume, primarily written and edited by scholars and researchers who are themselves members of minority groups, we reach a landmark in the history of American psychology. That this book appears in a series sponsored by the Division of Community Psychology of the American Psychological Association is most appropriate. The event occurs some 15 years after the birth of the division, and only a short time since the serious pursuit of affirmative action among university psychology programs. Yet today we have, for perhaps the first time, a multi-ethnic perspective on community mental health in a pluralistic society.

It is important to see this book as more than one written by researchers about minorities. It is also written by those who, as individuals, have personally lived with the ebb and flow of minority affairs in the practice of psychology.

For several years we have heard arguments for a minority perspective in psychology, yet even those of us who have supported the recruitment of minority students to psychology programs have often viewed the effort in paternalistic social justice terms: paramount in our attitude has been what *we* could "do for them" by allowing entrance to *our* profession. Few have been willing or able to recognize that the profession and the science of psychology badly need minority students and faculty, notwithstanding the question of achieving social justice *vis a vis* educational opportunities.

Like it or not, psychology is a modern religion, functioning as a moral and ethical enterprise deeply influenced by the ideology and belief systems of its priests and theologians (practitioners and academics). What must be understood is that the bias built into growing up in America as a member of a cultural or ethnic minority will unavoidably influence the way data, theory, and ideas are collected, collated, and communicated. A wide spectrum of cultural and ethnic bias is required in a discipline that pretends to understand human social, emotional, and cognitive behavior in a hetero-geneous world. It is simply the case that in both subtle and obvious ways individuals with a variety of sociocultural experiences will necessarily enrich the sociocultural understanding of our discipline. This was recognized several years ago when Stanley Sue and Thom Moore were asked by the executive committee of the Division of Community Psychology to serve as co-chairs of the Task Force on Minority Issues. This volume is one of the products of their work, and there is much for us to learn from it.

For many, the development of community psychology has been tied to the struggle for minority voices to be heard. Community psychology, always looking toward a pluralistic society, had championed the right to be the same, and the right to be different. The defining values of the com-munity psychology movement have been cultural relativity, diversity, and an ecological perspective that respects, indeed fosters, differences among people. We seek to avoid the single standard of competence. Measured against the prevailing cultural insulation and ethnocentrism of the mental health movement, this volume is a small step toward such values.

Today, at the onset of the 1980s, popular wisdom sees us entering a decade of economic and political conservatism. We know from historical precedent that social science explanations and actions are always influenced by such political-economic fluctuations. Those who have been in the struggle can feel ''in their bones'' the downturn of excitement and commit-ment by the majority to minority causes. This can be both depressing and invigorating: those who are to remain active must seize the time to continue significant gains by riding whatever the current cultural crest happens to be. Today it is most sensible to push for social policies that foster the development of natural support systems within minority communities. This stand is both realistic for current political-economic conditions, and makes social-psychological sense as minority communities begin to act on the realization, among themselves as well as among others, that they are indeed competent communities. This volume can be a stimulus for all of us to see more clearly the tremendous potential for mental health in a truly pluralistic society.

Julian Rappaport
University of Illinois
Urbana-Champaign

INTRODUCTION

Ethnic Minority Groups in Community Psychology

Stanley Sue
University of California, Los Angeles

Thom Moore
University of Illinois

Ira Iscoe
University of Texas

Donna Kiyo Nagata
University of Illinois

The study of social problems from a community psychology perspective and the development of interventions to promote more positive life experiences for people are inherently difficult. Part of the difficulty stems from the lack of consensus over what specifically constitutes "positive" life experiences. Targets of social interventions are collectives of people who tend to make judgments and evaluations of their own life conditions and to formulate individual opinions as to what is needed. In essence they have, and pursue, their own specific goals and values. Each group can be seen as a system in need of resources that can be transformed into products that correspond to its goals. The process of transforming resources into products is controlled in part by customs, traditions, or simply cultural preferences.

Ultimately, differences created by scarce resources and the processes of transforming them into social goods bring people together in either competitive or cooperative relations. Historically, ethnic minorities have received disproportionately small shares of resources and have constantly been unable to obtain a fairer share.

Problems in the quality of life of ethnic minorities can be found in a 1978 report from the United States Commission on Civil Rights. The report shows that, compared with the white majority, ethnic minorities have made only slight gains in education, income, housing, and unemployment since the 1960s. These findings are especially significant, because they demonstrate that even during a period when the country was particularly sensitive to minority issues, positive social and economic gains were difficult to achieve. Although there are many explanations of these data, one likely explanation is that centuries of patterned behavior is not to be changed in one decade. Furthermore, when the desired change does not occur, the mechanism to bring about that change should not be withdrawn and replaced by a sense of hopelessness. The plight of minorities cannot be treated as simply an experiment that can be abandoned when expected results are not immediately obtained.

The purpose of this book is to bring together the research, observations, and experiences of scholars concerned with ethnicity and community mental health. A strict definition has been avoided for ethnic group or race, although substantive discussion of American Indians, Asian Americans, blacks, and Hispanics does appear. What is important to recognize is the experiences associated with ethnic minority groups in society. In addition to being a forum for social scientists concerned with ethnic issues, this volume also serves as a model for recognizing the diversity of cultures and the enormous range of behaviors and beliefs that exist in our society. It calls attention to the need for respect, integrity, understanding, and compassion for all human beings. While most contributors address what may properly be called community mental health concerns, such as mental health needs and service delivery systems, broader issues in community psychology are also brought out.

Central to the organization of the book is the concept of diversity and pluralism. Throughout the early history of our country there have been repeated instances where cultures have clashed and attempted to resolve the conflict over distribution of goods in a pluralistic society. Unfortunately for the ethnic minorities of concern to this volume, many of these proposed solutions have maintained inequities and have failed to enhance their quality of life. The consequences of cultural conflict have not been powerful enough to eliminate from our society either cultural patterns of behavior and relating, or values. Thus the question remains as central as ever:

"How are we to live in a multicultural society?" Over time there have been "Grand Theories" that have approached the topic and moved our thinking, sometimes in more positive and, sometimes, in more negative ways. The authors of this volume, however, have been more inclined to address specific aspects of the question, and their answers involve a systematic and precise understanding of ethnic and racial minority life in America and strategies for improving that life.

The context for the works that follow is that of pluralism, and to appreciate the value of each contribution, the concept of pluralism must be examined.

Pluralism is an ideology which supports the rights of groups of things to be different within a common set. Cultural pluralism specifically suggests that cultural groups in a larger society should be allowed to retain both their unique identities and their membership in that larger social framework. Cultural pluralism is an ideology, as opposed to a theory. Newman (1973) distinguishes between theory and ideology in the following manner: A theory describes what *is*, and is an attempt to predict on the basis of available descriptive information; an ideology, on the other hand, is an attempt to state what *ought* to be and contains an evaluative or judgmental component. The "ought" in Newman's definition is important for this discussion, for cultural pluralism does not currently exist on a broad level.

Basic to the ideology of cultural pluralism is the principle of cultural relativity. Herskovits (1972) defines cultural relativism as ". . . the social discipline that comes of respect for difference—mutual respect. Emphasis on the worth of many ways of life, not one, is an affirmation of the values in each culture" (p. 11). In addition to this mutual respect is the notion of utilizing these differences as sources of strength rather than weaknesses (Rappaport, 1977). A culturally pluralistic view, then, includes (a) mutual respect for the existence of cultural differences, and (b) an awareness of the strengths inherent in those differences, which (c) work together in support of the rights of various cultural groups in society to maintain their uniqueness.

Cultural pluralism is a broad term. In our analysis we want to call particular attention to psychological and social interaction pluralism.

Psychological pluralism, with respect to mental health and disturbance, requires an understanding of differences in mental functioning and labels of normal/deviant mental health. It suggests a recognition of diverse standards of well-being and coping mechanisms formed by historical and participational identification. Gordon (1964) sees historical identification as a function of past or current historical events. For example, an interventionist attempting to understand Asian Americans should be aware that Japanese Americans, who experienced relocation camps during World War

II, would have a very different psychocultural outlook than Chinese Americans, who had not. Historical events may create a great deal of within group (e.g., Asian American) differences. Participational identification consists of feelings of sharing or mutual belongingness. Thus different ethnic groups with dissimilar cultures may share feelings of minority group status or alienation.

Social interaction pluralism, a second form, suggests an understanding of differences with respect to interpersonal styles of communication and behavior, while a third form, ethnic pluralism, concerns the understanding of differences in physical appearance, customs, foods, etc. Schermerhorn (1970) lists additional forms of pluralism such as ideological pluralism, political pluralism, and structural pluralism. The point is that *pluralism*, as a way to conceive the world, has wide implications for the perceptions of differences and interventions on a number of levels. The contributors to this volume point to strategies and concepts that enhance research and intervention in a pluralistic society.

Having given a broad description of pluralism, it is now possible to describe, more specifically, the term "culture": how it fits into a pluralistic ideology, and how it interacts with the roles of the social interventionist. Triandis (1972) makes a useful distinction between objective culture and subjective culture. Objective culture represents the material part of one's environment (e.g., money, cars, resources, or houses) while subjective culture is one's unique way of perceiving the social environment. Within the realm of subjective culture lie influences of the objective culture, as well as more vague and phenomenological factors such as past life experiences and future expectations. Gordon (1964) suggests that additional factors, such as geographical location, might also be included as a part of a subjective culture. On a basic level, there does exist an awareness of (Rice, Ruiz & Padilla, 1974), and often affinity for, one's own ethnic group (Clore, 1976; Glazer & Moynihan, 1975). While individuals or groups can potentially change their socioeconomic status or future expectations, there is less control over changing one's heritage or skin color. Race can be seen as a crucial part of *general* or *diffuse* subjective culture. However, the degree to which this basic factor is realized or manifested will be a function of the degree to which the other factors within the realm of subjective culture are emphasized. The final outcome is a specific subjective culture, composed of the diffuse subjective culture superimposed with specific individual and environmental influences.

When pluralism is discussed with respect to culture, as defined here, it becomes clear that a more complex and diverse view of society develops. Valentine (1971), for example, states that within a single urban community 14 culturally distinct Afro-American subgroups, plus nine other non Afroethnic groups, were revealed. The social interventionist must be aware that lumping ethnic groups together will become inadequate and that pluralism now takes on the meaning of an understanding of diversity not only between groups, but within groups as well.

In some sense, asking someone to look at an individual's subjective culture is like asking for recognition of that individual's context. The interaction of all the factors that make up one's subjective culture is important. Albers (1971) discusses the parallel importance of this recognition in the art world: "...a factual identification of colors within a given painting has nothing to do with sensitive seeing nor with an understanding of the color action in the painting" (p. 5). Similarly, stereotypes based only on skin color, or manner of speaking, offer little information about an individual's subjective culture.

Basically, cultural pluralism represents an issue of values in that it proposes that the social interventionist *value* differences and a plurality of cultures, as opposed to a mass or monoculture. Pluralism forces one to consider questions such as, "What constitutes a cultural difference? How do I view myself as a member of a special culture? Can I tolerate the right of others to be different from me?" Cultural pluralism requires social or community interventionists to examine and constantly reexamine the values they hold with respect to norm-setting, quality of life judgments, and the social causes considered important for intervention. It must be thoroughly understood that professional intervention carries with it implicit value statements. Pluralism asks that, in every possible setting for intervention, one adopts what Rein (1976) has called the "value critical" approach:

> In the value-critical approach, not only are the values treated as the subject of analyses, but it is assumed that analyses can never be independent of the values we hold. They constitute the network which helps us organize...And it is these frames, or modes, or values, or ideologies, or theories, or whatever we choose to call them, which are crucial for any creative work; for without them we have no question to ask. (p. 14).

Understanding these values enables social interventionists to do two things. First it would provide interventionists with an awareness of their "self-generated" values. Second, it also leaves them with a way to conceive other people's values.

Cultural pluralism, then, represents an ideological framework from which the social interventionist can develop a value-critical mode of thinking. This value-critical process of thinking, coupled with a culturally relativistic view, forms a useful model for social intervention in a pluralistic society.

The level at which pluralism exists in our society must not, however, be accepted as the final goal. We must recognize that cultural pluralism describes the strategies that people use to achieve a higher set of goals. For example, all automobile assembly lines do not employ the same strategies to produce cars. Likewise all families do not use the same techniques to raise their children. Systems theorists refer to this as equifinality; that is, there are a number of ways to achieve the same ends. In social life we can see that this same rule applies. Some people have perfected the art of hunting and gathering to provide the necessary resources to sustain their lives, and others have developed methods of farming. While it is important to attend to what people do, it is equally as important to understand why. We must guard against letting cultural differences serve as a manifestation of invariant social traits, and encourage those that are simply alternatives to realize the same goal. The contributions to this volume play an important role in establishing that the lives of ethnic minorities can only be understood as actions in pursuit of survival and quality of life.

Our view of mental health employs the notion of option. That is, in a pluralistic society individuals should be free to define and pursue their own goals and life styles, consistent with their cultural backgrounds. This statement does not deny that there may well be common mental health processes or skills that are functional across cultures in American society. Rather, it means that if there is a continuum ranging from recognition and appreciation of cultural diversity to the recognition and adoption of single standards, society has erred in the latter direction. The appreciation and utilization of cultural diversity in examining mental health, devising theoretical schemes, conducting research, and developing prevention and intervention programs must occur.

By stressing cultural pluralism, each of the chapters in this volume contributes some understanding to issues that have critical importance for community mental health and ethnic minority groups. The five chapters in Section One deal with mental health needs or resources of ethnic minority groups. Because of prejudice, discrimination, and the lack of opportunities, ethnic minorities are under a great deal of stress (Sue & Zane, 1980), a situation which was recognized by the President's Commission on Mental Health (1978). The mental health needs of these ethnic groups are presented in Section One. Several chapters indicate the development of culturally responsive programs of intervention, as well as the utilization of natural support systems already available in ethnic communities.

Section Two is mainly concerned with issues involving self-identity and competency in a pluralistic society. The failure to appreciate cultural diversity in society has at least two major consequences. First, individuals of minority group cultures are under stress, since there is a conflict between their own minority group's cultural or community values and those of the larger (majority) group. The resolution of conflict is of vital importance, and the strategies (e.g., ethnic or community identification and social change) that can be adopted are discussed. Second, the contributors argue that much of the diverse or different behavioral patterns used by ethnic minority groups should be viewed as competent and adaptive responses. Therefore, in a culturally pluralistic society, differences do not necessarily imply deficiencies in adaptation.

Finally, in Section Three the application of cultural pluralistic concepts in social change, development of theory, and training of community psychologists are discussed. Cultural diversity, then, can be seen as a guiding philosophy for research and theory, intervention, and training. Indeed, it is the very theme of this book.

REFERENCES

Albers, J. *Interaction of color.* New Haven: Yale University Press, 1971.

Clore, G. L. Interpersonal attraction: An overview. In J. W. Thibaut, J. T. Spence, and R. C. Carson (Eds.), *Contemporary topics in social psychology.* Morristown, N.J.: General Learning Press, 1976.

Glazer, N., and Moynihan, E. P. (Eds.). *Ethnicity: Theory and experience.* Cambridge: Harvard University Press, 1975.

Gordon, M. *Assimilation in American life.* New York: Oxford University Press, 1964.

Herskovits, M. J. *Cultural relativism: Perspectives in cultural pluralism.* New York: Random House, 1972.

Newman, W. H. *American pluralism: A study of minority groups and social theory.* New York: Harper & Row, 1973.

President's Commission on Mental Health. *Report to the President.* Washington, D.C.: U.S. Government Printing Office, 1978.

Rappaport, J. *Community psychology: Values, research, and action.* San Francisco: Holt, Rinehart and Winston, 1977.

Rein, M. *Social science and public policy.* New York: Penguin Books, Ltd., 1976.

Rice, A. S., Ruiz, R. A., and Padilla, A. M. Person perception, self-identity, and ethnic group preference in Anglo, Black, and Chicano preschool and third grade children. *Journal of Cross-Cultural Psychology,* 1974, *5,* 100-108.

Schermerhorn, R. A. *Comparative ethnic relations: A framework for theory and research.* New York: Random House, 1970.

Sue, S., and Zane, N. Learned helplessness theory and community psychology. In M. Gibbs, J. R. Lachenmeyer, and J. Sigal (Eds.), *Community psychology: Theoretical and empirical approaches.* New York: Gardner Press, 1980.

Triandis, H. C. *The analysis of subjective culture.* New York: John Wiley & Sons, Inc., 1972.

Valentine, C. A. Deficit, difference and bicultural models of Afro-American behavior. *Harvard Educational Review,* 1971, *2,* 137-157.

Part I

SERVICE NEEDS AND MENTAL HEALTH SERVICES

Service Needs and Mental Health Services

In the promotion of psychological well-being, it is essential that mental health needs be defined and that appropriate services be created to meet these needs. The five chapters in Section One address the issues concerning mental health needs and services.

As mentioned in the introduction, the President's Commission on Mental Health has played a substantial role in examining the mental health problems experienced by members of ethnic minority groups. As a member of the Commission, Charles V. Willie presents some of the testimonies given by the general public regarding ethnic concerns. It is clear that Willie's emphasis is not simply focused upon psychopathology, but also includes the general issue of the quality of life. His suggestions for enhancement of the lives of minority group persons include prevention approaches, improvements in service delivery systems, and the creation of innovative strategies.

Whereas Willie's chapter is devoted to testimonies and observations, Morton Kramer and Nolan Zane's contribution is an epidemiological-empirical approach to predict future service utilization and the incidence and prevalence of disorders among ethnic minority groups. They project that the proportionate increase of individuals at risk for mental health services will be greater among ethnic minority groups than among white Americans. The predictions are upsetting and are cause for deep concern. One important implication of the study is that attempts must be made to plan for the future—to be proactive rather than reactive. Social changes are rapidly occuring, so what is true today may not be true tommorow. For example, Hispanics are the fastest growing minority group and by the year 1990 they will be the largest; it is conservatively estimated that the Asian population in the United States will double from 1970 to 1980; in the state of California, as well as in Los Angeles and Chicago, nonwhite ethnic groups in the near future will outnumber whites. All of these changes indicate the necessity to address our efforts not only for today, but for the future. (It should be noted that the lag time between the preparation of the chapters and the publication of the book occurred when the 1980 census figures were being compiled. The figures are now available and support many of the population projections made by several of the contributors.)

Given that the need for mental health services is high, what kinds of resources are available? Amado Padilla and Susan Keefe's chapter deals with sources of help and help-seeking behaviors among the Mexican-American and Anglo communities. Differences in the use of formal mental health services and of social networks exist not only between these two groups, but within the segments of the Mexican-American community as well. The authors find that cultural factors and the structure of the community influence the perception of mental health needs and the availability of social networks—factors that are in turn related to specific patterns of help seeking behavior.

The chapters by Harriet Lefley and Evalina Bestman and by Carolyn Attneave provide insight into how formal mental health services can be designed to better serve ethnic communities. Translating community mental health ideology into practice, Lefley and Bestman describe their program to serve five ethnic groups in the inner-city area of Miami. The assumptions underlying their approach, the techniques used, and the consideration of the culture and life style of the five ethnic communities are clearly spelled out. The program may be seen as one model for intervention in ethnic minority communities. Attneave focuses on one group—the American Indians, she points to the problems in the provision of services to this group. New or more innovative directions for mental health services that incorporate American Indian participation and control are discussed.

Chapter 1

MENTAL HEALTH AND ETHNICITY

Charles V. Willie

On February 17, 1977, President Jimmy Carter established the 20 member President's Commission on Mental Health. The commission was asked to "identify the mental health needs of the nation" and was authorized by executive order to conduct "public hearings, inquiries and studies" necessary for identifying these needs. Subsequent public hearings held in the eastern and western United States provide the basis of this report.

At our organizing meeting in the White House, Julius B. Richmond, a member of the Commission, later appointed Surgeon General and Assistant Secretary for the Department of Health, Education and Welfare, reflected the attitudes of others on the commission when he said he wanted the people to appear and give testimony at the hearings and to know that "what they say will be taken seriously."

I also served as a member of the commission and sat with the hearing panel at sessions in Philadelphia and San Francisco. The hearings presented a unique opportunity for members of the majority as well as members of the various minority groups in this nation to identify mental health needs and issues from their own perspectives. A synthesis and an interpretation of what was said in these hearings by representatives of various minority groups—Hispanics, Blacks, Native Americans, and Asian Americans—and patients are presented and analyzed. My understanding, of course, derives from discussion with staff members and other commissioners.

Commission discussions have been particularly illuminating because of the diversified background of the participants. Rosalynn Carter, the First Lady, was Honorary Chairperson of the commission. Different races, ages, sexes, occupations, and geographical regions were represented among the 20 commissioners and staff. The commission included several former mental health patients who brought this particularly valuable perspective to its policy-making deliberations. The different points of view among the commissioners enabled them to tune in to various opinions and orientations, including those of professionals who provide services, those of patients who receive services, those of persons who need, but do not receive, help, and those of persons who receive, but do not want, the treatment they get.

A *Preliminary Report* of the commision that we presented to the president six months after the commission was created, indicated the broad dimensions of the mental disorder, not only in terms of the numbers of people affected, but also in terms of stress-producing circumstances in communities and how those contribute to illness or health (President's Commission on Mental Health, 1977). In the first paragraph the report stated that ''The mental health of a nation's people reflects the quality of individual lives, the strength of personal relationships, and the opportunities that exist for all people to participate fully in the national life.'' The *Final Report* elaborated further on these ideas and indicated some of the social circumstances that may produce stress that trouble the thoughts and emotions of individuals. It pointed out that ''American's mental health problems must include the damage associated with unrelenting poverty and unemployment and the institutionalized discrimination that occurs on the basis of race, sex, class, age, and mental or physical handicaps'' (President's Commission on Mental Health, 1978).

In addition, the Report mentioned ''disabilities in which psychological and emotional factors are directly involved.'' The report continued: ''These include certain physical handicaps, certain types of organic brain disease and the misuse of alcohol or other drugs. They also include many learning disabilities that affect children and the serious behavior disorders of children...'' (President's Commission on Mental Health, 1978). Alcohol abuse was labeled a serious social, physical, and mental health problem.

Knowledge that isolation, alienation, discrimination, and forms of arbitrary exclusion are harmful and tend to trouble the emotions and thoughts of individuals was not new. What was new was the acknowledgement by an authoritative group that this ''institutionalized discrimination'' ought to be seriously considered if the goal is to prevent as well as treat mental disorders.

The 1977-78 President's Commission on Mental Health had the benefit and the rich reservoir of materials, ideas, and recommendations assembled by the Joint Commission on Mental Illness and Health, whose report was published in 1961 (Joint Commission, 1961). Surveying the situation nearly two decades later, the President's Commission was building upon the breakthrough in establishing community mental health centers as the locus of treatment and was pointing toward prevention. Nevertheless, the President's Commission saw what it came to see because, figuratively, it stood on the shoulders of the Joint Commission. Prevention has come more clearly into focus. In the past there was little understanding of what, if anything, could be done in the field of prevention. Jack Ewalt, the Director of the Joint Commission, acknowledged that the Commission had been "heavily criticized for not making an all-out recommendation for preventative services."

The Joint Commission focused on community services. Specifically, it recommended "reduction in the size of state hospitals, and the provision of care near home in the community facilities" (Ewalt, 1977, pp. 17, 18). The Joint Commission recommended that these community mental health centers be established as medical facilities. Some members of the Joint Commission and its staff believed that centers that "attempted to attack broad social issues, such as racism, poverty, and education, would experience less success than those that adhered to a medical base (Ewalt, 1977, p. 17). While evidence was available when the Joint Commission was conducting its studies that "people who are deprived by reason of race or poverty have a higher incidence of all kinds of illness," it failed to make recommendations regarding these stress-producing circumstances, largely because many of the commission members and staff "did not feel that the improvement of general socioeconomic and racial conditions were the domain of preventative psychiatry," (Ewalt, 1977, p.18) although they thought the discipline could make a contribution in the area.

The President's Commission had to face the issues of racial discrimination and other forms of institutionalized oppression forthrightly. It had to do this, on the one hand, because of the kinds of individuals who were appointed by the President to serve on the Commission, and, on the other, because of the testimony it received from various minority group speakers at the public hearings. This testimony had to be taken seriously.

To deal with these issues, the Commission had to consider the prevention, as well as the treatment, of mental disorders and would not be able to limit its recommendations to only those that could be implemented through facilities that use a medical service model. Indeed, the Report of the Commission stated that useful approaches for prevention are "...reducing the stressful effects of life crisis experiences such as unemployment, retirement, and marital disruption due to death or other circumstances, and...analyzing and understanding the nature of social environments, including those of hospitals and other institutions, so that as an ultimate goal, environments may be created in which people achieve their full potential'' (President's Commission on Mental Health, 1978, p. 51). Another prevention strategy recommended was ''promoting the development of helping networks and mutual support groups that deal preventively with both everyday crises and extraordinary crisis situations'' (President's Commission on Mental Health, 1978, p. 76). To give organized directions to these efforts, it was proposed that a Center for Prevention be established in the National Institute of Mental Health, and that it focus on high-risk populations and high-risk situations. To indicate commitment to prevention, the commission recommended that within ten years the funding support for the Center for Prevention should be at least 10 percent of the total NIMH budget (President's Commission, 1978, p. 54).

Because of the new definitions of stress-producing circumstances offered by the minorities who testified at the commission hearings, the commission made prevention a priority item, and prevention had to be broadly defined as dealing with the alienation, depression, fear, and anger associated with poverty and oppression.

A Chicano from Santa Clara, California said, ''The traditional medical model has only a limited approach to the mental health problems when unemployment, low income, and other social problems are involved.'' This person added that ''social factors are the barriers to effective participation in the mental health services system for minorities.... Minorities need a measure of contol over their lives rather than endless talk therapies.'' An Asian American complained about the absence among the 20 Commissioners of anyone connected with Asian and Pacific islanders. Presumably, this protest was not only a desire ''to participate fully in the national life''—an opportunity the Commission flagged in its Preliminary Report as reflective of the mental health of a nation's people—but a desire to have a measure of control over one's existence, in determining what would be recommended, a need mentioned earlier that is appropriate for all, minorities as well as the majority.

Among Asian Americans, recent immigrants appear to be a high-risk population. The Pacific/Asian Coalition, which sent a representative to testify, wanted the Commission to be aware of the stresses that are experienced by this group. Doubt was expressed, however, that any treatment program for mental disorders among recent immigrants could be effective without a major training program to increase the number of bilingual mental health personnel. Several people affiliated with many different cultural groups stressed the importance of staffing mental health services with people who understand the culture of particular racial and ethnic groups. The commission was told that inadequate communication due to language and cultural barriers between patient and therapist affects diagnosis, treatment, and clinical disposition of patients.

A Chinese-American psychologist said that "services that improve the quality of life should be the definition of mental health services." This idea was echoed by a Hispanic person from Oakland, California, who identified "poverty, demeaning education, and racist governmental activity" as experiences that "stunt human potential" and must be addressed in any mental health program to help Spanish-speaking people. He also expressed doubt about the value of what he called "insight therapy" when it is not linked with other assistance—such as programs of advocacy that help prevent the rejection of Hispanics and other minorities by schools and community agencies—that contribute to the quality of life.

A black physician defined the quality of life issue in generic terms. He said that the nation's minorities suffer because we have placed property rights over human rights. He said this lack of concern for human rights has created a major problem and in part has resulted in three "isms": racism, sexism, and classism. As an example, this speaker pointed to the state of Louisiana, which he said, "has more black youth in institutions than it educates in colleges and universities."

A person from Alaska testified that "suicide and alcoholism are reaching epidemic proportions" there. We also heard that in black inner-city ghettos homicide is a major threat to the survival of many young male adults, particularly those 21 to 35 years of age. These disorders were identified as related in some ways to the social environmental conditions of life experienced by the people in these settings and demonstrated that more than a medical model of service delivery is needed.

The problems perceived were articulated with passion. Few participants were able to recommend what should be done. They simply said that "talk" or "insight" therapy seemed not to be the only answer. But one black professional, the head of a city school board, was sufficiently bold to assert that a causal relationship existed between the social problems enumerated above and mental disorders. He said that "unemployment, poverty, racism, and poor housing are conditions that could be altered with beneficial consequences in reducing mental illness." One speaker called for a mandated education for all children regardless of disability as a way of helping; others simply called for the involvement of the federal government, saying it had to get involved if the right to treatment was to be protected in the same way that civil rights are protected.

The black physician who mentioned the number of minorities in institutions in Louisiana was referring to people in detention facilities, as well as other institutions. Clearly, the prison population is an area of concern to minorities. They often are sent to jail instead of the hospital. Even in some state mental hospitals, one-third of the patient population is there because of penal commitments. A California legislator said this is the case in that state. Census Bureau figures for 1970 revealed that 19 percent of the 2,126,719 persons in institutions in the United States were in correctional institutions, training schools for juvenile delinquents, and detention homes. Indeed, the proportion of institutionalized persons in detention facilities (19.0 percent) was approximately the same as the proportion in mental hospitals and residential treatment centers. The proportion of institutionalized persons in detention facilities has remained a constant one in five for at least two decades.

The commissioners learned from a staff member of the Court of Common Pleas in Pennsylvania that "there is virtually no mental health treatment for prisoners in any state." There are diagnostic services, but little treatment. This person testified that "10 to 25 percent of all prisoners are in need of psychiatric care, according to some estimates." The treatment that is given, according to this representative of the court, is limited to chemotherapy or drugs. Moreover, former prisoners who are discriminated against in many sectors of society are rejected by the mental health care-giving system, too. The Commissioners were told that "community mental health centers sometimes are not willing to give follow-up care to released prisoners."

There is an old saying that the compassion of a community can be measured by the condition of its jails. If this statement is true or even partially true, there is much work to be done if the criminal justice system is to contribute to the quality of life and the mental health of people in this nation. One person, on the basis of his experience, believed that prisoners need "both educational and sociological counselors." He has found that many prisoners are functional illiterates and some do not understand "how others interpret (their) faults. . . ." At present, he said, "new prisoners are usually left to fend for themselves. In essence, this makes the prison yard little more than an extension of the inner-city slum street corner from which the person came." The prisoner who presented this analysis of the prison experience and the needs of inmates did not testify before the commission. His ideas were published in 1977 in Winter/Spring of *Core* magazine in an article entitled "Prison: A Big Business Plays Con Game of Rehabilitation," a copy of which was given to all commissioners by the writer (Washington, 1977, pp. 38, 40-41).

In his assessment of the programs in prison that were described as "the most important," this person mentioned "arts and crafts" along with others such as prisoner-organized groups "struggling to change the quality of prison life." This latter activity is another version of the theme of participation as reflective of mental health that was mentioned in the *Preliminary Report* of the President's Commission, and also the theme of the need to have a measure of control over one's environment repeatedly mentioned by representatives of different minority groups. The classification of "arts and crafts" as beneficial in the rehabilitation of prison populations is new information. But it seems to corroborate the testimony and claim of an officer of the American Dance Association that "art therapy and dance therapy (could be) used in mental health centers and prisons" to the benefit of persons with poor verbal skills. These were called "specialized therapies" which should be recognized along with more traditional therapies. The commissioners were urged to recommend "expanded research in the nonverbal aspects of therapy." In the light of the prisoner's report that many inmates are functional illiterates, arts and crafts are important, particularly in view of the doubt expressed by some minorities of the value of "talk" therapy for individuals. The commission held that new approaches that may facilitate the establishment of communication where other therapeutic approaches have failed or have been less successful must be explored.

Problems ethnic groups faced in finding adequate mental health care were noted in the *Final Report:*

> Appropriate services are not available to many of them, even though social, economic, and environmental factors render them particularly vulnerable to acute and prolonged psychological and emotional distress. Too often, services which are available are not in accord with their cultural and linguistic traditions. The number of Asian and Pacific Island Americans utilizing mental health services increases dramatically when services take into account their cultural traditions and patterns. Language barriers prevent many Hispanic Americans from seeking care, and when they do seek it the absence of bilingual personnel can reduce the effectiveness of treatment. Government funded or operated programs often ignore existing cultural, social, and community supports in the American Indian community. A frequent and vigorous complaint of minority people who need care is that they often feel abused, intimidated, and harassed by non-minority personnel. Like everyone else, minorities feel more comfortable and secure when care is provided by practitioners who come from similar backgrounds.... The common bond among these racial and ethnic minority groups is that all encompass people whose basic mental health needs have not been sufficiently understood by those involved in the planning and delivery of mental health services. (pp. 5-6)

The director of the Joint Commission that published its report in 1961 said that more than a decade and a half ago some of the staff and commission members "were a little uncertain as to whether a person from the ghetto, who is depressed or paranoid, was reacting normally to his life situation, or abnormally as compared to the person who might be adjusting and happy in similar surroundings." Because of this "uncertainty," what was described as "sweeping recommendations for socio-economic change" that were contained in that report were not, in the opinion of the director, given "any more attention than they deserved" (Ewalt, 1977, p. 18). We now know, on the basis of evidence presented, that many who inhabit slum ghetto communities and turn to harmful criminal activity are in fact "unable to cope with their daily responsibilities in rational ways." The President's Commission in 1978 could not claim "uncertainty" as the basis for not recommending socioeconomic changes in the lives of individuals in slum ghetto communities as a step toward prevention.

By alerting the President's Commission on Mental Health and, through it, the nation at large, of the need to marshall the joint efforts of many different institutional systems for the purpose of preventing mental disorder and disability, minorities who addressed the Commissioners spoke for themselves as well as the majority. The Joint Commission on Mental Illness and Health limited its priority recommendations to those that could be accomplished largely from a medical base. In public hearings held by the President's Commission, minorities indicated that this base was too narrow to accommodate a meaningful program of prevention. Moreover, they pointed out that exploration of new ways of delivering services must proceed in concert with priority programs of prevention. One approach need not wait on the other. Treatment and prevention programs tend to affect different populations in different ways. Once effective treatments programs are in place, interest in prevention tends to lag. In the past, effective treatment for various illnesses including mental disorders have been made available first to the affluent and members of the majority. Prevention, however, benefits both the majority and the minority, the affluent as well as the disadvantaged. Minorities, therefore, may help the majority as well as themselves by insisting that preventative efforts pertaining to mental disorders not be delayed.

Advocates of prevention have called for better employment, education, and housing opportunities, and a lessening of various forms of institutionalized discrimination that limit, in arbitrary and capricious ways, the participation of all Americans in available opportunities. The President's Commission was informed of the need to recommend action against mental disorder that includes, but transcends, the one-on-one relationship that characterize the interaction between   patient and professional in the medical care system.

By causing the commissioners to broaden their perspectives on what can and must be done to promote public mental health, the minority speakers helped the commissioners to understand the value of proposing therapeutic innovations that deal with groups as well as individuals. This is why we stated that the minorities spoke for themselves as well as for others.

For example, some who testified before the commission, including majority group members, said that psychiatric services in some instances are provided in ways that ignore the family. One speaker, the director of a child guidance clinic on the east coast, went so far as to say that "psychiatric services often usurp family perogatives." With reference to mental retardation, a state director of the Division of Mental Retardation said parents as well as their retarded youngster need help; but in his state, he said, "no agency deals with the anxieties of parents with retarded children." A woman from Delaware pointed out that "support for the family during a crisis is important."

The family was discussed not only as an area of stress but also as a life support system that may be interrupted by the premature death of a spouse. As stated by one person who addressed the commission, "the death of a spouse is one of the most stressful experiences of adults." The shorter life expectancy of black males compared with whites is an indirect mental health problem when one considers the stress generated by the premature death of a spouse. It was emphasized that one should not have to become a patient to receive help in such troubled times. Support groups were mentioned as one possible source of help, particularly community support groups consisting of some people who had coped with the troubling experience.

The family was mentioned both as a source of assistance for persons who are distraught and as a source of anxiety that may contribute to disturbed emotions and thoughts. A Los Angeles mental health clinic professional said that "Asians tend to take care of the mentally ill persons at home, that mutual interdependency within the family, as opposed to individuality, is their orientation." However, another speaker, a layperson and a homemaker, said, "psychiatrists do not make house calls so no one helps families who have mentally ill persons living at home." Psychiatrists, of course, are not the only professionals who could help a family that is trying to care at home for a member with a mental disorder. If there are other sources of help, this woman had not found them. Presumably she was speaking from experience and the anguish was sufficiently severe to motivate her to come to the public hearing, with no guarantee that she could speak. Fortunately, she was heard. Women were called to the commissioners' attention as an endangered group. In and out of family, said a San Francisco woman, they experience "sex-role stereotyping." A member of the Women's Health Concern Committee of a state department believed that: "Women are admitted to psychiatric facilities and to private care twice as much as men." Alcohol is used by some women as an attempt to escape those concerns that trouble their thoughts and emotions. The commission was told that alcohol abuse by women is increasing, that in one Middle-Atlantic state "drunk driving was the most frequent offense for which women were arrested." The evidence presented indicated that many women are troubled, that family life for some is terribly complicated, and that their role relationships with men offer less than what they desire and much that they do not want.

The commission was informed by a Pennsylvania woman that "15 percent of Philadelphia's homicides are a function of domestic strife." If homicide and other episodes of non-fatal violence in the home and elsewhere are recognized as a manifestation of troubled emotions and thoughts, there is clear and present need to work with groups as well as individuals in promoting mental health and in preventing mental disorder.

In summary, the minority speakers made three contributions: (1) they alerted us to the requirement for prevention as a way of attacking both the incidence and prevalence of mental disorders; (2) they indicated the possibility of effective therapeutic intervention at the community institutional level, such as reducing unemployment and strengthening families to cope with adversity; and (3) they called attention to premature death of adults, homicides, and other forms of violence as public mental health problems. Beyond these insights, we discovered that minorities probably have had greatest influence on human rights movement among patients and former patients of the mental health service system. This movement was repeatedly characterized at our hearings as being similar to the freedom movement among blacks of the 1950s and the 1960s in the United States. The human rights movement for patients has taken inspiration from the civil rights movement and has acknowledged its roots. Thus, the freedom movement initiated by minorities to guarantee their political rights has been a powerful influence on the mental health movement and its concern with human rights of patients.

In a democratic and open society, when institutional rights and individual rights come into conflict with each other, individual rights should be favored. Institutions exist to serve individuals. This philosophical principle is not easily comprehended and fully understood. It is frequently set aside by imperialistic institutions that are more powerful than individuals and therefore throw weight around to promote their survival, even at the expense of the survival of individuals.

In the past, the opinions of mental health professionals regarding the diagnosis, treatment, and even the incarceration of patients were supreme and seldom challenged. All of this is changing now. Patient advocacy groups are forming all over the country. The state of New Jersey has created a Department of Public Advocacy which has dealt with such issues as patients' rights to counsel, to retain control over assets, and to receive treatment. The New Jersey unit claims that since this "(advocacy) service has been underway, (mental health) services have been upgraded, many through negotiation and some voluntarily." Involuntary commitment of the mentally ill has long been an issue. It was raised again by a state senator who testified that this issue was in need of further investigation "so that the fundamental rights of mentally ill people are protected." An issue that surfaced during the hearing was mentioned by a west coast representative of the Network Against Psychiatric Assault and had to do with "the right to refuse treatment." This speaker insisted that persons should be protected against what he called "involuntary psychiatric intervention." The issue has surfaced because of the increased use of drugs in some institutions. Earlier, it was mentioned that such therapy is almost the only mental health treatment received by people with disturbed emotions and thoughts in jail. It was the belief of the Network representative that "drugs are used for the benefit of the staff and not the patients." Several representatives of patients' rights groups that included some former patients, described scenes in institutions in which patients were impassive because they were "zonked out" on drugs. Such treatment was described as having a negative effect upon the organic system of some individuals. Indeed, the west coast representative of the Network Against Psychiatric Assault classified "forced drugging" as "cruel and unusual punishment."

The President's Commission was sufficiently impressed by what it heard to state in the report that "mental health programs and services must not disregard these values (the protection of human rights and the guarantee of freedom of choice). Each client or patient must have the maximum possible opportunity to choose the unique combination of services and objectives appropriate to his or her needs. This must include the option of preferring no services as well as the option of selecting particular services in preference to others" (President's Commission on Mental Health, 1978, p. 42). To give legislative support to these ideas, we recommended that "each State have a 'Bill of Rights' for all mentally disabled persons" (President's Commission on Mental Health, 1978, p. 44). After listening to a number of horror stories at the hearing in San Francisco, a young psychiatrist in training felt compelled to address the commission for the purpose of offering an opinion that might provide a context for understanding the accusations. He said, "We talk about the best ways to care for people and the best place now only because there has been significant improvement in the treatment of severe mental illness."

On the basis of this analysis, the following conclusions are presented:

(1) Unemployment, inadequate education, poor housing, slum community environments, and various forms of institutionalized discrimination such as sexism, racism, and elitism are stress-producing circumstances and also are barriers to effective service, and, therefore, are associated with the high incidence and prevalence of mental disorders in some populations and must be dealt with in any effective program of prevention.

(2) Recent immigrants, poor people, older people, racial and ethnic minorities, and women are high-risk populations for the development of mental disorders because of their extraordinary stress, their lack of opportunity to participate in decision-making structures and gain a measure of control over their social environment, the absence of some institutional supports that sustain individuals during periods of difficulty, and their experience of cross pressures due to contradictory role expectations.

(3) Priorities for mental health programs may vary by cultural groups, majority or minority status in society, and professional or lay perspective so that one group may emphasize prevention over treatment while another group may have a reverse set of priorities. It is important to recognize that these differential sets of priorities are real and are based on the varying existential histories of each group, their social location and the varying ways society has adapted to them. Thus, each set of priorities should be accepted as valid and a way should be found to accomodate the differences.

(4) Various therapies are needed to reach people in varying social locations in society. Because different populations have differentially developed capacities for verbal communication, a variety of approaches are needed to establish contact, such as art and dance therapies, self-improvement and environmental control activities, and others.

(5) Community support groups are means of relieving anxiety and generating sufficient confidence to face new experiences that could be troubling to the thoughts and emotions of individuals if faced alone and without continuous consultation; these support groups should be recognized as a form of therapy that does not require one to assume the role of patient to receive help.

(6) Definition of the intervention unit for the purpose of rendering mental health care must be expanded to include groups as well as individuals, if prevention as well as treatment is to be accomplished. This conclusion is based on evidence that family strife, institutionalized discrimination, and premature mortality are associated with interpersonal violence, intergroup hostilities, and severe stress due to permanent separation because of death.

(7) Training programs for professionals at all levels of the mental health care-giving system must include people who are bilingual and people who have indigenous knowledge of the various racial, ethnic, and other subcultural populations in the society. This approach would

insure the availability of mental health professionals who understand the unique needs of people in various groups and would enable individuals in such groups to trust in and identify with the care-giving system and believe that it would not put the interests of the care-giving system above those of the patient.

(8) Institutional practices that some professional mental health personnel believe are necessary and essential for the protection of society as well as the care of the mentally disordered patients are on a collision course with what many patients see as an invasion of their freedom and a denial of their constitutional and human rights. Assertions of the right to prescribe treatment deemed to be appropriate in terms of conventional professional standards is countered with assertions of the rights to refuse treatment that is described as inappropriate by the patient. A philosophical issue is involved in how to resolve institutional and individual rights when they are in contention with each other. In a democratic society, individual rights take precedence over institutional rights. In those cases where the individuals' rights are limited for the sake of others, those individuals must still be granted due process of the law and other constitutional safeguards.

At the public hearings of the President's Commission on Mental Health, patients, professionals, and members of the minority and the majority were all present. Persons in each category spoke from their own perspective. Quite possibly the truth lay *between* the different perspectives. The public hearings provided opportunities for the confrontation of various perspectives that contributed to a range of understanding that the commissioners did not have before the hearings. In the end, therefore, the minority report presented in this discussion could become the majority report of the commission as the ideas of members of minority and majority groups, and lay and professional persons are merged into meaningful recommmendations that incorporate the thesis and antithesis in a new synthesis. What was unique about the approach of the President's Commission on Mental Health is that it provided an opportunity for the data of this synthesis to be offered by the public rather than merely be the limited perspectives of mental health professionals or the dominant people of power in the majority.

The work of the President's Commission on Mental Health proved again what sociologist Robert Merton of Columbia University said several years ago—"(the) nonconforming minority in society represents the interests and ultimate values of the (society) more effectively than the conforming majority". (Merton, 1968, p. 421).

REFERENCES

Ewalt, J. R. The birth of the community mental health movement. In W. Barton & C. Sanborn (Eds.), *An assessment of the mental health movement.* Lexington: Lexington Books, 1977.

Joint Commission on Mental Illness and Health. *Action for mental health.* New York: John Wiley & Sons, 1961.

Merton, R. K. *Social theory and social structure.* New York: The Free Press, 1968.

National Institute of Mental Health. *An interview with Rosalynn Carter,* Mental Health Matters, a national broadcast radio program, 1977.

President's Commission on Mental Health. *Preliminary report to the president. Washington, D.C.: U.S. Government Printing Office, 1977.*

President's Commission on Mental Health. Report to the president, Washington, D.C.: U.S. Government Printing Office, 1978.

Washington J. Prison: A big business plays con game of rehabilitation. *Core* magazine, Winter/Spring, 1977.

Chapter 2

PROJECTED NEEDS FOR MENTAL HEALTH SERVICES

Morton Kramer
Nolan Zane

Estimating current and future needs for mental health services is not a simple matter. Ideally, it would be desirable to develop specific estimates of such needs for each segment of our population—for whites, as well as for black Americans, Hispanic Americans, Asian/Pacific Americans, American Indians, and Alaska natives who comprise the minority segment of the population. Unfortunately, the basic data required to make detailed estimates of needs for each of these groups are simply not available now. The report of the President's Commission on Mental Health recognized this serious gap in knowledge and recommended:

> ...immediate efforts to gather reliable data (including socioeconomic and demographic data) on the incidence of mental health problems and the utilization of mental health services. Particular attention should be paid to population groups within our society known to have special needs such as children, adolescents, the aged, women, and racial and ethnic minorities.
> Increased research efforts designed to produce greater understanding of the needs and problems of people who are underserved or inappropriately served or who are at a high risk for mental disorders. (President's Commission on Mental Health, 1978, p. 49)

Although the required data are lacking, especially on minority groups, available data on the prevalance rates of mental disorders, rates of use of mental health services, and population projections for the United States can be used to provide some indication of the dimensions of the problem the nation will be facing.

BACKGROUND INFORMATION

Needs Assessment

Determination of the needs of a population for mental health services is an essential component of the processes involved in planning a program of such services. Assessment strategies vary depending on the information sought. Hagedorn, Beck, Neubert, and Werlin (1976) describe six such strategies. Three focus on the determination of needs at the community level. The other three—the rates-under-treatment, social indicators, and epidemiologic survey approaches—are more appropriate for the purpose of this chapter, that is, the assessment of needs on a national basis. Accordingly, data reported from studies using any of these latter three approaches will serve as the empirical base for this discussion.

The rates-under-treatment approach is based on utilization data for services in a given area. It is assumed that needs for services can be grossly estimated from data on those who have previously received care or treatment. *The social indicators approach* assumes that estimates of need are reflected in statistics of social descriptors that are highly correlated with rates of mental disorders such as population density, income, family status, living arrangement, the role a person occupies in a family, education, marital status, etc. (Rosen, 1977). *Epidemiologic surveys of the non-institutionalized population* can, under certain conditions, provide comprehensive needs assessment data. Such a survey would require an operational definition of what constitutes a person in need of mental health services; standard case finding techniques for determining—in a probability sample of the population of a catchment area, city, county or state—the number of people who meet this definition; and standard methods for determining the specific services such persons require and the type of facility in which such services can best be provided (Kramer, 1976). No such surveys, however, have ever been carried out, primarily because of the lack of standardized case finding methods that could be used in such a large scale endeavor.

Each of the above approaches has disadvantages (Hagedorn, et al., 1976). For example, utilization data cannot render information on unmet needs and are subject to selection biases associated with socioeconomic, administrative, and other nosocomial factors. The use of prevalence data for estimating need is limited by the lack of reliable and valid morbidity statistics on the mental disorders. As Frost (1941) states in his classic essay on epidemiology:

> ...since description of the distribution of any disease in a population obviously requires that the disease must be recognized when it occurs, the development of epidemiology must follow and be limited by that of

clinical diagnosis and of the rather complex machinery required for the systematic collection of morbidity statistics and mortality statistics. (p. 496)

Thus far, the absence of standardized case-finding techniques that can be uniformly applied in population surveys to identify persons with mental disorder, reliable differential diagnostic procedures for determining the specific type of mental disorders associated with each case, and methods for assessing the duration of the disorder have prevented the collection of systematic epidemiological data. Currently, considerable effort is being devoted to developing instruments which may eventually be used for such purposes (Spitzer & Endicott, 1977; Weissman, Meyers, & Harding, 1977; Wing, Nixon, Mann, & Leff, 1977). Such developments take time and it will be a while before these instruments are available for large scale use.

Available Data

In the meantime, it is possible to use the results of various community surveys of the prevalence of mental disorders, rates of use of psychiatric facilities obtained from national and local reporting programs, and population projections of the Bureau of the Census to provide some estimates of the needs for mental health services by whites and non-whites within the next few years. The results of these computations will provide useful indicators of the national state of affairs. As already stated, the lack of systematic morbidity data based on standardized techniques for determining the presence of a mental disorder, its type, and its severity and uniform procedures for specifying types of services needed by the patient prevent a more definitive assessment of need for mental health services. A detailed discussion of these problems and their implications for mental health services research has been presented elsewhere (Kramer, 1976). This chapter hopes to give the reader some appreciation of the extensive research and development activities needed to develop a comprehensive data base for effective planning, monitoring, and evaluation of mental health services.

DEFINITIONS

To aid interpretation of the epidemiological and other data on mental disorder used in this chapter, definitions of several terms and concepts are given.

Mental health services.   Services established by governmental and non-governmental agencies, including those in the private sector, which apply available knowledge to accomplish the following tasks: (1) prevention of mental disorders and their associated disabilities; (2) detection of persons with mental disorders (case finding); (3) diagnosis, treatment, and rehabilitation of persons with such disorders; and (4) promotion of mental health.

Mental disorder.   Disorders defined and listed in the Diagnostic and Statistical Manual of the American Psychiatric Association, second edition, (1968).

Need for mental health services.   For purposes of the computations to be presented later, every person with a mental disorder will be considered in need of mental health services.

Epidemiology.   Epidemiology has been variously defined. Greenwood (1935) defined it simply as the study of mass aspects of disease. Clark (1953) defines it as a science that is concerned with the study of factors influencing the occurence and distribution of disease, defect, disability, or death in aggregations of individuals. Mechanic (1969) has described epidemiology as the study of distributions of disease, defects, and disabilities in populations and the various personal and environmental factors that affect the manifestation of such conditions. Gruenberg (1968) states that epidemiology relates observed distributions of disorders to the physical, biological, and social environments in which people live (Gruenberg, 1968).

Statistical ratios used in epidemiology.   Morris (1955) states: ''By contrast with clinical medicine, the unit of study in epidemiology is the group (including both the sick and the well), not the individual. Deaths, or any other event, are studied only if information can be obtained, or inferred, about the group in which the events occurred. The clinician deals with the cases. The epidemiologist deals with cases in their population. He may start with a population and seek out the cases in it, or start with cases and refer them back to a population, or what can be taken to represent a population. But always the epidemiologist ends up with some estimate of cases/population. In consequence, he can sometimes ask questions which the clinician may also ask, and get better or different information in reply. Sometimes he can ask questions that cannot be asked in clinical work at all'' (p. 395).

Epidemiological research uses a great variety of statistical methods. However, two basic ratios of cases to population used in epidemiologic studies of disease require some elaboration—the incidence rate and the prevalence rate (Kramer, 1957).

Incidence refers to the number of new cases of a disease occurring in a population during a specified interval. Thus, incidence determines the rate at which new cases occur in a group of individuals. "New" cases must be carefully defined—as, for example, the first or initial attack of a disease during an individual's lifetime. The rate is computed by taking the ratio of the number of "new" cases in the specified interval to the appropriate population group exposed to risk of attack. This rate may be made specific for a variety of factors—such as age, sex, marital status, and socioeconomic status—so as to describe the rates at which a disease develops in specific segments of the population. Such computations require classification of the total population and of cases of the disease by age, sex, etc.

Prevalence refers to the total number of cases of a disease present in a population group during a specified interval—the number of cases existing at the start of an interval plus the new cases that developed during the interval. The interval of observation must always be specified if a prevalence rate is to be correctly interpreted, for we may speak of the number of persons who are sick at any time during a given day, week, month, or other arbitrary interval (Dorn, 1951). The characteristics of individuals who are to be counted as cases (for example, all persons who have "active" disease within the interval of study) must also be carefully defined. The prevalence rate is computed by taking the ratio of the number of cases in the specified interval to the number of people in the appropriate population group for which the rate is being determined. In studies of chronic disease there are two commonly used prevalence rates: *point prevalence,* the number of cases of disease as of a given date, and *interval prevalence,* the number of cases present during a year. These rates may also be made specific for such factors as age, sex, geographic area, and socioeconomic status.

Rates of utilization of psychiatric facilities are modeled after the above rates. Thus, the treated incidence rate (the TI rate) is defined as the number of *new* admissions to a specified facility during a year per 100,000 population. The treated prevalence rate (the TP rate) is defined as the number of persons under care of the specified facility as of a given day per 100,000 population (point prevalence) or the number of persons under care of the facility during a year per 100,000 population (interval prevalence).

The relationship of the "true" rates (as determined in an epidemiologic survey) to the "treated" or administrative rates is described in detail in another reference (Kramer, 1969).

Race.   The morbidity, facility utilization, and population data used in this chapter specific for race follow the definitions of the Census Bureau. In the 1970 Census of Population persons were asked to indicate their race by selecting one of the following categories: white; Negro or black; (American) Indian; Japanese, Chinese, or Filipino; Hawaiian; Korean; or other (specify). The white population includes persons who indicated the "other race" category and furnished written entries that should correctly be classified with the white category. As of the 1970 census, the white population was 178,098,000 and the non-white, 25,138,000. Blacks constitute the largest part of the non-white population, accounting for 90 percent of this group. The remaining 10 percent of this category includes the other racial groups listed above. The reader should note that Hispanic-Americans are not a separate group of this classification. The Census Bureau did prepare separate tabulations for the Spanish language population, but morbidity data and population projections required for this chapter are not available for this category of persons.

Until recently, the collection of data on utilization of mental health facilities by race was opposed by various governmental, professional, and lay organizational groups who feared that such data would be used in detrimental ways (Kramer, 1973). The realization that such data are required for the planning of mental health programs resulted in periodic sample surveys carried out on the federal level to determine the patterns of use of psychiatric facilities by race in the United States.

CHANGES IN PATTERNS OF USE OF PSYCHIATRIC FACILITIES

According to the census returns from 1950, 1960, and 1970, about 1 percent of the United States population were inmates of institutions (U.S. Bureau of Census, 1953, 1963, 1973). There was a change between 1950 and 1970 in the number of persons in institutions per 100,000 population by type of institution. Overall, there was a slight increase in the rate for all institutions combined (from 1,035 to 1,047 per 100,000). Sizeable decreases occurred in resident rates for two classes of institutions—a 47 percent decrease for mental institutions (from 405 to 214 per 100,000) and an 84 percent decrease in hospitals for the tuberculous (from 50 to 8 per 100,000). There was an 8 percent decrease in the rate for correctional institutions (from 175 to 161 per 100,000). A 38 percent increase occurred in the resident rate of training schools for juvenile delinquents (from 24 to 33 per 100,000), and an 11 percent increase in homes and schools for the mentally handicapped (from 89 to 99 per 100,000). A 133 percent increase occurred in the population of homes for the aged and dependent (from 196 to 456 per 100,000). The rate for all other institutions—detention homes, homes for unwed mothers, homes for neglected and dependent children, chronic disease hospitals, and homes and schools for the physically handicapped—decreased from 96 to 75 per 100,000.

Although persons in mental institutions accounted for the largest portion of the institutional population in both 1950 and 1960—39 and 33 percent, respectively—by 1970 they represented only 20 percent of the institutional population, with persons in homes for the aged and dependent accounting for the largest portion (44%) and inmates of correctional institutions the third largest portion (15%).

The trends in the composition of the institutional population varied markedly by race and sex. This is shown in Table 1, which demonstrates the changes that occurred in the percent of the total population of each race-sex group in institutions by type of institution between 1950 and 1970.

The number of people in state and county mental hosptals continued to decrease quite rapidly, so that by the end of 1975 the number of resident patients in those institutions (191,391) was 34 percent of the number at the end of 1955 (558, 922), the year in which the mental hospital population was at its highest level (President's Commission on Mental Health, Vol. III, 1978). This striking decrease was brought about by a series of events that followed upon the enactment of the National Mental Health Act of 1946. The succeeding years witnessed an extraordinary amount of activity in basic, clinical, field, applied, and administrative research in the mental health field (Segal, Boomer, & Bouthilet, 1975) in the application of the resultant findings to the planning and implementation of community mental health programs (Kramer, 1975) and in the training of all types of mental health personnel who were required to meet the manpower needs resulting from these increases in research and service activities (Arnhoff & Kumbar, 1973).

Several events occured during the 1950s and 1960s which were responsible for sizable reductions in the population of state mental hospitals. During these years increasing numbers of outpatient clinics, inpatient psychiatric services of general hospitals (National Institute of Mental Health, 1972), and nursing homes for the ages were established. Innovations in treatment of the acutely ill (Galioni, Adams, & Tallman, 1953), psychosurgery (National Intitute of Mental Health, 1951; 1952; 1954) and group psychotherapy, the open hospital, and other programs were designed to counteract the dehumanizing effect of long-term institutionalization in the large mental hospitals. There were also exposés of the shameful state of affairs in many of the large state institutions. These changes helped professionals, lawmakers, and the laity develop an interest in finding alternative ways of providing care for the mentally ill. The introduction of tranquilizers brought about still further changes in programs for the care of the mentally ill and the locus where such care would be provided (Gallant & Simpson, 1976; Swazey, 1974). The increasingly widespread use of psychoactive drugs since 1955 in inpatient

Table 2-1
Number and Percent of Persons in Institutional Population
by Type of Institution, Race & Sex, U.S. 1950, 1960, 1970

Type of Institution	White			Non-White		
	1950	1960	1970	1950	1960	1970
	Males					
	Number					
Total	791,150	889,156	871,554	158,478	227,669	254,773
	Percent					
Total	100.0	100.0	100.0	100.0	100.0	100.0
Mental Institutions	36.4	32.9	23.0	25.6	21.7	17.4
Homes for the Aged & Dependent	17.8	20.0	32.4	4.6	4.6	8.5
Correct'l. Institutions	20.9	23.1	20.6	54.4	54.5	52.7
Training Schools for Juvenile Delinquents	2.3	2.6	3.5	3.9	4.8	8.6
Homes & Schools for Mentally Hand'cp'd.	8.2	9.8	11.5	2.3	3.2	5.1
Tuberculosis Hospitals	5.0	3.8	0.9	5.0	5.3	1.4
All Other	9.4	8.5	8.1	4.1	5.9	6.2
	Females					
	Number					
Total	560,002	692.455	913,531	57,216	77,687	86,861
	Percent					
Total	100.0	100.0	100.0	100.0	100.0	100.0
Mental Institutions	45.2	37.3	17.5	55.1	46.3	33.3
Homes for the Aged and Dependent	25.8	39.5	65.5	6.9	11.0	29.2
Correct'l. Institutions	1.3	1.2	0.8	9.9	10.6	7.4
Training Schools for Juvenile Delinquents	1.9	1.2	1.0	3.8	4.4	5.5
Homes & Schools for Mentally Hand'cp'd.	11.1	10.7	8.7	5.6	8.0	10.5
Tuberculosis Hospitals	4.1	1.8	0.4	10.5	8.5	1.9
All Other	10.5	8.3	6.0	8.2	11.2	12.2

NOTE: U.S. Bureau of the Census, Persons in Institutions, 1950, 1960, and 1970 and outpatient care of the mentally ill and, indeed, in all aspects of medical practice, provided much of the impetus for accelerating the pace of development of improved methods for the treatment and rehabilitation of persons with mental disorders and in the development of community programs for the prevention and control of mental disorders (Mechanic, 1969).

Also in 1954, the New York State Legislature enacted the Nation's first Community Mental Health Services Act (Forstenzer, 1964). Finally, the passage of the Mental Health Study Act in 1955 established the Joint Commission on Mental Illness and Mental Health for the purpose of analyzing and evaluating needs and resources of the mentally ill in the U.S. as a basis for making recommendations for a national mental health program (P.L. 84-182, 1955). This eventually led to the passage, in 1963, of the Mental Retardation Facilities and Community Mental Health Centers Construction Act (P.L. 84-164, 1963). This law, and similar ones enacted by various states, stimulated the development of programs that accelerated the shift in the primary locus of care of the mentally ill from state hospitals to facilities located in the community.

In effect, these programs have discouraged the use of state hospitals for the treatment and rehabilitation of persons with mental disorders by encouraging the creation and use of community mental health centers and other community-based services (Arnhoff, 1975; Becker and Shulberg, 1976). These programs have also discouraged the use of mental hospitals for elderly patients with chronic brain syndromes associated with cerebral arteriosclerosis and senile brain disease by encouraging the use of nursing homes and other facilities for the aged (Kramer, Taube, and Redick, 1973). Medicare and Medicaid legislation reinforced these administrative decisions so that there are now far more aged mentally ill in nursing homes than in mental hospitals (President's Commission on Mental Health, 1978). These policies played a major role in bringing about the large increase in the number of residents of homes for the aged and dependent noted earlier.

There were dramatic changes in locus of delivery of mental health services, as well, beginning in 1955—the year in which the first decrease occurred in the state mental hospital population after more than 100 years of continuous increase. In 1955, state and county mental hospitals accounted for almost half of the total patient care episodes[1], provided by all the psychiatric facilities in the U.S., with a rate of 505 per 100,000. By 1973, this portion had decreased to 12 percent of the total episodes, with a rate of 313 per 100,000. By then, only ten years after the passage of the original Community Mental Health Centers Act, community mental health centers accounted for 23 percent of the total episodes, almost twice the inpatient episodes provided by state hospitals. The shift in the primary locus of delivery of mental health services from the state mental hospitals to community mental health centers and other community-based facilities reflects a major modification of service programs and the initiation of new services within the mental health field. Use of the community and its resources as the medium for the treatment and rehabilitation of persons with mental disorders represents a significant step toward adequate mental health care for minorities (Sue and Sue, 1971; Morales. 1976). The President's Commission found, however, that significant barriers to appropriate mental health care for minority groups still exist and emphasized that "many patients needing treatment will not seek care if providers are not sensitive to their culture or unable to speak their language." To meet the particular needs of minority populations, the Commission recommended that:

"Mental Health Service programs should:

a. actively involve ethnic and racial minorities in planning and developing services;
b. provide culturally relevant services and staff them with bilingual, bicultural personnel; and
c. contract with minority community-based organizations for delivery of services." (President's Commission on Mental Health, 1978, p. 21)

Thus, much still remains to be done, and a needs assessment should maximize the possibility of planning services for minority populations in accordance with their needs (Siegal, Attkisson, and Cohn, 1977). Moreover, one of the essential services a community mental health center is required to provide involves the screening of residents in the center's catchment area to determine their needs for mental health services and whether those in need should be treated at a center or at some other type of facility. In their review of needs assessment in the mental health field, Siegal, *et al.* (1977) recommend that local mental health programs should not undertake prevalence studies to assess needs due to their cost, complexity, and methodological difficulties. However, they indicate that a familiarity with findings of the major psychiatric epidemiology studies will enhance the community assessment procedure. These findings from prevalence studies of the non-institutionalized population and from other studies of patterns of use of psychiatric facilities provide rates specific for age, sex, race, socio-economic status, other demographic variables, and diagnosis that identify high risk groups. The following sections of this chapter will illustrate how available data can be used to identify high risk groups and to develop projections of needs for mental health services on a nationwide basis. These examples will provide models that may aid in planning community-based programs which may be of most utility to minority individuals with mental disorders.

PROTECTION OF NEEDS FOR MENTAL HEALTH SERVICES

Illustrative high risk groups

Redick and Johnson (1974) have reported results from their survey study of admission rates to state and county mental hospitals and outpatient facilities from the U.S. for the year 1970 specific for marital status, living arrangements, and family characteristics. They found high admission rates for female, heads of families, as well as for children living in female-headed families, in families headed by a non-parental relative, and with non-related individuals. Two other high risk groups consistently identified in other studies were children from low income families and those from broken homes (Pollack, 1968). Kramer, Rosen, and Willis (1973) highlighted these observations in their discussion of high risk groups that should be singled out for special attention in the planning of community mental health services.

Many of these high risk conditions are closely related. For instance, female-headed families are, by definition, broken families, and a high proportion of them subsist on incomes below the poverty level. For each of the high-risk groups listed, a greater portion of non-White children than White children are represented. In 1970, a greater percentage of non-White children than White children were in families with a female head (28.5 vs. 8.5), an "other relative" head (7.0 vs. 1.5), a poverty level income (40.0 vs. 10.7), a broken home (31.4 vs. 10.3), and only nonrelated individuals (1.1 vs. .5). Except for the last category, the proportion of non-White children in each high risk group is at least three times greater than the respective portion of White children. These data suggest that minorities will continue to constitute a high-risk group with an increasing need for mental health services.

Implications of expected changes in the composition of the population for the mental health services

The preceding section suggested that the need for mental health services, for minorities in particular, will increase. An estimation of the magnitude of this increase can be made by considering the impact population changes in the U.S. are likely to have on the number of White and non-Whites who may be expected to use mental health services.

Estimated population changes
for the U.S. 1970-1985

The 1985 population estimate used in these computations is the
Census Bureau's Series II projection (U.S. Bureau of Census, 1975). The
projection is a moderate one. It is based on the estimated July 1, 1974
population and assumes a slight reduction in mortality, an annual net
immigration of 460,000 per year and an ultimate cohort fertility level at the
replacement level of 2.1[2] average lifetime births per woman.

Table 2 indicates the expected changes in the composition of the
population of the U.S. between 1970 and 1985 specific for age and race. By
1985, the population will have increased to about 234.1 million people, an
increase of 15.2 percent from 1970 (203.2 million). The increase will be 13
percent for Whites (from 177.7 to 200.5 million) and 32 percent for non-
Whites (from 25.5 to 33.5 million). Non-whites are expected to constitute
about 14 percent of the population in 1985, compared to 13 percent in
1970. The relative increases expected in the size of each age group of the
non-White population range from 87 percent in the age group 25-34 years
to seven percent in the age group under 15 years. These increases are
considerably in excess of those in the White population, which range from
56 percent in the age group 25-34 years, to three percent in age group
45-64 years. The number of White children under 15 will decrease by nine
percent. Of particular importance is that large relative increases will be
occurring in those age groups which characteristically have high—usually
the highest—incidence and prevalence rates of mental disorder and high
rates of use of mental health facilities. For instance, in 1972 th highest rates
first admissions to state and county mental hospitals were reported for the
age groups 25-34 and 35-44 years. These groups also account for the largest
relative increases in persons (25-34: 60 percent; 35-44: 35.7 percent). The
non-White population will experience a greater percent increase than the
White population for both of these high-risk age groups (87.2 vs. 56.1 and
44.8 vs. 34.5, respectively).

Table 3 demonstrates how the greater relative population increase for
non-Whites compared to Whites for each age group from 1970 to 1985
would be reflected in future annual admission to psychiatric facilities. The
overall relative increase in non-White annual admission will be more than
twice that of the White population. This differential rate of increase in
annual admissions suggests, that in terms of the number of individuals
developing a mental disorder which will require mental health services by
1985, a much greater portion of the non-white population compared to the
white population will require such services.

As noted previously, the approximate nature of data collected by state
and national reporting programs as a means of estimating the need for
mental health services must be underscored. The primary problem centers
on the difficulty such programs have in obtaining unduplicated counts of

Table 2-2
U.S. populations, actual 1970[a] and estimated 1985[b], and
numerical and percentage change in U.S. populations:
1970-1985, by age and color

Age (Years)	1970			1985		
	Total	White	Nonwhite	Total	White	Nonwhite
	Population in Thousands					
Total	203,212	177,749	25,463	234,069	200,548	33,521
Less than 15 years	57,900	49,002	8,898	53,892	44,382	9,510
15-24 years	35,441	30,652	4,789	38,496	32,087	6,409
25-34 years	24,907	21,779	3,128	39,846	33,989	5,857
35-44 years	23,089	20,328	2,761	31,332	27,334	3,998
45-64 years	41,810	37,658	4,152	43,844	38,673	5,171
65 years & over	20,065	18,330	1,735	26,659	24,083	2,576
	Change in No. of Persons (in thousands) 1970-85			Percent Change in No. of Persons 1970-85		
Total	30,457	22,799	8,058	15.2	12.8	31.6
Less than 15 years	-4,008	-4,620	612	-6.9	-9.4	6.9
15-24 years	3,055	1,435	1,620	8.6	4.7	33.8
25-34 years	14,939	12,210	2,729	60.0	56.1	87.2
35-44 years	8,243	7,006	1,237	35.7	34.5	44.8
45-64 years	2,034	1,015	1,019	4.9	2.7	24.5
65 years and over	6,594	5,753	841	32.9	31.4	48.5

[a] U.S. Bureau of the Census, *U.S. Census of Population, 1970, General Population Character-istics* PC(1)-B1, Table 52.
[b] U.S. Bureau of the Census, *Current Population Reports,* Series P-25, No. 601, Oct. 1975, Table 8 (Series II projection — projection based on the estimated net immigration of 400,000 per year and an ultimate cohort fertility level (average number of lifetime births per woman) at the replacement level figure of 2.1.

individuals who receive services, compared to counts of episodes of care and admission actions. The psychiatric case register of Monroe County, New York,[3] is now the only data collection operation in the U.S. that can provide systematic unduplicated counts of people who receive services for mental disorders. It thus serves as a source of basic data for answering a variety of questions that cannot be answered in national and state reporting programs. Such data are still subject to the limitation that they are administrative-type epidemiologic data rather than so-called "true" epidemiologic data. Another limitation of register data is that the diagnoses

Table 2-3

Effect of population changes expected to occur in the U.S. between 1970 and 1985 on annual admissions to psychiatric facilities,[a] assuming no change in annual age-color specific admission rates during interval

Age (Years)	1970 (Estimated)[b]			1985 (Projected Estimate)[c]		
	Total	White	Nonwhite	Total	White	Nonwhite
	Number of admissions					
Total	2,529,586	2,095,927	443,659	3,134,753	2,506,087	628,666
Less than 18 yrs.	450,036	370,555	79,481	419,090	333,607	85,483
18-24 years	453,686	376,319	77,367	538,807	425,734	113,073
25-44 years	961,734	770,053	191,681	1,442,245	1,121,475	320,770
45-64 years	543,391	472,118	71,273	573,608	484,843	88,765
65 years and over	120,739	106,882	13,857	161,003	140,428	20,575
	Change in No. of Admissions 1970-85			Percent change in No. of Admissions 1970-85		
Total	605,167	410,160	195,007	23.9	19.6	45.0
Less than 18 years	-30,946	-36,948	6,002	-6.9	-10.0	7.6
18-24 years	85,121	49,415	35,706	18.8	13.1	46.2
25-44 years	480,511	351,422	129,089	50.0	45.6	67.3
45-64 years	30,217	12,725	17,492	5.6	2.7	24.5
65 years and over	40,264	33,546	6,718	33.3	31.4	48.5

[a]Psychiatric facilities include State and county mental hospitals, private mental hospitals, V.A. psychiatric inpatient services, general hospital psychiatric inpatient services, community mental health center inpatient and outpatient services and all other outpatient psychiatric services except those of the Veterans Administration.

[b]Calculated by applying the admission rates for 1971 to the U.S. population for 1970. (Source: U.S. Bureau of the Census, U.S. Census of Population, 1970, General Population Characteristics, PC(1)-B1, Table 52).

[c]Calculated by applying the admission rates for 1971 to the projected U.S. population for 1985 (Source: U.S. Bureau of the Census [1975]: Current Population Reports, Series P-25, No. 601, Table 8, Series II Projection).

reported to it are dependent on the diagnostic practices and biases of the mental health personnel in the various facilities that report to the register.

The following example demonstrates how expected population changes have implications for the treated incidence and treated prevalence of a major mental disorder, schizophrenia. Although only schizophrenia is considered in this example, the same reasoning applies to the treated incidence and treated prevalence of affective disorders, organic brain syndromes, neuroses, and personality disorders.

*Treated incidence and prevalence of schizophrenia
for Monroe County, New York, 1970*

The treated incidence and treated prevalence rates were categorized by race, sex, and age for Monroe County, N.Y. (Babigian, 1975). The age-adjusted incidence rate for non-White males (1.6 per 1,000) is 2.16 times that for white males (.74 per 1,000), while the rate for non-white females (1.31 per 1,000) is 2.43 times that for white females (.53 per 1,000). The non-White rates are considerably in excess of the White rates in every age group for both males and females. Except for the age group 15-24 years, the non-White rate is more than twice that of the White rate. The rates rise to a maximum in the age group 15-24 years for both White males (2.56 per 1,000) and non-White males (3.58 per 1,000). Female rates reach maximum in the age group 25-34 years (1.30 per 1,000 for Whites and 3.22 per 1,000 for non-White females) (Kramer, 1978).

With respect to prevalence, the age adjusted rate for non-White males (7.89 per 1,000) is 1.77 times that for White males (4.46 per 1,000) and that for non-White females (6.15 per 1,000) is 1.34 times that for their White counterparts (4.59 per 1,000). Except for the female age group 15-24 years, non-White rates for males and females greatly exceed the corresponding White rates in every age group. Maximum rates for males and White females occur in the age group 35-44 years (17.11 per 1,000 for non-White males, 9.30 per 1,000 for White males, and 9.30 per 1,000 for White females). The non-White female rate reaches a maximum in the age group 45-54 years (16.50 per 1,000). The higher treated incidence and prevalence rates for the non-White population compared to the White have been noted by many other investigators (Yolles and Kramer, 1969; Malzberg, 1940; Pasamanick, 1964; President's Commission on Mental Health, Vol. III, 1978).

Probability of developing schizophrenia

The consequences of treated incidence rates of the level reported for Monroe County may be further illustrated by using these rates to determine the probability of a person born in 1970 having at least one admission to a psychiatric facility at some time during his or her lifetime. This index has been used frequently to estimate the probability of a person developing schizophrenia at some time during its lifetime. This probability is a function of the treated incidence rates and of the mortality rates of the life table used in the computation. When the age-sex-race specific treated incidence rates are applied to their respective life tables, the following probabilities are obtained.

White males	4.8%	Non-white males	10.0%
White females	3.9%	Non-white females	8.9%

Thus, the probability of a non-white males developing schizophrenia which requires psychiatric services is 2.1 times that of White males, while the corresponding probability ratio for females is 2.3.

The hypothetical nature of these estimates must be noted. They are based on the assumption that an individual born in Monroe County will live in a stable population subjected throughout his/her lifetime to the stated levels of mortality and the stated treated incidence rates of schizophrenia for the year 1970. The probabilities of developing schizophrenia, particularly for the non-White population, are among the highest reported. It is impossible, however, to determine the extent to which such racial differences may be due to a bias on the part of psychiatrists to diagnose blacks and other minorities as schizophrenics more frequently than whites and to diagnose them less frequently as affectively ill. Babigian, Gardner, Miles, and Romano (1965) studied the consistency with which specified diagnostic terms are applied by psychiatrists in the multiple agencies that report to the registrar. For patients with one or more episodes of psychiatric services following their initial one, 79 percent of them received the same diagnosis on the second contact as on the first. Chronic brain syndrome was the most reliable diagnostic category (92 percent). For schizophrenia, the diagnostic consistency was 70 percent and for affective psychosis, 40 percent. The time interval between consecutive contacts did not materially affect consistency. Unfortunately, racial differences in diagnostic consistency were not reported. Tarter, Templer, and Hardy (1975) found that apart from organic disorders, inter-judge agreement between highly experienced psychiatrists on other major diagnostic categories was poor. There was less than 50 percent agreement on neurotic and personality disorders and slightly more than 50 percent agreement on psychotic disorders. Simon, Fleiss, Gurland, Stiller, and Sharpe (1973) examined the differences between a hospital staff diagnosis and a project staff diagnosis using techniques developed in the US-UK Diagnostic Study (Cooper, Copeland, Brown, Harris, and Gourlay, 1972). According to the hospital staff diagnosis, a diagnosis of schizophrenia rather than affective illness was given far more frequently to Blacks than to Whites. There was no significant association between race and the project staff diagnosis. Studies of this type are needed to determine the extent to which schizophrenia may be over-diagnosed and affective disorders underdiagnosed in the minority population in the Monroe County facilities as well as other psychiatric facilities in the nation.

Estimated incidence, 1970 and 1985

Table 4 shows the estimated number of new cases (incidence) of schizophrenia in the U.S. that would have entered treatment in 1970, if

Monroe County T. I. rates specific for age-sex-race applied, and the corresponding number expected in 1985, *assuming no change in T.I. rates.* There would be an overall increase of 26.2 percent in the annual number of new cases, of which the relative increase for non-Whites (42.9 percent) is over twice that for Whites (20.7 percent). The relative increases vary in each age group and are the same as the corresponding relative increases in the population of the U.S. in the specific age group. For example, in the age group 25-34 years, the annual number of new cases in the White population would have increased by 56 percent and for the non-White population by 87 percent. Of particular interest is the change in the population under 15 years. While there would be a decrease of nine percent in White cases, a seven percent increase is expected for non-Whites.

Although the relative increases for each race-age group correspond to their respective population gains, a noteworthy point is that the overall percentage increase in expected numbers of new cases of schizophrenia exceeds the overall percentage increases for the general population. This occurs because the higest treated incidence rates for schizophrenia are in those age groups in which the expected relative increases in population are also the highest: 15-24 years; 25-34 years; 35-44 years (see Table 4 for increases). For this reason, the expected relative increase in total population for whites is 13 percent and for non-Whites is 32 percent, but the corresponding increases in new cases of schizophrenia would be 21 percent and 43 percent, respectively.

Indeed, it cannot be emphasized too strongly that the incidence of schizophrenia will continue to increase until research produces the knowledge needed to prevent its occurance. This prediction is based on the assumption that there will be no radical change in the diagnostic system or in the way it is applied by mental health professionals. As of now, it is impossible to forecast the date by which sufficient knowledge about the etiology of this disorder and, equally important, the methods needed to apply this knowledge, will have been developed. Even if a major research breakthrough did occur, the likelihood of achieving significant reductions in the number of new cases quickly seems quite small in view of the large increases expected in the size of the population groups in which the risk of acquiring this disorder is known to be high. Very effective and efficient methods of prevention would be required to counterbalance the increases in annual numbers of new cases that can be expected to occur as a result of the population gains shown in Table 2 (Kramer, 1978).

Estimated prevalence, 1970 and 1985

A consideration of factors that affect the treated prevalence of mental disorders (e.g., the number of cases under care in the population as of a given moment in time) indicates that prevalence will increase. Prevalence is

Table 2-4

Effect of population changes expected to occur in the U.S. between 1970 and 1985 on annual number of new cases of schizophrenia coming under care, assuming no change in annual age-color specific treated incidence rates during interval.[a]

Age (Years)	1970 (Estimate)[b]			1985 (Projected Estimate)[c]		
	Total	White	Nonwhite	Total	White	Nonwhite
	New cases during year					
All ages	147,139	110,982	36,157	185,649	133,998	51,651
Less than 15 years	5,297	2,450	2,847	5,262	2,219	3,043
15-24 years	64,596	51,495	13,074	71,403	53,906	17,497
25-34 years	35,388	27,224	8,164	57,773	42,486	15,287
35-44 years	17,919	14,026	3,893	24,497	18,860	5,637
45-64 years	22,866	14,687	8,179	25,269	15,082	10,187
65 years and over	1,100	1,100	—	1,445	1,445	—
	Change in number of new cases 1970-85			Percent change in number of new cases 1970-85		
All ages	38,510	23,016	15,494	26.2	20.7	42.9
Less than 15 years	-35	-231	196	-0.7	-9.4	6.9
15-24 years	6,834	2,411	4,423	10.6	4.7	33.8
25-34 years	22,385	15,262	7,123	63.3	56.1	87.2
35-44 years	6,578	4,834	1,744	36.7	34.5	44.8
45-64 years	2,403	395	2,008	10.5	2.7	24.6
65 years and over	345	345	—	31.4	31.4	—

[a]Computations are based on the assumption that the 1970 age-color specific treated incidence rates for Monroe County, N.Y., applied to the actual population of the United States in 1970 and the projected population of the U.S. in 1985.

[b]Calculated by applying the 1970 age-color specific treated incidence rates for Monroe County, N.Y., to the age-color specific population of the U.S. for 1970, (U.S. Bureau of the Census, U.S. Census of Population, 1970 General Population Characteristics, PC(1)-B1, Table 52).

[c]Calculated by applying the 1970 age-color specific treated incidence rates for Monroe County, N.Y., to the projected U.S. age-color specific population for 1985 (U.S. Bureau of the Census, 1975: Current Population Reports, Series P-25, No. 601, Table 8 [Series II Projection]).

dependent not only on the incidence, but also on the duration of the disorder. Table 5 illustrates the changes to be expected in treated prevalence merely as a result of shifts in the size and age distribution of the population of the U.S. between 1970 and 1985. Again, assume that the age-race specific treated prevalence rates of Monroe County apply to the corresponding age-race population groups in 1985 as well as in 1970. Here, again, the relative increases in the various age groups would be the same as those in the general population. Racial comparisons resemble those for incidence. The percent increase in prevalence for non-Whites greatly exceeds that for Whites in each age category with the overall non-White increase (45 percent) being almost two times that for the Whites (25 percent), compared to those increases expected to occur in the general population (32 percent for non-Whites and 13 percent for Whites).

Demand for mental health services: Need vs. resources

The preceding discussion demonstrates the increase in the prevalence and incidence of mental disorders that will occur by 1985 as a result of population changes and advances in clinical medicine. The most striking and consistent finding is the dramatic percent increase in the number of non-White individuals who will have or will develop mental disorders and, consequently, require mental health services. The corresponding White increases are also significant, but of a lesser magnitude. In view of the increasing need for mental health services, it is of interest to speculate on the numbers of persons who would need these services and the extent to which available services will meet such needs. As mentioned previously, the basic instruments required for collecting the data needed to provide an answer have not been developed. However, it is possible to hypothesize varying levels of need (e.g., 2 percent, 10 percent, 20 percent) based on community surveys of prevalence of mental disorders, in which it is assumed that every person identified as a case "needs" mental health services (Pasamanick, Roberts, Lemkau, and Krueger, 1957; Dohrenwend and Dohrenwend, 1969). The comparison of these levels of needs with the utilization data on psychiatric facilities provides some rough estimates of the extent to which the demand for mental health services will be met. In addition, the application of these levels of need to data on mental health personnel yields various estimates of the intensity of care provided by the available sources of manpower.

Estimates of unmet needs for 1980 can be made assuming three levels of need for services: 2 percent, 10 percent, 20 percent, and assuming also that the utilization rates of the population will remain at the 1971 levels. Except for the two percent level of need, the percentage of unmet needs will

Table 2-5

Effect of population changes expected to occur in the United
States between 1970 and 1985 on annual number of cases of
schizophrenia under care (hospitalized and unhospitalized)
assuming no change in annual age-color specific treated
prevalence rates during interval.[a]

Age (Years)	1970 (estimate)[b]			1985 (Projected estimate)[c]		
	Total	White	Nonwhite	Total	White	Nonwhite
	Number of cases receiving care during year					
All ages	974,972	809,668	165,304	1,247,806	1,008,622	239,184
Less than 15 years	21,199	16,661	4,538	19,940	15,090	4,850
15-24 years	189,878	163,682	26,196	206,402	171,345	35,057
25-34 years	229,675	194,704	34,971	369,343	303,862	65,481
35-44 years	255,108	211,208	43,900	347,568	284,000	63,568
45-64 years	258,474	206,366	52,108	276,824	211,928	64,896
65 years and over	20,638	17,047	3,591	27,729	22,397	5,332
	Change in number of cases receiving care, 1970-85			Percent change in number of cases receiving care, 1970-85		
All ages	272,834	198,954	73,880	28.0	24.6	44.7
Less than 15 years	-1,259	-1,571	312	-5.9	-9.4	6.9
15-24 Years	16,524	7,663	8,861	8.7	4.7	33.8
25-34 Years	139,668	109,158	30,510	60.8	56.1	87.2
35-44 Years	92,460	72,792	19,668	36.2	34.5	44.8
45-64 Years	18,350	5,562	12,788	7.1	2.7	24.5
65 years and over	7,091	5,350	1,741	34.4	31.4	48.5

[a]Computation based on the assumption that the 1970 age-color specific treated
prevalence rates for Monroe County, N.Y., applied to the actual population of the United
States in 1970 and the projected population of the United States in 1985.

[b]Calculated by applying the 1970 age-color specific treated prevalence rates for Monroe
County, N.Y., to the age-color specific population of the U.S. for 1970 (U.S. Bureau of
the Census, U.S. Census Population, 1970 General Population Characteristics, PC(1)-B1,
Table 52).

[c]Calculated by applying the 1970 age-color specific treated prevalence rates for Monroe
County, N.Y., to the projected U.S. age-color specific population for 1985 (U.S. Bureau
of the Census, 1975: Current Population Reports, Series P-25, No. 601, Table 8 [Series II
Projection]).

be quite high in 1980. The assumption that 10 percent of the U.S. population is in need of psychiatric services appears to be a moderate estimate in view of the findings of a frequently quoted prevalence study (Pasamanick, *et al.*, 1957) and more recent studies by Regier, Goldberg, and Taube (1978), and Weissman, Meyers, and Harding, (1978). Assuming a 10 percent level of need more than 8 out of 10 people requiring mental health services in 1980 will not receive them through these agencies. With a 20 percent need of services, the proportion not receiving such services increases to 9 out of 10. A certain number will be treated by private psychiatrists, psychologists, and social workers, but these resources are quite limited. Of the 25,700 active psychiatrists in the U.S., only about one-half (13,000) are in office-based practice (National Center for Health Statistics, 1975). Private psychologists and psychiatric-social workers account for approximately seven and three percent of their respective professions (Cates, 1970; National Institute of Mental Health, 1973).

Prevalence rates of mental disorders can also be used to demonstrate the numbers of so-called "core" mental health professionals-psychiatrists, psychologists, psychiatric social workers, and nurses-that would be needed to provide varying levels of service to the population in need of mental health services. Assume that 10 percent of the population of the U.S. is in need of mental health services. Assume also that each person identified as a case of mental disorder required *six hours per year* of service from each member of a specialty team consisting of a *psychiatrist, psychologist, social worker,* and *psychiatric nurse.* This would require the following personnel for each specialty.

Year	Table 2-6 No. of persons in need	No. of personnel of each specialty required to provide six hrs. per patient per year
1970	20,321,000	81,284
1975	21,532,400	86,310
1980	22,867,600	91,470

Comparison of these numbers with those reported by the Task Panel on Mental Health Personnel for the President's Commission for the current supply of mental health personnel emphasizes the extreme shortages that exist. In the absence of more precise data, the panel used numbers of members in the respective professional societies and other data collected by the NIMH on manpower in mental health facilities to estimate the numbers of persons in each discipline (President's Commission on Mental Health, Vol. II, 1978). Thus, as of *1975* there were:

> Psychiatrists: 25,700 members of the American Psychiatric Association plus non-members of the APA who report a psychiatric specialization to the American Medical Association:
>
> Psychologists: 19,000 licensed/certified psychologists providing health services and an additional 3,700 qualified to do so;
>
> Social Workers: about 31,212 social workers working in mental health facilities;
>
> Psychiatric Nurses: about 39,000 registered nurses working in mental health facilities.

The Task Panel on Special Populations found that minorities are poorly represented in the mental health disciplines and that the supply of qualified professionals continues to lag behind the increasing demand for services (Presidents Commission on Mental Health, 1978). The Commission stated that:

> Fewer than 2 percent of all psychiatrists are Black, and data on other minorities are difficult to interpret because of the large number of foreign medical graduates of Asian or South American origin. A recent survey by the American Psychological Association estimates that of all doctoral level health service providers in psychology, 0.9 percent are Black, 0.7 percent Asian, 0.4 percent Hispanic, and 0.1 percent are American Indian. Social work and nursing are more representative of the population, with an estimated 15 percent of National Association of Social Workers members and 7 percent of nurses belonging to the American Nurses Association, Division of Psychiatric and Mental Health Nursing, coming from minority groups (p. 63).

The President's Commission was particularly concerned about the underrepresentation of racial minorities in mental health disciplines and recommended that a high priority be given to a multilevel effort to increase the number of minority mental health professionals who provide service as well as the number who are involved in teaching, research and administration.

DISCUSSION

The above findings delineate the dimensions of need for mental health services for specific population groups in the U.S. It should be noted that the projections based on utilization data are understated in that they have taken into account only the effect of expected population changes of various age, sex, and racial groups. If increases do occur in the rates of use of mental health facilities, the proportions presented would be increased over and above those described. In general, the trends reviewed present convergent evidence of the increasing need for mental health services for all segments of our population in the near future. It is also apparent that the resources required to meet this need adequately will not be available. At present, the portion of of non-White children living in family arrangements associated with a high risk of mental disorder is two to three times that for White children. These conditions partially account for the greater relative increase expected for non-Whites as compared to Whites with respect to the use of mental health services.

The Special Populations Subpanel on Mental Health of Black Americans has pointed to another major problem that must be taken into account in needs assessment for community programs:

> The thrust of many states toward deinstitutionalization has resulted in the discharge of thousands of long term state hospital patients all of whom are poor and many of whom are Black. They are returning to communities already underserved, without the concomitant transfer of resources to assist these communities in the development of new programs to address the needs of this new population. As noted above, the existing programs in these same communities are already deficient and faced with mandates which require additional staff and facilities will fall short in meeting needs they have been delegated to address unless some anticipatory action takes place (President's Commission on Mental Health, Vol. III, 1978, pp. 838-839).

All of the foregoing emphasizes that present and future demand for mental health services will be especially great for members of the minority population.

It is also important for planners and educators to take special note of the point highlighted by Regier, et al. (1977) "that mental disorder represents a major U. S. health problem, which although requiring active specialist attention, is beyond that which can be managed by the specialty mental health sector alone. Hence, there is a need both for a further integration of the general health and mental health care sectors and for a greater attention to an appropriate division of responsibility that will maximize the availability and appropriateness of services for persons with mental disorder. Given the limitations of specialty resources, improvements in the mental health training of primary health care providers are needed to maximize the quality of mental health care for those fully or partially dependent on the general medical practice sectors. In addition, greater attention must be focused on the human services sector and on the social and economic costs incurred by those with mental disorder who receive no mental health services from the 'health' arena—concerns which relate, at a minimum estimate to more than 3% of the population" (p. 693). Again it is the minority population which will be particularly affected.

The projection of large numbers of persons requiring mental health services emphasizes the need for morebasic and applied research on the biological, genetic, psychological, behavioral, social, and political factors that affect the etiology, duration, and outcome of mental disorders in persons from various age, sex, socioeconomic, and cultural groups. Such knowledge can facilitate the achievement of primary prevention and the development of more effective treatment and rehabilitation programs. Both of these purposes require more epidemiologic, statistical, and demographic research to acquire the relevant data. Indeed, these data are essential for the planning, monitoring, and evaluation of effective community mental health programs.

Despite the progress made in epidemiologic and biostatistical research on mental disorders, there remains a considerable agenda of unfinished business (Kramer, 1976). Besides the aforementioned difficulties associated with needs assessment, there are other high priority problems involving such areas as follow-up studies of former patients; attitudinal, cultural, and related factors affecting service utilization; classification of psycho-social and other factors related to mental disorders; development of social indicators on family units within which more than one social problem exists concurrently; data on mental health service delivery by mental health professionals in private practice and by medical practitioners; cost effectiveness research; the interrelationship of morbidity, social, and economic problems; simultaneous use of mental and other health services at the local level; and the development and utilization of automated mental health information systems.

Of particular importance for epidemiologic research is the establishment of several field research units with adequate and stable, long-term financing to design and implement studies that determine the extent to which community mental health programs are affecting the level of disability from mental disorders found in their respective catchment areas. Indeed, efforts to evaluate the effectiveness of such programs will continue to suffer many of the same shortcomings associated with past research projects if adequate resources—financial, manpower, scientific, and administrative—are not made available.

Other alternative delivery and treatment programs should be designed in response to the various needs of specific minority groups. Cass (1976) and Castro (1977) recommend the use of an action problem-oriented approach with a behavioral focus in treating Chicano and other minority and lower socio-economic clients. This approach is consistent with the low income client's expectations that emphasize the therapist as an active helper, the physical working through of mental problems, interpersonal as opposed to intrapersonal difficulties, and the importance of external environmentally-based factors in the instigation or exacerbation of such problems. A similar treatment model has been proposed by Brown, Stein, Huang, and Harris (1973) for Chinese-Americans. They also underscore the advantages of treating the Chinese-American patient in community based facilities close to its family residence and of utilizing paraprofessionals to compensate for the shortage of mental health professionals. Wilcox (1973) advocates more patient control over the treatment process in mental health programs serving Black communities. He suggests that this change invests the patient in both his/her own treatment and that of others.

These approaches are but a few in the growing number of innovative programs designed to improve mental health care for minorities. However, most of them will retain their hypothetical nature until the mental health needs of the various minority groups and the effectivenes of such efforts to meet those needs can be reliably assessed through research. This demand for basic and applied research as well as for qualified personnel in the mental health field becomes all the more pressing with the realization that the minority need for such services will increase dramatically in the near future. Indeed, this need represents a major challenge to the mental health profession, one with which it must reckon if it hopes to make a significant contribution to the realization of a healthy, pluralistic society.

FOOTNOTES

[1]Patient care episodes are defined as the sum of the number of patients under care of a specific type of facility at the beginning of the year and all the admission actions to these facilities during the following 12 months.

[2]Replacement level fertility is that level of fertility required for the population to replace itself with the projected mortality rate and in the absence of net immigrations.

[3]Babigian (1972) describes the historical development of the register.

REFERENCES

American Psychiatric Association. *Diagnostic and statistical manual of mental disorders.* 2nd ed. (DSM-II), 1968.

Arnhoff, F. N. Social consequences of policy toward mental illness. *Science,* 1975, *188,* 1277-1281.

Arnhoff, F. N. & Kumbar, A. H. *The nation's psychiatrists—1970 survey.* Washington, D.C.: American Psychiatric Association, 1973.

Babigian, H. M. The role of psychiatric case registers in the longitudinal study of psychopathology. In M. Roff, L. Robins, & M. Pollack (eds.) *Life history research in psychopathology,* Vol. 2 Minneapolis: University of Minnesota Press, 1972.

Babigian, H. M. Schizophrenia: Epidemiology. In A. M. Freeman, H. Kaplan, and B. J. Sadock (eds.), *Comprehensive textbook of psychiatry* (II), Vol. 1, ed. 2. Baltimore: Williams and Wilkins, 1975.

Babigian, H. M., Gardner, E. A., Miles, H. C., and Romano, J. Diagnostic consistency and change in a follow-up study of 1215 patients. *American Journal of Psychiatry,* 1965, *121,* 898-901.

Becker, A. and Schulberg, H. C. Phasing out state hospitals—a psychiatric dilemma. *New England Journal of Medicine,* 1976, *294,* 255-261.

Brown, T. R., Stein, K. M., Huang, K., and Harris, D. E. Mental illness and the role of mental health facilities in Chinatown. In S. Sue and N. Wagner (eds.), *Asian-Americans psychological perspectives.* Palo Alto, California: Science and Behavior Books, Inc., 1973.

Cass, J. M. Applicability of a behavioral model in serving the mental health needs of the Mexican American. In M. R. Miranda (ed.), *Psychotherapy with the Spanish-speaking: Issues in research and service delivery.* Monograph no. 3. Los Angeles: Spanish Speaking Mental Research Health Center, 1976.

Castro, F. G. *Level of acculturation and related considerations in psychotherapy with Spanish-speaking/Surnamed clients.* Occasional Paper no. 3, Los Angeles: Spanish Speaking Mental Health Research Center, 1977.

Cates, J. Psychology's manpower: Report on the 1968 national register of scientific and technical personnel. *American Psychologist,* 1970, *25,* 254-263.

Clark, E. G. An epidemiologic approach to preventive medicine. In H. R. Leavell, and E. G. Clark (eds.), *Textbook of preventive medicine.* New York; McGraw-Hill, 1953.

Cooper, J. E., Copeland, J. R. M., Brown, G. W., Harris, T., and Gourlay, J. A. Further studies on interviewer training and inter-rater reliability of the Present State Examination (PSE). *Psychological Medicine,* 1972, *7,* 517-523.

Cooper, J. E., Kendall, R. E., Gurland, B. J., Sharpe, L., Copeland, J. R. M., and Simon, R. *Psychiatric diagnosis in New York and London.* Maudsley Monograph no. 20. London: Oxford University Press, 1972.

Dohrenwend, B.P. and Dohrenwend, B. S. *Social status and psychological disorder.* New York: John Wiley & Sons, Inc., 1969.

Dorn, H. F. Methods of measuring incidence and prevalence of disease. *American Journal of Public Health*, 1951, *41*, 271-278.

Forstenzer, H. M. New York's new directions in mental health services. *State Government*, Autumn, 1964.

Frost, W. H. Epidemiology. In K. F. Maxcy (ed.), *Papers of Wade Hamptom Frost: A contribution to epidemiological method.* New York: Commonwealth Fund, 1941.

Galioni, E. F., Adams, F. H., Tallman, F. F. Intensive treatment of backward patients: A controlled pilot study. *American Journal of Psychiatry*, 1953, *109*, 576-583.

Gallant, D. M. and Simpson, G. M. (eds.). *Depression: Behavioral, biochemical, diagnostic and treatment concepts.* New York: Halstead Press, 1976.

Greenwood, M. *Epidemic and crowd diseases: An introduction to the study of epidemiology. and psychopathology.* Washington, D. C.: U. S. Government Printing Office,

Gruenberg, E. M. Epidemiology and medical care statistics. In M. M. Katz, J. O. Cole, and W. E. Barton (eds.), *The role and methodology of classification in psychiatry and psychopathology. Washington, D.C.: U.S. Government Printing Office,* 1968.

Hagedorn, H. J., Beck, K. H., Neubert, S. F., and Werlin, S. H. *A working manual of simple program evaluation techniques for community mental health centers.* DHEW Publication no. (ADM) 76-404. Rockville, MD: National Institute of Mental Health, 1976.

Kramer, M. A discussion of the concepts of incidence and prevalence as related to epidemiologic studies of mental disorders. *American Journal of Public Health*, 1957, *47*, 826-840.

Kramer, M. *Applications of mental health statistics.* Geneva: World Health Organization, 1969.

Kramer, M. Some perspectives on the role of biostatistics and epidemiology in the prevention and control of mental disorders. *Milbank Memorial Fund Quarterly*, 1975, *53*, 279-336.

Kramer, M. Issues in the development of statistical and epidemiological data for mental health services research. *Psychological Medicine*, 1976, *6*, 185-215.

Kramer, M. Population changes and schizophrenia, 1970-1985. In L. C. Wynne (ed.), *The nature of schizophrenia.* New York: John Wiley & Sons, Inc., 1978.

Kramer, M., Rosen, B. M., and Willis, E. M. Definitions of mental disorders in a racist society. In C. V. Willie, B. M. Kramer, & B. S. Brown, (eds.), *Racism and mental health.* Pittsburgh: University of Pittsburgh Press, 1973.

Kramer, M., Taube, C. A., and Redick, R. W. Patterns of use of psychiatric facilities by the aged: Past, present, and future. In C. Eisdorfer and M. P. Lawtan (eds.), *The psychology of adult development and aging.* Washington, D.C.: American Psychological Association, 1973.

Kramer, M., Taube, C. A., and Starr, S. Patterns of use of psychiatric facilities by the aged. Current status, trends, and implication. In *Aging in modern society.*

Psychiatric Research Report no. 23. Washington, D. C.: American Psychiatric Association, 1968.

Malzberg, B. *Social and biological aspects of mental disease*. Utica, N.Y.: State Hospitals Press, 1940.

Mechanic, D. *Mental health and social policy*. Englewood Cliffs, NJ: Prentice-Hall, Inc., 1969.

Morales, A. The impact of class discrimination and white racism on the mental health of Mexican-Americans. In C. A. Hernandez, M. H. Haug, and N. N. Wagner (eds.), *Chicanos: Social and psychological perspectives*, 2nd edition. St. Louis: C. V. Mosby Co., 1976.

Morris, J. N. Uses of epidemiology. *British Medical Journal*, 1955, *2*, 395-401.

National Institute of Mental Health. *Proceedings of the first research conference on psychosurgery*. DHS no. 16. Washington, D.C.: U.S. Government Printing Office, 1951.

National Institute of Mental Health. *Second research conference on psychosurgery*. DHS Publication no. 156. Washington, D.C.: U.S. Government Printing Office. 1952.

National Institute of Mental Health. *Third research conference on psychosurgery*. DHS Publication no. 221. Washington, D.C.: U.S. Government Printing Office, 1954.

National Institute of Mental Health. *Psychiatric services in general hospitals, 1969-1970*. Mental Health Statistics Series A, no. 11. DHEW Publication no. (HSM) 73-9099. Washington, D.C.: U.S. Government Printing Office, 1972.

National Institute of Mental Health. *Financing mental health care in the United States*. HEW Publication no. (HSM) 73-9117. Rockville, MD: National Institute of Mental Health, 1973.

Pasamanick, B., Roberts, D. W., Lemkau, P. V., and Krueger, D. E. A survey of mental disease in an urban population. I. Prevalence by age, sex, and severity of impairments. *American Journal of Public Health*, 1957, *47*, 923-929.

Pasamanick, B. Myths regarding prevalence of mental disease in the American Negro. *Journal of the National Medical Association*, 1964, *56*, 6-17.

Pollack, E. S. Monitoring a comprehensive mental health program. In L. M. Roberts, N. S. Greenfield, and M. H. Miller (eds.), *Comprehensive mental health: The challenge of evaluations*. Madison, Wisconsin: University of Wisconsin Press, 1968.

The President's Commission on Mental Health. *Report to the President: The Commission's Report and Recommendations*. Volume I, Washington, D.C., 1978, and Task *Panel Reports* submitted to The President's Commission on Mental Health. Appendix, Volumes II-IV, Washington, D.C., 1978.

Public Law 84-182—84th Congress, July 28, 1955. *Mental health study act of 1955*.

Public Law 88-164—88th Congress, October 31, 1963. *Mental retardation facilities and community mental health centers construction act of 1963*.

Redick, R. W. *Referral of discontinuations from inpatient services of state and county mental hospitals. United States, 1969.* Statistical Note 57. Rockville, MD: Biometry Branch, National Institute of Mental Health, 1971.

Redick, R. W. and Johnson, C. *Marital status, living arrangements and family characteristics of admissions to state and county mental hospitals and outpatient clinics, United States, 1970.* Statistical Note 100. Rockville, MD: Biometry Branch, National Institute of Mental Health, 1974.

Regier, D. A. Goldberg, I. D., and Taube, C. A. The de facto U.S. mental health services system: A public health perspective. *Archives of General Psychiatry,* 1978, *35,* 685-693.

Rosen, B. M. *A model for estimating mental health needs using 1970 Census socioeconomic data.* NIMH, U.S. Dept. of HEW, Series C., No., 9, DHEW Publications No. (ADM) 77-63, 1977.

Segal, J., Boomer, D. S., and Bouthilet, L. (eds.), *Research in the service of mental health—report of the research task force of the National Institute of Mental Health.* DHEW Publication no. (ADM) 75-236. Washington, D.C.: U.S. Government Printing Office, 1975:

Siegal, L. M., Attkisson, C. C., and Cohn, A. H. Mental health needs assessment: Strategies and techniques. In W. A. Hargreaves, C. C. Attkisson, and J. D. Sorenson (eds.), *Resource materials for community mental health evaluation.* 2nd edition. DHEW Publication no. (ADM) 77-328. Rockville, MD: National Institute of Mental Health, 1977.

Simon, R. J., Fleiss, J. L., Gurland, B. J., Stiller, P. R., and Sharpe, L. Depression and schizophrenia in hospitalized black and white mental patients. *Archives of General Psychiatry,* 1973, *28,* 509-521.

Spitzer, R. L. and Endicott, J. *Schedule for affective disorders and schizophrenia—Lifetime version (SADS-L).* Supported by NIMH Grants MH-21411 and MH-23864. Third edition, 1977.

Sue, S. and Sue, D. W. Chinese-American personality and mental health. *Amerasia Journal,* 1971, *1,* 36-49.

Swazey, J. P. *Chlorpromazine in psychiatry—A study of therapeutic innovation.* Cambridge, Massachusetts: Massachusetts Institute of Technology Press, 1974.

Tarter, R., Templer, D. W., and Hardy, C. Reliability of psychiatric diagnosis. *Diseases of the Nervous System,* 1975, *36,* 30-31.

U.S. Bureau of the Census. *U.S. census of population: 1950, Vol. IV, special reports, part 2, chapter C, institutional population.* Washington, D.C.: U.S. Government Printing Office, 1953.

U.S. Bureau of the Census. *Census of population: 1960 subject reports. Inmates of institutions.* Final Report PC (2) -8A.

U.S. Bureau of the Census. *Census of population: 1970 subject reports. Persons in institutions and other group quarters.* Final Report PC(2) -4E. Washington, D.C.: U.S. Government Printing Office, 1973.

U.S. Bureau of the Census. *Current population reports. Projections of the population of the United States: 1975-2050.* Series P-25, no. 601, Washington, D.C.: U.S. Government Printing Office, 1975.

Weissman, M. M., Meyers, J. K., and Harding, P. S. Psychiatric disorders in a U.S. urban community: 1975-1976. *American Journal of Psychiatry,* 1978, *135,* 459-462.

Wing, J. K., Mann, S. A., Leff, J. P., and Nixon, J. M. The concept of a 'case' in psychiatric population surveys. *Psychological Medicine,* 1978, *8,* 203-217.

Wing, J. K., Nixon, J. M., Mann, S. A., and Leff, J. P. Reliability of the PSE (ninth edition) used in a population study. *Psychological Medicine,* 1977, *7,* 515-516.

Yolles, S. F. and Kramer, M. Vital statistics. In L. Bellack and L. Loeb (eds.), *The schizophrenic syndrome.* New York: Grune & Stratton, In., 1969.

Chapter 3

THE SEARCH FOR HELP
Mental Health Resources for Mexican Americans and Anglo Americans in a Plural Society

Amado M. Padilla
Susan E. Keefe

Part of the human condition is to experience emotional problems and, at times, to seek help for those problems. Yet the perception of the nature of emotional problems, the particular sources appealed to for help, and reasons for consulting or failing to consult with various helping agents may all vary within and between cultural groups. This is true both when comparing cultures within a single society and cultures of diverse societies. Here we will examine the way in which members of two cultural groups in the United States, Mexicans and Anglos, confront their emotional problems and attempt to resolve them. Special attention is given to the sociocultural context encompassing the two groups and its impact on the way in which emotional problems are addressed.

Previous studies present evidence of specific differences between Mexican Americans and Anglos regarding utilization of mental health services. These studies (Bachrach, 1975; Jaco, 1960; Karno and Edgerton, 1969; Keefe, Padilla, and Carlos, 1978; Torrey, 1972) all demonstrate that Mexican Americans use professional mental health services at a lower rate than Anglos. To explain the difference, Jaco (1957, 1960) and Madsen (1969) contend that Mexican Americans are more likely than Anglos to rely on the extended family for support when experiencing emotional problems. Extensive reliance on the family by Mexican Americans is believed to be the result of a reluctance to expose personal problems to non-family mem-

77

bers, as well as strong attachment to the kin group in particular (Madsen, 1964; Rubel, 1966). Anglos, on the other hand, are assumed to be more willing to discuss their problems outside the family circle. Other researchers have suggested that Mexican Americans are more likely than Anglos to consult physicians about emotional problems (Karno and Edgerton, 1969) and that Mexican Americans have resources unavailable to Anglos such as ethnic community workers (Grebler, Moore and Guzman, 1970; Moll, Rueda, Reza, Herrera, and Vasquez, 1976; Torrey, 1972) and *curanderos* or "folk healers" (Creson, McKinley, and Evans, 1969; Kiev, 1968; Madsen, 1964; Torrey, 1972).

An exception to the studies cited above is that of Bloom (1975), who investigated utilization patterns of residents in Pueblo, Colorado for the time periods of 1960 and 1970. Bloom observed that in 1960, Mexican Americans underutilized mental health services, whereas, in 1970, he noted an overutilization of such services. After considering many of the standard explanations to account for the underutilization of services in 1960 (e.g., Karno and Edgerton, 1969), Bloom argued that the overutilization in 1970 could be explained by one or more of the following: (a) In 1970 Mexican Americans' improved image of the mental health delivery system due, possibly, to the shorter length of hospitalization; (b) The larger number of Chicano staff members employed throughout the service delivery system, which possibly made services more accessible to Mexican Americans; (c) The availability of financial assistance to low income individuals that made it possible for persons to receive inpatient care in a private facility; and (d) The increased number of referrals from the criminal justice system. Although these explanations are probably all true to varying degrees, there is no empirical data that suggest any one explanation is more plausible than the others. In short, although Bloom's findings show a change in utilization rates between 1960 and 1970, we are still left to speculate on the cause(s) for the change over the ten year period.

As well as demonstrating differential use of various sources of emotional support, researchers argue that Mexican Americans, especially lower class and rural, have a separate system of health care compared to Anglos (Clark, 1959; Madsen, 1964; Saunders, 1954; Weaver, 1970). Lower class and mostly rural Mexican Americans are found to believe in supernatural causation of physical and emotional illness, utilize folk medicine and folk healers, and regard professional physicians, psychotherapists, and modern hospitals with suspicion. In one study, it was found that attitudes toward hospitalization are associated more with level of education than ethnicity for Mexican Americans than Anglo Americans (McLemore, 1963). Thus, there is reason to believe that, regardless of socioeconomic attributes, the ethnic subcommunity is influential in shaping attitudes towards health care and use of professional health facilities. Nall and Speilberg (1967) in a study of tubercular Mexican Americans found, for example, that Mexican Americans integrated into the ethnic subcommunity are more likely to reject modern medical treatment. It is possible, in other words, that the Mexican American community offers a collective source of support for its members in time of physical and emotional stress, in turn shaping and perpetuating certain attitudes and behaviors which may differ from other ethnic communities. Furthermore, many of these attitudes and behaviors may persist across acculturation and socioeconomic strata within an ethnic group, differentiating the group as a whole from other ethnic segments of society.

Taking into account these differentiating characteristics, the concept of pluralism has been developed in the social sciences to aid in the investigation of societies with multiple sociocultural components. Pluralism has been applied to societies where there has traditionally been little contact between ethnic groups, such as South Africa, as well as in societies with greater degrees of intergroup contact and mobility, including the United States (Kuper and Smith, 1969). In our research on the relationship between ethnicity and mental health care, we have found it helpful to interpret the results within a pluralistic framework. We will begin with an examination of the concept of a plural society. Following this, we will discuss the data gathered on emotional support systems among Mexican Americans and Anglos in three Southern California cities and analyze the results in the context of pluralism.

PLURAL SOCIETY IN THE UNITED STATES

The concept of pluralism was first used by Furnivall (1939; 1948) in the context of colonial tropical societies in the Far East. Since then, it has been developed and has gained favor in the study of other societies, including the United States. In general, pluralism refers to the maintenance of separate institutions (set forms of activity, grouping, rules, ideas, and values) by distinct social groups encompassed within a single political unit—in other words, vertical as opposed to horizontal stratification. Smith (1960) introduced the concept of pluralism to a wider audience in his article, "Social and Cultural Pluralism." In a later revision of the concept, Smith (1969) made a useful distinction between cultural, social, and structural pluralism:

> Briefly, we must first distinguish three levels or modes of pluralism: structural, social, and cultural. By itself the last consists solely in institutional differences to which no corporate social differences attach.

> Social pluralism is the condition in which such institutional differentiations coincide with the corporate division of a given society into a series of sharply demarcated and virtually closed social sections or segments. Structural pluralism consists further in the differential incorporations of specified collectives within a given society. . . . (p. 440)

Smith goes on to state that structural pluralism presupposes social and cultural pluralism and establishes inequality in access to social, political, and economic resources through segregation and subordination by the dominant segment.

Smith has been criticized by Leons and Leons (1977) and others for failing to recognize the dynamic modifying influences of acculturation and miscegnation in a plural society. In time, they submit, cultural differences may all but disappear given constant contact between the segments of a plural society. Leons and Leons argue that while acculturation may do away with cultural pluralism, social and structural pluralism may persist. Gordon (1964) was first to elaborate on this process with regard to ethnic groups in general in the United States. Gordon argues that, even though American minority ethnic groups are adopting mainstream cultural patterns, they are prevented from assimilating into the primary groups and institutions of the White Anglo American Protestant majority. Gordon emphasizes the exclusion of ethnics from mainstream American society, while Kramer (1970) develops the idea of the ethnic minority community as a separate social subsystem—complete with norms, roles and statuses, values, and expectations. Kramer's work deals primarily with non-White ethnic and racial groups, but Novak (1971) demonstrates that White ethnics from southern and eastern Europe are similarly "unmeltable."

Research with Mexican Americans has proceeded mostly from an assimilationist perspective (Graves, 1967; Grebler, et al., 1970; Madsen, 1964; Moore, 1968, 1970a; Rubel, 1966). In these studies, acculturation and social and economic assimilation are assumed to be interdependent variables, each of which lies on a continuum ranging from traditional Mexican orientation to mainstream American orientation. Little attempt is made to isolate the processes of acculturation and assimilation. As a result, researchers who find cultural change in values and family life infer that Mexican Americans are gradually assuming the American way of life. At the same time, however, these studies document that Mexican Americans are not making great socioeconomic strides. More recent studies confirm, in fact, that Mexican Americans have very low rates of upward educational, residential, occupational, or income level mobility (Shannon and Shannon, 1973). Assimilationists assume that, with acculturation, more Mexican Americans will interact on intimate social levels with Anglo Americans, but little evidence is presented to support this.

Although assimilation theory dominated early research, a few scholars in the 1970's have dealt with the Mexican American condition as an example of internal colonialism (Almaguer, 1971; Blauner, 1972; Moore, 1970b; Barrera, Munoz, and Ornelas, 1972). First designed by Franz Fanon (1968) and Albert Memmi (1965) to describe the French occupation of their Algerian homeland, internal colonialism is typified by political and socioeconomic subordination of a group of people set apart socially and marked as culturally inferior by the dominant colonizers. While the concept of internal colonialism may represent the Mexican American experience, it cannot, as Murguia (1975) points out, make sense of the socioeconomic mobility (however limited) achieved by some Mexican Americans; neither can it account for widespread acculturation within the minority group.

Thus, while both assimilation and colonialism deal with social, cultural, and structural aspects of the relationship between various ethnic groups in society, neither explanatory model examines these aspects independently. It would be best to examine the evidence for pluralism in such a way that the social, cultural, and structural relationships between the two groups were done separately.In this paper, we will attempt such an analysis. Our point of departure will be an examination of how Mexican and Anglo Americans deal with emotional problems and to whom they turn during times of crisis. It is our contention that this data will lend themselves to some insights about pluralism in the United States.

Research Design

The research on which this paper is based was conducted in three Southern California cities chosen for their variation in population and ethnic density and their differing economic profiles.[1] Santa Paula, with a population of about 18,000, located in the agriculturally-rich Santa Clara River Valley, is primarily known for its citrus industry. Oxnard is a metropolitan center for outlying towns in Ventura County, including Santa Paula. It has a population of about 80,000 people and the economy is based on retail trade, light industry, and agricultural field crops. The third city, Santa Barbara has over 72,000 residents and relies on tourism, retail sales, and research and development firms as economic mainstays and is situated in Santa Barbara County which is adjacent to Ventura County. The Spanish-surname population makes up 21% of the population in Santa Barbara, 34% in Oxnard, and 41% in Santa Paula. In Santa Barbara, Mexican Americans are employed primarily as operators (20 percent) and service workers (26 percent); only one percent are farmworkers (U.S. Bureau of the Census, 1972a). Mexican Americans in Oxnard, on the other hand, are employed as operators (25 percent) and farmworkers (21 percent) (U.S. Bureau of the Census, 1972b). The same is true in Santa Paula, where 26 percent of the Mexican Americans are operators and 25 percent are farmworkers (U.S. Bureau of the Census, 1972c). While the economic profiles vary, the Mexican Americans in all three towns are overwhelmingly blue collar workers, with levels of income and education well below those of the general population.

A large survey was undertaken in the first year of research (1975-6). Sampling was designed to gather an equal number of respondents in each of the cities, with the Mexican American respondents stratified by cultural background and socioeconomic status. To obtain the stratified Mexican American sample, three census tracts were chosen in each town for sampling. The information provided by the U.S. Bureau of the Census is primarily socioeconomic and it was on the basis of this information, the ethnic density of the tract, and first-hand observation in three cities, that particular census tracts were selected. It was assumed that cultural characteristics would be associated to some extent with socioeconomic status and ethnic density and, thus, a range of variation would be obtained. The three census tracts in each city were selected, therefore, to fit as closely as possible the following ideal types: (1) high ethnic density and low socioeconomic status, (2) mid ethnic density and mixed socioeconomic status, and (3) low ethnic density and high socioeconomic status. The census tract with the highest ethnic density in each city covers the locally designated Mexican American *barrio*.

Because of the need for comparative data to evaluate the impact of ethnicity, both Mexican Americans and Anglo Americans in each census tract were interviewed. The samples of the two ethnic groups were selected using a city directory which lists residents by address. Spanish-surname and non-Spanish-surname heads of household were selected randomly from the streets enclosed by each of the nine tracts. The Spanish-surname households were contacted by bilingual interviewers of Mexican descent and the non-Spanish-surname households by interviewers of Anglo American descent. The questionnaire was designed to be given quickly to a large number of people. It contained 123 items, took 20 to 30 minutes to administer, and covered four general topics: Extended family structure; attitudes toward and use of alternative sources of help for emotional problems; attitudes toward and knowledge and use of public mental services; and cultural and socioeconomic background information on the respondent. On the whole, Mexican Americans were the most willing to participate; 77% of the persons of Mexican descent contacted agreed to be interviewed compared to 55% of the Anglos. The final sample included 666 Mexican Americans and 340 White Anglo Americans.

The stratified sampling produced Mexican American respondents with a range of socioeconomic traits that was desired. The repondents interviewed in the census tracts designated as high ethnic density/low socioeconomic stat in each town are most likely to be first generation, Spanish-speaking, and of low socioeconomic status, The low ethnic density/high socioeconomic status census tracts, in contrast, produced more respondents who are third generation, English-speaking, and of high socioeconomic status. The mid ethnic density tracts in Santa Barbara and Oxnard produced a mixed range of cultural types and respondents who are somewhere between the *barrio* and the Anglo-dominated census tracts in educational achievement, but more like the *barrio* census tracts in occupational level.

While it was not the intent of the survey to produce a statistically random sample of Mexican Americans, the sample obtained has socioeconomic characteristics much like those of the Mexican American population as a whole in urban areas of California (as well as Mexican Americans in the three cities studied). Most of the Mexican Americans surveyed are of low socioeconomic status; 86 percent of the male heads of household are blue collar workers and the respondents' median years of education are 9.1. Likewise, Mexican Americans in urban parts of California have a median of 9.9 years of education and 77 percent of the males are employed in blue collar occupations (U.S. Bureau of the Census, 1972c).

A second survey was initiated the following year in order to explore the research interests in more depth. This questionnaire took two to three hours to administer and many respondents required more than one interview to complete it. The schedule contained 807 items in four basic areas of interest: Social interaction with relatives, friends and others; use of alternative sources of help for emotional problems and a description of the help received; awareness of cultural heritage and loyalty to the ethnic group; and socioeconomic background information. In order to facilitate data gathering, the first year sample was re-interviewed during this phase. An attempt was made to contact all of the previously interviewed respondents who had indicated they would participate in a second interview (including 98 percent of the Mexican Americans and 97 percent of the Anglos). Of the first Mexican American sample, 486 respondents were contacted for the second interview. The remaining respondents either had declined to be re-interviewed after the first interview, had moved outside the survey area, or were never home when the interviewer came to call. Of those contacted, over 75 percent (or 372 respondents) agreed to be re-interviewed and 25 percent declined. For the white Anglo American sample, 200 respondents from the first survey were able to be contacted, 82 percent (or 163 respondents) of whom agreed to complete the second interview, while 18 percent declined. Distribution of the samples by town and census tract remained much the same as for the first survey.

Because of our desire to compare Mexican American mental health clinic users with non-users and given the extremely small number of users uncovered in the first sample (N = 16), additional clinic users were solicited to answer the second questionnaire. With the approval of local public mental health clinics in the three cities, and operating under guidelines established to guarantee the client's rights to confidentiality, clinic users of Mexican descent were asked to be volunteers in the study. Despite our rigorous efforts, only nine volunteers could be located and the total sample for the second survey thus consists of 381 Mexican Americans as well as the 163 Anglo Americans.

Data from the first survey have been discussed at length elsewhere (Keefe, 1978; Keefe, Padilla, and Carlos, 1979; Padilla, Carlos, and Keefe, 1976). Therefore, the present paper will be concerned with data from the second survey, unless otherwise noted. Since the second survey covers a subset of the respondents in the original survey, the results of the two questionnaires are, to a great extent, complementary. For this reason, only those areas in which results of the two surveys diverge will be called to attention. It should be noted that our presentation of the data is informal and has been more technically discussed in our previous works cited above.

No systematic differences were found in analyzing the data concerning mental health care by town or census tract; therefore, the ethnic samples are considered here as aggregates. The two ethnic samples in the second survey are fairly similar in age, sex, and marital status. Over two-thirds of the respondents in both samples are women and about three-quarters or more of each group are married. The Anglos average 45 years of age and the Mexican Americans average 43 years of age. Respondents. from both ethnic groups are also likely to have been urban dwellers for most of their lives. The Mexican Americans, on the other hand, differ from the Anglos in being much more residentially stable; the average Mexican American has lived in the same town for 22 years, compared to 15 years for the average Anglo. Moreover, many of the Mexican Americans are natives of the city in which they were interviewed; 19 percent of the Mexican Americans are city natives compared to 6 percent of the Anglo Americans.

The Mexican American sample exhibits considerable intra-ethnic diversity. Forty percent of the Mexican American respondents are first generation, that is born in Mexico; 37 percent are second generation, born in the United States, with one or both parents born in Mexico; and 19 percent are third generation, born in the United States, with both parents born in the United States. Generation can be used as a rough index of the acculturation and assimilation of an ethnic group (Warner, and Srole, 1945). Much of the data in the following sections, therefore, is broken down by generation to indicate directions of change within the Mexican

American population. The generation level could not be determined for four percent of the sample and these respondents have been deleted from the generation figures, but included in statistics for the ethnic group as a whole.

THE ETHNIC COMMUNITY: CULTURAL, SOCIAL, AND STRUCTURAL BOUNDARIES

Before comparing the mental health systems of the two ethnic groups, let us first examine the evidence for cultural, social, and structural pluralism generally in the communities studied. In all three cities, the Mexican American segment is readily visible and for the most part distant from the Anglo segment. Santa Barbara was founded as a mission-*presido* (garrison) in the eighteenth century. Until the mid-ninteenth century, it remained in the control of the Spanish and Mexican descendents, but with the discovery of gold in California and the tremendous population influx of Anglo Americans, socioeconomic and political power quickly came to reside with the Yankee newcomers. The towns of Santa Paula and Oxnard were founded by Anglo Americans during this period of intense growth. Both developed into agricultural centers and relied at first on Chinese and Japanese labor.

The twentieth century brought a new wave of Mexican immigration to the American Southwest in general and to these three towns in particular, which continues to the present. While the orginal settlers from Mexico represented a range of socioeconomic levels, later arrivals have been primarily poor, at first seeking to escape the havoc of the Mexican Revolution and later in search of jobs. Being different from the Anglo community both culturally and socioeconomically, the Mexican immigrants have been segregated within separate neighborhoods, schools, and places of recreation. In addition, they were and are employed mostly in a relatively few low-skilled job categories, such as farm workers, gardeners, construction laboreres, cooks, maids, and so on, both because of their limited skills and discrimination by employers.

World War II marked a change in opportunities for the residents of Mexican descent. The second generation of Mexicans in the United States, more fluent in English, more educated, and more sophisticated about the majority culture had grown in numbers. With economic expansion, industrial jobs opened up for these Mexican Americans. Many Mexican Americans joined the armed services and later used G.I. benefits to buy homes, go to college and otherwise better their lives. Overt discrimination against Mexicans has been limited since the 1950's, but while native-born second and third generation have successfully acquired higher-paying skilled and semi-skilled blue collar jobs, there has been little mobility into white collar occupations. Prejudice and ethnic stereotypes are still prevalent and primary relationships tent to be restricted within ethnic boundaries. Despite their increasing association with Anglos in the schools, neighborhoods, the workplace, and areas of mass recreation, Mexican Americans continue to act as a distinct ethnic community.

CULTURAL PLURALISM

Data collected in our survey bear out the existence of cultural, social, and structural boundaries between the Mexican American and Anglo communities. With regard to the cultural factor, the boundary between both cultures is by no means impenetrable. In fact, most Mexican Americans are aware to some extent of the two cultural systems. For example, 96 percent of the Mexican American respondents speak some Spanish and 84 percent carry on conversations in Spanish every day, while, at the same time, 78 percent also speak some English and 70 percent carry on English conversations daily. Rather than being cultural isolates, Mexican Americans are involved to varying degrees in two cultures, and, while participation in the two cultures is not mutually exclusive, only the Mexican Americans, as opposed to the Anglos, interact as members of both in any great numbers. Their cultural distinctiveness compared to Anglos thus lies in this acceptance of two cultures, not in cultural opposition.

The idea of the loss of traditional culture and gain of new cultural patterns from a host society (acculturation) is usually discussed as an all-encompassing process in which the group in time loses the traditional traits and acquires new traits (Social Science Research Council, 1954). If this is so, we should expect the three generations of Mexican Americans to reveal a gradual attrition of Mexican traits, on the one hand, and the acquisition of American traits on the other. The adherence of three generations of Mexican American respondents to certain cultural patterns, however, indicates a somewhat different process (see Table 1). As might be expected, the immigrant Mexicans appear the most traditional in their cultural affiliation. They are most likely to be fluent in Spanish, have a Spanish first name, have visited the interior of Mexico, identify themselves as "Mexican," acquire Mexican cultural items such as art objects or records, and posseses attitudes such as agreement that "The best music is Mexican music" or "In Mexico, the people are friendlier than in the United States."

In some ways, the second and third generations together present a contrast to the first generation. For example, the native-born are much more likely to prefer English language radio and television programming than the foreign-born. The native-born also tend to disagree with the statement that Mexican people are "friendlier" than Americans or that Mexican music is "best." In addition, they are unlikely to identify themselves as "Mexican." In other words, there appears to be a gradual replacement of Mexican cultural traits over generation with new ones. This change is reflected by a decline in Spanish language fluency and preference, a concomitant increase in English language fluency and preference, the acquisition of and preference for an English first name as opposed to a Spanish first name, and the declining tendency to travel in Mexico or have Mexican cultural items in the home. Finally, there are several similarities across all three generations. Perhaps most important, Mexican Americans remain Catholic from generation to generation and thus are members of a both a religious and an ethnic minority in the United States. They also agree that living in the United States is preferable to living in Mexico, primarily because of the higher standard of living. Furthermore, all generation stress the importance of maintaining certain aspects of Mexican culture in the United States such as learning Mexican history and the Spanish language. Finally, there is a strong tendency to retain the Mexican cuisine, which serves as a symbolic as well as real indicant of their ethnicity.

The answers to questions about knowledge of cultural heritage represent all of these various responses to cultural cntact and change. Contrast between foreign and native-born is provided by the questions about Thomas Jefferson and Los Ninos Heroes de Chapultepec (military cadets who died defending the Castle of Chapultepec in Mexico City against American troops in 1847). Gradual decline in knowledge about Mexico is evident in the question requesting identification of Luis Echeverria, the former President of Mexico, 1970–1976. Fairly consistent knowledge of both Mexican and American culture across generations is found in the ability to identify pictures of Abraham Lincoln and Benito Juarez (mid-nineteenth century leader of the rebellion against the French in Mexico and subsequent Mexican President).

In sum, the process of acculturation is by no means uniform or inevitable. Instead, there appears to be elimination and retention of some cultural traits. Although there is gradual acquisition of American culture traits over time, it is inaccurate to infer that Mexicans simply become more American from generation to generation. At the same time, certain Mexican cultural patterns are held fast. Furthermore, there is modification and adaptation of Mexican culture to American life so that in some ways Mexican Americans have adopted unique cultural characteristics such as the use of *pochismos* (Mexican American slang), have acquired an individual

Table 3-1
Generational Adherence to Selected Mexican and American
Cultural Traits

Cultural Trait	Mexican American by Generation		
	First (N = 153) %	Second (N = 42) %	Third (N = 0) %
1. Language			
a) Speak Spanish	100	98	82
Good/excellent Spanish fluency	71	55	39
Prefer to speak Spanish	82	21	7
Prefer Spanish television	65	10	6
b) Speak English	50	97	99
Good/excellent English fluency	24	69	78
Prefer to speak English	3	31	63
Prefer English television	11	65	79
2. First Name			
Given Spanish first name	89	69	44
Prefer Spanish first name	79	48	24
3. Visited Mexico (after settling in the United States)	85	48	24
4. Catholic religion	91	84	93
5. Knowledge of cultural heritage			
a) Identify Luis Echeverria	91	70	35
Answer question on Ninos Heroes de Chapultepec	76	34	17
Identify picture of Benito Jaurez	of 71	63	Benito
b) Answer question on Thomas Jefferson	38	69	68
Identify picture of Liberty Bell	56	92	99
Identify picture of Abraham Lincoln	84	99	99
6. Ethnic Identification			
"Mexican"	82	15	9
"Mexican American or American of Mexican descent"	12	64	64

Table 3-1 Continued

Cultural Trait	Mexican American by Generation		
	First (N = 153) %	Second (N = 142) %	Third (N = 70) %
"Chicano"	1	11	5
"American"	1	4	9
7. Attitudes toward U.S. and Mexico			
"Mexican people are friendlier"	71	35	20
"Child growing up in U.S. luckier than in Mexico"	66	79	85
"Better chance of getting ahead in U.S."	76	81	84
8. Attitudes toward Mexican Culture			
"Mexican music is best"	60	39	32
"Should learn Mexican history in U.S. Schools	87	91	87

history as an ethnic group in the United States, and have begun to develop a new and separate identity as Chicanos. Whether or not these characteristics are truly indicative of an unique Mexican and American culture *per se* is debatable. For example, only 6 percent of the Mexican American respondents in our sample identify as "Chicano." Nevertheless, there is no indication that Mexican Americans begin to assume an identity free of their ethnic heritage, for example, only a small percentage of respondents hold an identity of simple "American". We can conclude, therefore, that despite a certain degree of acculturation, Mexican Americans as a whole contribute to the cultural pluralism in American society.

SOCIAL PLURALISM

Before turning to an examination of the social ties between Anglos and Mexican Americans, let us briefly compare the social organization of the two ethnic groups. The literature abounds with descriptions of the Mexican

American community as an integrated kin-based network that contrasts with the loose ties found in the Anglo community (Clark, 1959; Madsen, 1969; Rubel, 1966). Data from our first survey confirm the striking difference in extended family structure between Anglos and Mexican Americans (Keefe, 1978; Keefe, Padilla, and Carlos, 1978). Anglos are likely to have fewer kin in town, while Mexican immigrants are more likely to settle near a number of kin. Native-born Mexican Americans are likely to have the largest networks of nearby relatives. Moreover, the differences between the two ethnic groups remain when controlling for occupation, education, and geographic mobility. In other words, Mexican Americans as a group appear more family-oriented than Anglos.

The variation in social organization between the two groups is even more evident in data from the second survey. In addition to questions about relations with kin, respondents were also asked about friends, fictive kin, co-workers, neighbors, and membership in voluntary organizations. The local networks of Anglos and Mexican Americans differ both qualitatively and quantitatively. Mexican Americans respondents have social relations with many more people in town than Anglos; on the average Mexican Americans have 40 local friends, relatives, neighbors, and so on, while the Anglos know about 27 people. Analysis by generation indicates real differences between the Mexican American generations. The first generation tends to have fewer social contacts in town (21) than Anglos. But the social circle enlarges with subsequent generations to more than twice the size of the Anglos; on the average second generation people know 47 people socially, and the third generation has a network averaging 67 contacts in town.

Kinsmen are primarily responsible for the increase in social contacts across generations among Mexican Americans. Numbers of fictive kin, friends, co-workers, and neighbors tend to remain constant across generations, while number of relatives increases substantially. At the same time, kin make up a larger and larger proportion of the total social network. Forty-eight percent of the first generation's social networks consist of kinsmen compared to 57 percent of the second generation and 74 percent of the third generation networks. Anglos, on the other hand, are likely to have social circles made up primarily of non-kin; only 11 percent of the average Anglo network consists of relatives.

This ethnic difference in social networks has important implications for the way in which respondents deal with their emotional problems as we shall see later. It will suffice to point out here that the Mexican American community is primarily kin-based and, as such, is more tightly integrated and group-oriented than the Anglos. Most people in the networks of Mexican American respondents tend to know each other by virtue of kin ties. Likewise, the social relations tend to be of a long standing nature, since birth for consanguinal relatives and since marriage for affines. Furthermore, some of the kin ties are likely to have been strengthened by *compadrazgo*, the ritual bond between godparents and real parents of a godchild. The social network of most Mexican Americans is thus a primary group with strong loyalties among members and a basis for the sharing and maintenance of cultural traits and norms. Anglos lack this kind of local network. Most Anglo social contacts are with friends or co-workers. These ties tend to be shorter in duration than kin ties and it is almost certain that not all members of the social network know each other. More likely, there are several sets of friends seen on different occasions as well as the set of co-workers who are likely to be seen mainly on the job. In addition, unlike Mexican Americans, Anglos are more likely to belong to voluntary organizations, which further segments their social relations. Thus, Anglos, are likely to have specialized sets of social contacts, rather than having an integrated primary group. As a result, they have more privacy and more choice in their social relations than Mexican Americans.

Turning to the interaction between the two ethnic groups, data from the second survey indicate the presence of social pluralism to varying degrees. Judging from responses to questions about the ethnicity of associates in the past, associates at present, and intermarriage, Anglos and Mexican immigrants demonstrate the greatest ethnic enclosure of social relationships. About 90 percent of the Anglos had mostly Anglo childhood friends and schoolmates, and more than 80 percent had mostly Anglo friends and schoolmates as a teenager. The ethnic boundaries are somewhat less distinct for the Anglos' associates at present, but more than 60 percent of the respondents have mostly Anglo friends, neighbors, co-workers, and leisure-time associates. The same pattern appears among the first generation Mexicans. Since most of them grew up and were educated in Mexico, it comes as no surprise that the vast majority had mainly childhood and teenage friends and schoolmates of Mexican descent. Although residing in the United States, the first generation continues to associate mostly with other Mexicans; 70 percent or more have friends, neighbors, co-workers, and leisure-time associates who are mostly of Mexican descent.

Second and third generation Mexican Americans interact more outside their ethnic group, but still tend to maintain strong ties with the Mexican American community. This is most obvious in their response to questions about their associates in the past. For example, while the majority had some Anglo schoolmates and schoolfriends as children and as teenagers (if they continued in school), their neighborhood friends were mostly Mexican Americans. At present, the native-born are likely to have some Anglo friends, co-workers, and neighbors. But only about one-third indicate that they interact with most Anglo co-workers and only about one-quarter say the same for neighbors. Less than one-sixth interact mainly with Anglo friends or leisure-time associates, the more intimate relationships. In other words, the increased contact with Anglos tends to be confined to less intimate interaction.

The data on intermarriage serve to emphasize this generalization. The first generation Mexicans are not ethnically enclosed with regard to intermarriage. Only one percent of the first generation respondents have married Anglos, have an Anglo father or have an Anglo mother. Similarly, the Anglos tend to be restricted to parents of Anglo ethnicity; only 1 percent have a Mexican father and none have a Mexican mother. Nevertheless, they are somewhat more likely to have a Mexican spouse, as seven percent are married to a Mexican American. The second generation follows the Anglo pattern: one percent have an Anglo father, none have an Anglo mother, and six percent have an Anglo spouse. The third generation reports the highest rates of ethnic inter-marriage among parents; six percent have an Anglo father and two percent an Anglo mother, but the proportion married to Anglos (seven percent) remains about the same as the second generation. In sum, there appears to be no great tendency to marry outside the ethnic group among either Anglos or Mexican Americans, and the sphere of kinsmen, the most intimate of social circles, tends to remain ethnically enclosed for the most part.

The tendency to associate with members of one's own ethnic group appears to be related to both individual preference and perceptions of group discrimination. Given a series of questions about preference for ethnically similar or different associates in a restaurant, at a party, as neighbors, or as marriage partners for family members, the first generation and Anglos are most likely to prefer their own ethnic group. With regard to perceived discrimination against people of Mexican descent, all three generations of Mexican Americans are likely to believe that discrimination exists, but the first generation tends to recognize it the most frequently. Thus, both external and internal factors appear to be important in determining the social pluralism of the two ethnic groups.

STRUCTURAL PLURALISM

Anglos and Mexican Americans are not equally incorporated into the political and socioeconomic institutions of the three communities studies. Further, there is variation between the foreign-born and native-born Mexican Americans in the extent of exclusion from the mainstream. With regard to politics, the first generation is systematically excluded from the political arena because of their lack of facility with English. The native-born fare only somewhat better. Before the 1960's, Mexican Americans rarely ran for public office in the three cities and never won when nominated. Since then, a few Mexican Americans have been elected to the city councils of Santa Barbara and Santa Paula, and to the school boards to Santa Paula and Oxnard, but their representation is nonetheless minimal. More informal representation through voluntary associations is not afforded the Mexican American either. Less than 30 percent of the respondents belong to one or more organizations and these tend to be religious, fraternal, or recreational groups, with little political impact. The Mexican American political organizations that exist in the communities have relatively small memberships and their success as pressure groups has been limited. While the Mexican Americans have somewhat more political visibility in Santa Paula, the smallest town with the highest density of Mexican Americans, Anglos are unquestionably dominant in community politics in all three towns.

Mexican Americans have also tended to be residentially separate from the Anglo population, although there has been movement out of the *barrio* in all three towns since the late 1940's. Still, over one-half of the Mexican American population in Santa Paula lives in the census tract covering the *barrio*, as do one-third of the Mexican Americans in Oxnard and one-quarter in Santa Barbara. First generation immigrants are the most likely to settle in the *barrios* and, thus, are the most segregated segment of the Mexican American population. The *barrio* offers goods and services that are hard to find elsewhere, such as Spanish language records and publications, special cuts of meat, and nightclubs offering Mexican style music and dancing. Moreover, the *barrio* symbolizes the structural separation of the Mexican American population from the larger community.

Data on income, occupation, and education demonstrate the socioeconomic gap between Anglos and Mexican Americans. First generation Mexicans are most obviously subordinate on all three counts. Fifty-four percent of the first generation male heads of household are unskilled laborers; a total of 88 percent are blue collar workers. In contrast, only eight percent of the Anglo respondents are unskilled laborers and 46 percent in all are blue collar workers. With regard to education, 69 percent of the Mexican immigrant males have no more than an eight year elementary education, compared to 10 percent of the Anglos. On the other hand, 56 percent of the Anglos have one or more years of college versus seven percent of the Mexican immigrants. As might be expected, the annual family income reflects the disproportionate occupational and educational distribution of the first generation and the Anglos. While 60 percent of the first generation Mexicans make less than $10,000 a year and eight percent make $15,000 or more, only 39 percent of the Anglos make less than $10,000, while 41 percent make $15,000 or more.

Second generation Mexican Americans have made significant gains in occupation, education, and income compared to the first generation. For example, 26 percent of the second generation male heads of household are white collar; 22 percent have had one or more years of college; and 29 percent earn $15,000 or more annually. But there is no similar gain between the second and third generations; in fact, there is a slight decline with respect to all three indicators. Only 18 percent of the third generation male heads of households are white collar workers; 19 percent have had one or more years of college; and 20 percent make $15,000 or more a year. These data indicate clearly that Mexican Americans are not attaining equal status with Anglos. Instead, there is a pattern of limited mobility between the first and second generations, which declines again for the third generation. Moreover, the population across generations is overwhelmingly blue collar, the majority of whom have not completed high school and earn a family income of less than $12,000 annually. This contrasts with the average Anglo, who is white collar, has one or more years of college, and makes over $12,000 a year. Clearly, the Mexican American population forms a structurally subordinate segment of the plural society in the three communities.

Summarizing data on the cultural, social, and structural pluralism, Mexican Americans differ significantly from Anglos. There is acquisition of mainstream culture in some ways, but acculturation is not uniform and many Mexican traits are retained. Considering the adoption of numerous American cultural patterns, however, it is perhaps most accurate to characterize the Mexican American population as participants to varying degrees in two cultural system. Furthermore, there is no evidence that acculturation is complete in three generations; in fact, so long as social and structural pluralism continues, there is no reason to expect it to be complete. The maintenance of ethnically-enclosed primary groups, combined with diversified interactions in settings such as school and work, creates a situation in which two cultural systems can continue to coexist indefinitely. Rather than a strict process of acculturation, then, we find more evidence of "situational ethnicity" (Nagata, 1974). In other words, Mexican Americans tend to be more "Mexican" at home and more "American" at school and at work. The subordination of the Mexican American population in blue collar occupations further imposes a class-based difference in behavior and life style between the two ethnic groups, which contributes to their social and cultural differentiation.

Although general distinctions can be made between Anglos and Mexican Americans, it cannot be emphasized too strongly that there are equally marked distinctions within the Mexican American population itself. Clearly, first generation Mexicans are different, both culturally and socioeconomically, from the native-born Mexican Americans. In fact, this internal division is recognized by the ethnic group members themselves. The immigrants disdain the inability of the native-born to speak proper Spanish as well as their disregard for many important Mexican customs. Furthermore, the first generation tends to be shocked and outraged by many of the moral standards by the more Americanized native-born, such as teenage dating patterns. The native-born, in turn, consider the immigrants to be uneducated and "old-fashioned." They point out that the immigrants have a different accent, use different gestures, wear different clothes, and even walk differently (slower and more nimbly). Sometimes, the native-born refer to the immigrants with derogatory terms such as "broncs" (derived from *"bronco"* or rough and unsophisticated) or "TJs" (referring to the border town of Tijuana where many immigrants first gain entrance to the United States). In some respects the boundary between native-born and foreign-born Mexican Americans is almost as distinct as between Mexican Americans and Anglo Americans, but, of course, there is interaction between native and foreign-born within the extended family circle. Even here, however, the "generation gap" frequently creates conflict. In any event, one can make the case for intra-ethnic as well as inter-ethnic pluralism.

MENTAL HEALTH RESOURCES IN THE ETHNIC COMMUNITY

The way in which an individual reaches the decision to seek help for an emotional problem and the sources of help subsequently contacted are in large part a result of the ethnic boundaries just discussed. In this section we describe the process of emotional problem solving within the two ethnic groups. Included is a comparison of the perception of mental illness among Mexican Americans and Anglos, the types of emotional problems experienced by respondents, the sources asked for help, and additional sociocultural factors which affect the choice of sources of help. In the following section the relationship between the search for help and cultural, social, and structural pluralism will be discussed in detail.

Perceptions of Mental Illness

The first step in seeking help for an emotional problem is the individual's decision that there is indeed a problem which requires treatment. This, in turn, rests on cultural perceptions of mental or emotional health and illness. Studies have demonstrated that the nature and content of mental illness may be perceived differently across cultures (Opler, 1956). Our research indicates that different perceptions exist for

Mexican Americans and Anglo Americans. In an exploratory study of perceptions of mental illness among a small sample of Mexican Americans by an associate in our research (Newton, in press), it was found that Mexican Americans conceive of mental health and illness as a continuum ranging from: (1) a stable level or the theoretical absence of emotional problems, to (2) "emotional" problems which range from minor, temporary problems that can be endured, to serious persistent problems that cannot be handled by the individual alone, and finally (3) problems which involve an inablility to cope with life, a loss of self-control, and a loss of contact with reality. These problems are considered more serious than emotional problems and are believed to be the result of a culmination of emotional problems that are not treated and continue to grow worse.

The inclination toward mental and emotional stability or malfunctioning is believed by Mexican Americans to be related to an individual's enduring strength of character. Individuals with a strong character (strong will power, strong mind, strong spirit) are independent, self-sufficient, self-confident, and self-controlled. A strong person faces problems head-on and works actively to solve them; although a strong person may get depressed over certain problems, he or she can endure the pain and still function. Self-help for problems is preferred, but a strong person should be able to recognize when professional help is necessary and take corrective action. In contrast, individuals with a weak character are believed to be easily influenced, unable to make decisions, dependent, emotional, and lacking confidence. Weak people hide from their problems; they feel helpless and give up easily. Instead of trying to solve their problems, weak people worry about them and are likely to become nervous as a result; they tend to be sensitive and unstable and react by going to extremes. Because of this personality set, a weak person is more likely to encounter an emotional problem and, thereafter, to have it develop into a more serious type of problem. A weak person is incapable of recognizing when professional help is needed and does not seek it. Once they have a mental disorder, weak people are less likely to recover because of their basic inability to maintain control of themselves.

Proper treatment for mental and emotional problems is considered to be a direct function of the problem's severity. Minor emotional problems are expected to be met with self-help. This is more easily accomplished, however, by strong people compared to weak people. If the problems persist and become serious and pervasive, it is best to "talk it out" with a relative or close friend. Generally, the next step should be to consult with a physician. This is primarily a result of the fact that physicians are the only widely known professional health specialists. In addition, because of the physical symptoms which usually accompany emotional problems (such as nervousness, insomnia, and muscle aches), medical specialists are consulted in order to accurately determine whether or not the cause of the problem is physical or emotional. If the cause is emotional, the physician may also be expected to recommend a therapist. The final stage, at which psychiatric care should be sought, arises when the problem is beyond the individual's control, all other sources of help have failed, and the individual is on the brink of mental incapacitation.

Clearly, professional mental health care is perceived by Mexican Americans as a last-ditch effort to help an individual contend with his or her problems, which are likely to be long-standing and at an advanced stage. Furthermore, while Mexican Americans' perceptions of therapists are generally positive and there is agreement that therapy should be undertaken to prevent mental breakdown, actual recourse to a psychotherapist is complicated by the belief that seeing a therapist is a sign of weakness. As a result, even people who consider themselves strong (and thus perceptive about the need to seek help) are likely to either put off seeking therapy until they have lost all control and must be taken by others for treatment, or consult a mental health professional privately, without telling anyone. Mexican Americans take pride in a self-image of strength and are unwilling to risk the shame of admitting they cannot handle their own problems. They see themselves as stronger than Anglos, and they take as a sign of Anglos' weakness their greater use of mental health services. The implication is that Mexican Americans wait substantially longer than Anglos before turning to therapy.

Notably absent from this model of mental illness is any reference to supernatural causation or help in treatment. Despite abundant evidence in the literature that Mexican Americans believe many mental disorders are the result of supernatural interference in the form of witchcraft or folk illness and cure is best effected by folk healers with knowledge of the supernatural (Madsen, 1964; Rubel, 1966), we find little evidence of this in our research. Perhaps the difference in regional location of the population under study or the era in which the research was conducted explains this anomaly. Most of the earlier research was done over 15 years ago in rural areas, largely in south Texas. Whatever the reason, the folk medical system appears to be of little importance among Mexican Americans in the three communities studied here.

In an exploratory study of a small sample of Anglo Americans done following that of the Mexican Americans, we found a somewhat similar continuum model of mental illness ranging from minor, temporary problems to chronic lack of self-control and lack of contact with reality. While Anglos do not tend to distinguish between the terms "emotional" and "mental" (both indicate a serious illness), they perceive differences, as do the Mexican Americans, in the degree to which a person experiences problems. Similarly, Anglos also perceive self-help as the best cure-all, recommending friends, relatives, and other informal sources of help when this fails and, as a third step, consultation with the family physician. Lastly, Anglos feel that psychotherapy should be sought as the final effort to find help. Thus, the treatment model is much the same for both Anglos and Mexican Americans.

The two ethnic groups differ in their perception of causation of mental or emotional illness. They also differ in the concomitant attitudes toward people who develop such problems and who require psychiatric help. Instead, Anglos regard environmental factors, such as maltreatment by family members or lack of money or trouble on the job, as most important in causation. There is no reference made to a person's character if the individual has an emotional problem, or if he or she requires help. Many Anglos feel professional psychiatric care is a last resort, since it is believed to be expensive and not very effective. In fact, many Anglos consider therapy a luxury and, in some ways, a sign of affluence. Although stigma is associated with use of a therapist for extremely severe problems (such as excessively violent behavior), little stigma is attached to consultation for less severe problems. In all, seeing a therapist is not considered to be a sign of weakness. On the other hand, Anglos believe a person can develop a weak character as a result of prolonged mental or emotional illness. For Anglos then, psychotherapy represents the last in a series of helping agents; for Mexican Americans, it represents the first admission of weakness and failure.

Confronting the Emotional Problem

The process of recognizing the presence of an emotional problem and subsequently seeking help is extremely complex. As discussed above, there is the cultural factor in how such problems are perceived. In addition, there are a number of factors that influence this process. For example, there are negative social attitudes toward treatment, treatment delivery personnel, and people in treatment. Other relevant variables include the actual and perceived availability of helping personnel, the self-concept of the individual in question, and the person's willingness to assume a "sick" role. The effect of these factors, by and large, is to inhibit self-referrals for help. At this point, we turn to an examination of data bearing on the "recognition of emotional problems" as a means of documenting differences which were found between Anglos and Mexican Americans, and especially between Anglos and first generation Mexican Americans.

Respondents were asked whether they had ever consulted a number of alternative sources of help with an emotional problem; the list included friends, relatives, neighbors, co-workers, voluntary organization members, clergymen, physicians, community workers, group meetings, private therapists, and public mental health clinics. In addition, Mexican Americans were asked if they had ever gone to a *compadre* (literally co-father, the kin name between men, one of whom has baptized the other's child; *comadre* is the equivalent term for women), *padrino* (god-parent), or *curandero* (folk-healer). Seventy-two percent of the Anglos indicated that they have contacted one or more of these sources at one time or another about an emotional problem. Similarly, 71 percent of the second generation and 66 percent of the third generation Mexican Americans have sought help. In contrast, only 46 percent of the first generation have done so. This is surprising since we would have expected the immigrants to have more problems since they experience more characteristics associated with emotional problems: poverty, lack of education, unskilled and boring jobs, crowded living conditions, migration, and lack of facility with the culture of mainstream society. First generation respondents may have just as many, if not more, problems as other Mexican Americans and Anglos. That they do not seek help as readily suggests the existence of an intervening sociocultural pattern. From the data presented so far, several alternatives emerge. First, we might assume that the value of strength of character affects the first generation most, so they are probably least likely to be willing to admit to problems. This is necessary not only for their own self-image but for their public image. Since emotional sickness is equated with weakness, which, in turn, brings about lack of respect by others, it is to be avoided in order to maintain normal social relations. Second, the first generation has the smallest social circle and, therefore, simply has less availability of potential informal supports. Further reasons for the low rate of seeking help among immigrants will be suggested later in this section.

At the same time the individual decides he or she is in need of help, there is an awareness of the nature of the problem at hand. The way in which the problem is perceived in turn has some effect on the type of helping agent chosen. It is also indicative of ethnic perceptions of "appropriate" problems and the individual's role in the dynamics of the problem. Respondents who indicated they had consulted with someone about an emotional problem were asked to briefly describe the nature of the problem. Responses were categorized according to the primary locus of responsibility for the problem as perceived by the respondent: internal, external family-related, external non-family, and alcohol/drug related problems. Problems believed to stem from personal inadequacies in handling emotional problems (internal locus) included such things as grief over the death of a loved one, general depression or nervousness, nightmares, and inability to cope with "everyday" problems. Family-related problems include those specified as marital problems, problems mainly involving the children, and problems involving the entire family (parents and children). Non-family problems include those brought on by such things as sickness of the respondent or a family member, financial worries, or job-related troubles. Any problem specified by the respondent as alcohol or drug related was categorized separately.

Table 2 indicates the distribution of the types of problems reported by respondents. For Mexican Americans, by far the most commonly reported problems are family-related, especially marital problems. Family problems are also most often cited by Anglos, but there is no similar emphasis on marital problems. Moreover, Anglos are about twice as likely to specify internal problems as are Mexican Americans. The fact that Mexican Americans are unlikely to report internal-locus problems can be interpreted as a reflection of their reluctance to take personal responsibility for emotional problems. Like the recognition that an emotional problem exists in the first place, perception of the problem as self-induced is further admission of weakness of character.

Sources of Help

Once the individual perceives the need to seek help for a problem, a particular helping agent must be chosen. For both Anglos and Mexican Americans, the sources most commonly consulted include relatives, friends, physicians, and clergymen. Anglos are also likely to go to group meetings (such as Alcoholics Anonymous, church groups, and encounter groups) and private therapists for help. Neither ethnic group is inclined to consult with community workers, co-workers, or voluntary organization members.[2]

For Mexican Americans, relatives are the most important source of support in times of trouble. In the first survey, 36 percent indicated they spoke to a relative about an emotional problem in the last year and in the second survey, 29 percent reported confiding in a relative at one time in their life. Other informal types of helping agents, including friends, co-workers, neighbors, and *compadres,* are much less important for Mexican Americans. This is understandable, considering the preponderance of kinsmen in their circle of associates. Yet, it also appears to be due in part to a preference for discussion of private matters with the extended family. Anglos also consult frequently with relatives about their emotional problems, but they tend to appeal to friends just as often, if not more so. In the first survey, 34 percent of the Anglos saw a friend and 22 percent a relative about an emotional problem in the last year; in the second survey, 35 percent reported talking to a friend and 37 percent to a relative at one time in their life. This difference is in part a result of the fact that Anglos are less

Table 3-2
Types of Emotional Problems Reported by
Mexican and Anglo Americans

Mexican American Generation

Emotional Problems Reported	First	Second	Third	Mexican Americans	Anglos
Total number of Problems	155	232	88	488	351
Locus of Problem by Percentage					
1. Internal	20	16	17	18	35
2. Family-Total	62	62	62	61	49
a. marital	28	30	28	28	15
b. children	18	16	14	16	17
d. family	16	15	19	16	17
3. Non-family	12	13	14	13	11
4. Alcohol/Drugs	6	9	7	8	5
Total	100	100	100	100	100

NOTE — The Mexican American total column reflects three generations plus 13
Mexican American respondents who could *not* be classified by generation.

likely to have relatives nearby. Yet, even when kin are accessible, Anglos rely equally on friends and relatives (Keefe, Padilla, and Carlos, 1979). In other words, Anglos do not distinguish between the bonds of friendship and familism in the search for emotional support. This is further evident in the significantly greater number of Mexican Americans as opposed to Anglos who believe it is a good idea to seek advice for an emotional problem from a relative (49 percent vs. 34 percent; x^2 = 9.18; $p < .01$).

The role of both physicians and clergymen should be mentioned. One-fourth of the Mexican Americans and one-third of the Anglos in the second survey asked their physician for help with an emotional problem at some time in their life. There is a tendency for first generation Mexican Americans to consult with physicians much less frequently than native-born Mexican Americans, presumably because of the expense. With regard to clergymen, one in four Mexican Americans and more than one in five Anglos in the second survey sought help from a clergyman.

Finally, and not unexpectedly, we find professional psychiatric services are used much more often by Anglos than Mexican Americans. Whereas one in five Anglos in the first survey saw a private counselor, psychologist, or psychiatrist at some time in their life, this is true for only one in twenty-five Mexican Americans (x^2 = 76.4; $p < .001$). Similarly, over twice as many Anglos as Mexican Americans went to a public mental health clinic in the past two years (five percent vs. two percent; x^2 = 4.0; $p < .05$). In the second survey, the proportion of Mexican Americans who had ever contacted a private therapist or public mental health services had increased slightly (12 percent and 7 percent respectively), primarily because we had actively solicited additional mental health clinic users who were also more likely to have used private professional services. Nonetheless, even in the second survey, Anglos are much more likely to utilize private services (23 percent vs. 12 percent; x^2 = 11.4; $p < .001$). Again, as might be expected, the first generation is least likely to make use of psychotherapists; 11 percent have had some contact with public or private psychotherapy versus 16 percent of the second generation and 19 percent of the third generation.

In sum, informal sources of help such as kin and friends are preferred for help and also tend to be consulted most often. Second-level helping agents include clergymen and doctors. Anglos frequently consult with psychotherapists as a final attempt to find help, while Mexican Americans, especially the first generation, tend to *avoid* conventional mental health facilities and therapists or are *not aware* of the services offered.

Factors Affecting Choice of the Helping Agent

There are additional factors affecting the search for emotional support and the differentiation between the type of help available from informal sources such as relatives and friends, more formal sources such as clergymen and doctors, and professional psychiatric services, including private therapists and public mental health clinics. The factors affecting selection from these potential sources of help are four types: (1) the perceived nature of the emotional problem itself; (2) the perceived qualities of the source of help selected; (3) language ability and preference; and (4) social patterns and their accompanying information networks.

As was made clear previously, Anglos and Mexican Americans perceive the nature of their problems somewhat differently, more Anglos perceiving them as mainly self-related. The way in which problems are perceived also affects the source of help chosen. The way in which problems are perceived also affects the source of help chosen. For example, both Anglos and Mexican Americans tend to go to relatives and friends for all sorts of problems: internal, family-related, non-family, and those related to alcohol and drugs. Mexican Americans with a marital problem, for instance, first talk to a relative or friend and then turn to a priest, or perhaps a physician. Problems which involve the family as a whole follow somewhat the same pattern. Child-related problems, however, are very often treated by professional therapists. Internal problems are dealt with by informal helpers and physicians. As a matter of fact, 35 percent of all the internal problems described by the Mexican American respondents were treated by physicians compared to only 23 percent of the Anglos' internal problems. With respect to psychotherapists, Mexican Americans only turn to these professionals with any frequency for child-related problems; Anglos utilize them for all sorts of problems. For problems which are marital, child-related, and related to the family as a whole, Anglos turn first to their family and friends and then to either a clergyman, physician, or therapist with equal frequency. For internal problems, Anglos are not likely to go to a clergyman after talking with informal sources, but are equally likely to see a physician or professional therapist. Again, it is apparent that Anglos regard psychotherapy as a ubiquitous source of help, while Mexican Americans seem to consider it only for their children who may have no choice in the matter.

The second factor to be discussed is the individual's perception of the significant qualities of the particular source of help chosen. Both Anglos and Mexican Americans turn to family and friends because they are trusted to provide confidential support and because they are believed to be familiar with either the specific problem or the respondent's life in general, thus perhaps having some insight to help in resolving the problem. Both ethnic groups tend to consult with clergymen because they believe the problem will remain confidential and because the clergy is believed to be informed on how to best deal with life's problems. Of course, the clergy tends to be considered competent in this regard mainly by those respondents who have strong religious convictions and attend church regularly. Physicians are most often consulted by Anglos because they believe medication is required to relieve their emotional problems and because they view their problem as physical in origin. First generation Mexican Americans also go to physicians, perceiving the need for medication and, additionally, because they respect the physician's knowledge. The native-born are more likely to say they have a family physician who is familiar with their situation. Both Anglos and Mexican Americans consult with psychotherapists because they were referred, although Anglos are much more likely to be self-referrals than Mexican Americans. For example, almost half of the Anglos using a public mental health clinic were self-referrals, compared to one-fifth of the Mexican Americans. Moreover, first generation Mexican Americans are least likely to be self-referrals. This again would appear to corroborate other data indicating that Mexican Americans, especially immigrants, do not voluntarily seek out professional psychiatric services.

Mexican Americans who consult psychotherapists do not have a negative opinion of therapists. On the contrary, Mexican Americans appear to be quite satisfied with the services they receive. In fact, they are somewhat more satisfied than Anglos. Of respondents who consulted a private psychotherapist, 74 percent of the Mexican Americans, but only 50 percent of the Anglos, indicated they were helpful with their problems (x^2 = 3.34; p = .07). And 87 percent of the Mexican Americans, compared to 56 percent of the Anglos who went to a public mental health clinic, thought it was helpful (x^2 = 4.26; $p <$ .05). In a way, it can be taken as proof of strength of cultural values that Mexican Americans do not consult psychotherapists despite favorable attitudes by former clients.

Perhaps the most significant cultural factors to affect choice of a helping agent among Mexican Americans is language ability and preference. In the discussion of acculturation patterns, it was clear that first generation Mexican Americans are overwhelmingly Spanish-speaking. Only one-fourth of the first generation respondents consider themselves fairly fluent in English. This is further reflected in the language in which they discuss their emotional problems. About 80 percent or more of the immigrants use mainly Spanish in talking to relatives, *compadres,* and friends about their emotional problems. The same pattern occurs in their choice of language when discussing emotional problems with their priest; 88 percent of those seeing a priest spoke mainly in Spanish. Since 71 percent of the first generation who attend church go to a Catholic church located in the *barrio* staffed by Spanish-speaking priests, religious help in their own language is easily accessible.

Accessibility of other formal Spanish-speaking helpers is not easy because of their relative absence in the communities studied. A count of the number of physicians (all specialties) as well as psychiatrists in the three communities confirms the fact that the Mexican American population is forced to seek out physicians and psychiatrists with whom they must discuss their problems in English. As a matter of fact, the lack of medical care from physicians who speak Spanish is severe. For example, using 1970 population census figures, the ratio of Anglo physicians to the non Spanish origin population in Santa Barbara, Santa Paula, and Oxnard is respectively 1:193, 1:948, and 1:774. On the other hand, the ratio of Spanish surname physicians to the Spanish origin population in Santa Barbara and Oxnard is 1:3732 and 1:6081 respectively. A ratio for Santa Paula cannot be computed because of the absence of Spanish surname physicians in this town.

A similar lack of Spanish speaking professionals exists in the area of mental health care in the three communities. While 36 Anglo psychiatrists are found in private practice, only one Hispanic (but not Mexican American) psychiatrist can be found in three communities. In terms of public mental health therapists (psychiatrists, psychologists, psychiatric social workers, and psychiatric nurses), there were 25 Anglos and only 5 Hispanics (not necessarily Mexican Americans) in our sampling of mental health centers and clinics. This situation, then, poses a dilemma for those Spanish dominant Mexican Americans who need mental health care, especially immigrants. They can seek assistance and discuss their problems in English, they can choose not to seek professional help, or they can return to Mexico. Our data indicate that of those first generation respondents who sought help from a public mental health clinic, 50 percent were forced to speak English. Similarly, of the 15 first generation respondents who acknowledged that they had consulted a professional for counseling, three had traveled to Mexico for consultation, while a fourth had received such aid in Mexico prior to immigrating to the United States.

We do not believe that the communities studied are atypical in regard to the small number of Spanish surnamed physicians or mental health specialists. On the contrary, we believe that the communities, if not representative, possibly have greater access to Spanish speaking professionals than other communities of similar size. These data highlight two points that we have been making: first, that culturally-relevant services for non-English speaking clients are essential; and, second, that the very small number of Spanish speaking professionals attests to the absence of structural pluralism of Mexican Americans in the United States. In sum, Spanish speakers who are forced to discuss their problems in a language that is not their own or through an interpreter make communication about sensitive problems difficult. It also means that Spanish speakers are unlikely to receive help of the quality they deserve.

Language considerations are also important for the second generation respondents who tend to use Spanish to some extent in their discussions of emotional problems with relatives, *compadres,* friends, and priests. Physicians and mental health specialists tend to be spoken to in English. Third generation respondents use predominantly English regardless of the source of help.

Finally, we must consider the effect of social patterns on the choice of helping agents. In the previous discussion of ethnicity of the respondents' associates, we found that Anglos and Mexican Americans interact within ethnic boundaries. In the search for help with emotional problems, this pattern tends to continue. Anglos talk to friends and relatives of their own ethnic group and more than nine out of ten who consult a clergyman, physician, or professional therapist see an Anglo American. Mexican Americans also remain within ethnic boundaries at least for informal sources of help, including friends and relatives. First and second generation respondents also tend to see priests of Mexican descent, while the third generation (who are most likely to go to English services in a church located outside the *barrio*) consult mainly with Anglo priests. The ethnicity of other sources of help also varies by generation. One in four of the first generation went to a physician of Mexican descent and over half went to a professional therapist of Mexican descent to talk about an emotional problem. Most of the second generation went to an Anglo physician and an Anglo private therapist, while over half consulted with a public mental health therapist of Mexican descent. Lastly, the third generation went primarily to physicians, private therapists, and public mental health therapists of Anglo descent.

In sum, Mexican Americans tend to remain within ethnic boundaries when seeking informal support. More formal and professional ethnic sources of help are limited in availability. Nevertheless, the first generation seeks out priests who are of Mexican descent and makes an effort to do the same with physicians and psychotherapists. Language limitations are probably foremost in motivating the immigrants to search for helping agents of the same ethnicity. Even so, second generation respondents are likely to turn to priests and public mental health therapists of Mexican descent, though language would not appear to be much of a motivating factor. If there were equal availability, chances are there would probably be more choice of formal and professional helping agents of the same ethnicity among second and third generations.

One of the consequences of ethnic enclosure, at least on an informal level, is variation in the level of information about psychotherapy available to respondents. In the first questionnaire, respondents were asked if they could tell the interviewer where the nearest local mental health clinic was located. The following question asked respondents if they recognized the name and location of the nearest clinic when it was given by the interviewer. Almost half of the Anglos and more than half the native-born Mexican Americans indicated some knowledge of mental health facilities in answering these two questions. Only 37 percent of the first generation Mexican Americans, on the other hand, had similar knowledge of available mental health facilities. Data from the second survey indicate that the first generation is also least likely to know of someone who has made use of professional psychiatric services; 28 percent know of someone who has seen a psychiatrist and 33 percent know someone who has been a patient in a mental hospital. For native-borns, the majority are acquainted with someone who has been in a mental hospital. Anglos are most familiar with people using these sources of help; 80 percent know someone who went to a psychiatrist and 65 percent know someone who has been in a mental hospital. Thus we find, not unexpectedly, familiarity with professional mental health resources is related to their use by each group and that it is the first generation, those who use professional services least, who are least likely to know where they might be located, or have any indirect knowledge about the services provided. Of course, there may be considerable knowledge about the services and yet relatively little use of them, as is demonstrated by the native-born Mexican Americans. Nontheless, there is a general pattern of some increase in use with increased knowledge of the services available, which excludes first generation Mexican Americans, who, because they interact primarily among themselves, do not have access to information concerning professional psychiatric care.

THE CONSEQUENCES OF PLURALISM IN THE SEARCH FOR HELP

Anglo Americans make up the dominant segment of the larger community. They are the numerical majority; their cultural patterns take precedence over others; and they control the social, economic and political life of the community. As a group, they are fairly well educated, make a good living, live in middle class neighborhoods, and have many of the comforts in American society. The social relationships among Anglos are predominantly based on friendships between individuals. Most Anglos have lived in town less than 15 years and their ties to the community and to other members of the community are relatively undeveloped. In addition, they have little personal contact with members of other cultural groups. Although they may have some contact with ethnic minorities in secondary relationships, such as co-workers, most of their significant interactions are with others of Anglo descent. This pattern is maintained in their search for emotional support as well.

Anglos tend to perceive emotional problems as primarily the result of environmental factors—the individual's strength of character having little to do with causation. Though problems begin with external causes, they may become internalized with time and attributed to self more than to other factors. Thus, if the original cause can be found, the individual can be helped. Concomitantly, there is public approval of most any helping agent that might ease the problem at hand. While not responsible for the problem itself, the individual is held responsible for recognizing that the problem exists and finding help.

Anglos first tend to discuss their problems with family and friends. Friends tend to be most readily available, but Anglos also seek out specific close relatives, who may live at a distance, for emotional support. If the problem continues, other more formal and professional helping agents are consulted. Many Anglos join special groups designed to help individuals with various and assorted kinds of problems. For family-related problems in particular, Anglos turn to a clergyman, or perhaps a physician, and then a professional therapist. Internal problems are likely to call for a physician's help, followed by professional therapy. Anglos often believe they should receive medication for the somatic symptoms they experience. There is little tendency, however, to perceive the physician as one competent to provide psychotherapy. Furthermore, while they may also expect the physician to refer them to a psychotherapist if necessary, Anglos are almost as likely to seek professional therapy without being referred. Their attitude towards therapy is not extremely positive, but they will eventually seek it out if it appears that other sources have not helped. In many ways, Anglos perceive psychiatric care as a service available to the consumer looking for treatment; it is expensive and there is no guarantee it will help, but it is relied upon when there is no other alternative.

Mexican Americans make up a subordinate segment in the communities dominated by Anglos. While many of their Mexican cultural traits are lost over generations, Mexican Americans retain certain cultural patterns and have added new ones unique to their ethnic group in the United States. Mexican Americans lack socioeconomic and political power as a segment of the community. Some individuals have achieved high status, but compared to Anglos, Mexican Americans have lower levels of education, a lower standard of living, and generally have fewer of the luxuries available to their Anglo counterparts. Mexican Americans tend to be long-standing members of the community and their social relationships are predominantly kin-based. By virtue of kinship, Mexican Americans are part of intimate social groups providing structure and support for all members. The kin group provides an ethnically-enclosed circle of associates and, while members of other ethnic groups may be contacted in the course of making a living, or chatting with neighbors, the most meaningful relations are kinship and friendship—those bounded by ethnicity. Moreover, it is within these intimate social groups that help is first sought for emotional problems.

Mexican Americans believe the tendency to have emotional problems is a direct result of the individual's strength of character. Regardless of the situation imposed by the environment, an inherently strong person is believed able to overcome problems, while a weak person will inevitably break under pressure and require help. A strong person should also be able to recognize the need for help when the time comes, but the value placed on self-help and the ability to withstand pressures and problems contradicts this. Therefore, problems are not willingly admitted and once they are, help is sought from the least threatening sources. Formal sources of help such as priests and physicians are acceptable because they offer a range of services other than the treatment of emotional problems. Thus, the individual need not admit that an emotional problem exists, or expose to others the real nature of the problem in order to consult with a physician or priest. Psychotherapists, in contrast, offer just one service and are avoided because the need for therapy reflects a weakness of character. In the same way, Mexican Americans are unlikely to perceive their problems as primarily internal, a further admission of weakness. Mexican Americans seek help for problems that are mostly related to familial difficulties, especially difficulties with a spouse.

When the need for help is recognized, Mexican Americans usually talk with a kinsman, the most available and most preferred source of help. Sometimes a close friend may be consulted. In either case, the first contact is with another member of their own ethnic group. For persistent problems, help is sought from a priest or a physician, either of whom are considered competent to deal with varying sorts of emotional problems. Priests are especially important sources of help for Mexican Americans with marital problems and physicians for internal problems. Psychotherapists are not often consulted, but, when they are, their services are most commonly requested for children's problems.

Few physicians or professional therapists of Mexican descent are available (Martinez, 1977; Padilla, 1977; Ruiz, 1971; Stang and Peale, 1977). This shortage is due largely to the structural pluralism that exists and the relatively small number of Mexican Americans who are in professional occupations of any kind. Nevertheless, many individuals, particularly those who speak Spanish, seek out the few Mexican American physicians and therapists who are available. Other evidence of structural pluralism is the absence, until recently, of mental health clinics relevant to the Mexican American population (Padilla, et al., 1976). Since 1970, mental health services in two of the three communities studied have made some attempt to provide bilingual staff and culturally appropriate services to meet the needs of Mexican Americans. Multi-service centers were built recently in the barrio of each of the two large cities. The mental health clinic branches in these centers all have bilingual staff. These are recent developments and, before they were established, mental health services were inadequately organized for the Mexican American community. The third town in the study (Santa Paula) has no permanent mental health clinic and is served by two non Spanish-speaking therapists who staff the clinic two days a week. Mexican Americans in this town who use public mental health services are likely to travel over ten miles to one of the larger cities nearby in order to receive treatment—an obvious deterrent to mental health care.

One of the implications of the ethnically-enclosed social patterns at the informal level is the distinct nature of information exchanged by ethnic group members. Unlike Anglos, who more commonly exchange information about professional psychiatric care, Mexican Americans are less likely to talk about such services, simply because fewer of them have utilized these more formalized services of help. Without such experience, there is even less reason to seek out and utilize these services. While many of the native-born know the location of a mental health clinic, it is much like an Anglo knowing where the local Mexican American community center is located; very little is known about the purpose or function of the establishment, nor is there any motivation to investigate it.

First generation Mexican Americans are due special consideration in the discussion of pluralism because they form a separate, distinct segment of the Mexican American community. They are the most socioeconomically depressed and the most residentially segregated. They are the least educated and not integrated into the larger community. They are culturally distinct from both Anglos and other Mexican Americans; they are largely Spanish-speaking; and they have very little contact with Anglo Americans, even in secondary relations. While their social relations, like other Mexican Americans, tend to be with kin, they are not likely to have very large local kin groups, having immigrated to the United States, and as a result are more socially isolated than either Anglos or native-born Mexican Americans. When they experience emotional problems, therefore, they have fewer informal sources of support to rely on for help.

It is among the immigrants that cultural pressure to maintain an image of strength persists. They are also the least able to afford to seek the help. When problems occur, they have few resources at hand, lack information about resources that may be available in the community, and, because of language limitations, find it difficult to seek out potential resources. Consequently, foreign-born Mexican Americans are least likely to expose their problems, seek help voluntarily, or consult with a physician or psychotherapist. Although they try to work within a Spanish-speaking network of help, many are forced to speak with their physician or professional therapist in English, and some travel to Mexico in order to find culturally-relevant services. Finally, the fairly rigid ethnic boundaries within which they interact serve to reinforce their distinct cultural beliefs, making them more resistant to change than the native-born Mexican Americans.

CONCLUSIONS

Our research on mental health and ethnic communities leads us to several conclusions. Most previous research has been done with rural people who tend to be fairly uneducated, unacculturated, and less sophisticated about medical systems and psychological disorders. Results from these studies include characterization of the Mexican American population as ignorant of modern medicine, afraid of physicians and hospitals, retaining belief in folk medicine and supernatural causation, and maintaining a preference for traditional folk healers. Our data indicate that such is not the case with urban Mexican Americans in Southern California. Instead, this population readily consults with physicians, while folk healers are rarely utilized, even among immigrants. Considering that the Mexican American population in the Southwest is predominantly third generation and urban-dwelling, it is extremely misleading to extrapolate from much of the existing literature. Future research must be directed towards urban populations and must include consideration of full range of helping agents available in the community, not merely the more colorful folk healing specialists.

A second conclusion indicated by our research is the need to analyze the Mexican American population according to its socioculturally significant segments. We have found generation to be the most useful, but other indicators are important as well, such as socioeconomic status, immigrants from Mexico, ethnic identity and loyalty, and the type of neighborhood and city of residence. This list is not inclusive, but it demonstrates the range of variables that must be taken into consideration in doing research with Mexican Americans. Research that does not identify which specific segment of the Mexican American population is being studied yields questionable results. In our own data, simple analysis of the Mexican American group as a whole would have obscured much of its rich variation, as well as any indication of the process occurring within the population. By comparing the three generations, aspects which are truly characteristic of the entire ethnic group can be ascertained with confidence. It is important to add that it is only with the comparative Anglo data that we are able to evaluate inter-ethnic, as well as intra-ethnic similarities and differences.

The recognition of intra-ethnic differences is especially important for mental health practitioners who service the Mexican American community. First, mental health service agencies must be aware of the specific characteristics of the local Mexican American population they serve. Second, mental health specialists must recognize that needs may vary between segments of the Mexican American population and services should be designed to accommodate these variations. To reach some of these segments, it may be necessary to step outside the traditional bounds of mental health services. This is already being done by clinics in some areas, where staff provide many services, including finding housing or jobs, besides psychotherapy (Burruel and Chavez, 1974). Combining services in this manner should increase the number of Spanish-speaking people, especially first generation Mexican American, using public mental health clinics.

While the immigrants form the most culturally distinct segment of the Mexican American population, it must not be assumed that, with each generation, Mexican Americans are gradually acculturating to the mainstream society. Many Mexican traits are retained over generations and some new ones specific to Mexicans in the United States are added. There is no simple process of change. Moreover, the adoption of certain Anglo American traits, such as the English language, should not be confused with the assimilation into Anglo American primary groups. Mexican Americans interact within an ethnic community in each successive generation. Kinship establishes the core of this ethnic community and the close, integrated social networks ensures the continuation of many cultural patterns distinct from the mainstream.

Just as there are ethnic communities, there are also ethnic systems of mental health. Each ethnic group has an integrated set of perceptions, attitudes, and behaviors associated with mental health and illness. Thomas and Garrison (1975) demonstrate this with the case study of a Dominican migrant in New York. They argue for a general systems view of community mental health that can incorporate the many ethnic and minority group systems making up the whole. This model is advocated for both research and practice in the field of community mental health. We find strong evidence for this viewpoint in our research. Only with a better understanding of ethnic systems will community mental health professionals successfully reach out to all peoples in need of help.

FOOTNOTES

[1]This research was supported by Grant MH 26099 from the National Institute of Mental Health, Center for Minority Group Mental Health Programs.

[2]The sources of emotional support of Anglos and Mexican Americans have been analyzed in more depth elsewhere (Keefe, Padilla, and Carlos, 1979).

REFERENCES

Almaguer, T., Toward the study of chicano colonialism. *Axtlan—Chicano Journal of the Social Sciences and the Arts*, 1971, *1*, 7-21.

Bachrach, L.L. *Utilization of state and county mental hospitals by Spanish Americans in 1972.* (Statistical Note 116). Rockville, Md.: National Institute of Mental Health, Division of Biometry, 1975.

Barrera, M., Munoz, C., and Ornelas, C. The barrio as an internal colony. In Harlan H. Hahn (ed.), *People and politics in urban society, urban affairs annual review*, Vol. 6 Beverly Hills, Ca.: Sage Publications, 1972.

Blair, P.M. *Job discrimination and education: An investment analysis, a case study of Mexican Americans in Santa Clara County, California*. New York: Praeger, 1972.

Blauner, R. Colonized and immigrant minorities. In P.I. Rose (ed.), *Nation of nations*. New York: Random House, 1972.

Bloom, B.L. *Changing patterns of psychiatric care*. New York: Human Science Press, 1975.

Burreul, G. and Chavex, N. Mental health outpatient centers: Relevant or irrelevant to Mexican Americans? In A.B. Tulipan, C.L. Attneave, and E. Kingstone (eds.) *Beyond clinic walls*. University, AL: University of Alabama Press, POCA Perspectives, 1974.

Clark, M. *Health in the Mexican American Culture*. Berkeley: University of California Press, 1959.

Creson, D.L., McKinley, C., and Evans, R. Folk medicine in Mexican American subculture. *Diseases of the Nervous System*. 1969, *30*, 264-266.

Fanon, F. *The wretched of the earth*, New York: Grove Press, 1968.

Furnivall, J.S. *Netherlands India: A study of plural economy*. Cambridge: The University Press, 1939.

Furnivall, J.S. *Colonial policy and practice: A comparative study of Burma and Netherlands India*, London: Cambridge University Press, 1948.

Gordon, M.M. *Assimilation in American life: The role of race, religion, and national origins*. New York: Oxford University Press, 1964.

Graves, T.D. Psychological acculturation in a tri-ethnic community. Southwest Journal of Anthropology, 1967, *23*, 337-350.

Grebler, L., Moore, J.W., and Guzman, R.C. *The Mexican American People: The nation's second largest minority*. New York: The Free Press, 1970.

Jaco, E.G. Social factors in mental disorders in Texas. *Social Problems*, 1957, *4*, 322-328.

Karno, M. and Edgerton, R.B. Perception of mental illness in a Mexican American community. *Archives of General Psychiatry*, 1969, *20*, 233-238.

Keefe, S.E. Why Mexican Americans underutilize mental health clinics: Fact and fallacy. In J.M. Casas and S.E. Keefe (eds.) *Family and Mental Health in the Mexican American Community*. Los Angeles: Spanish Speaking Mental Health Research Center, UCLA, Monograph No. 7, 1978.

Keefe, S.E., Padilla, A.M., and Carlos, M.L. *Emotional support systems in two cultures: A comparison of Mexican Americans and Anglo Americans*. Los Angeles: Spanish Speaking Mental Health Research Center, UCLA, Occasional Paper No. 7, 1978.

Keefe, S.E., Padilla, A.M., and Carlos, M.L. The Mexican American extended family as an emotional support system. *Human Organization*, 1979, *38*, 144-152.

Kiev, A. *Curanderismo: Mexican American folk psychiatry*. New York: Free Press, 1968.

Kramer, J.R. *The American minority community*. New York: Thomas Y. Crowell, 1970.

Kuper, L. and Smith, M.G. (eds.) *Pluralism in Africa*. Berkeley: University of California Press, 1969.

Leons, M.B. and Leons, W. The utility of pluralism: M.G. Smith and plural theory. *American Ethnologist*, 1977, *4*, 559-574.

Madsen, W. *The Mexican American of South Texas*. New York: Holt, Rinehart, and Winston, 1964.

Madsen, W. Mexican American and Anglo Americans: A comparative study of mental health in Texas. In S.C. Plog and B. Edgerton (eds.), *Changing Perspectives in Mental Illness*. New York: Holt, Rinehart and Winston, 1969.

Martinez, C. Hispanics in psychiatry. In E.L. Olmedo and S. Lopez (eds.), *Hispanic mental health professionals* (Monograph No. 5). Los Angeles: University of California, Spanish Speaking Mental Health Research Center, 1977.

McLemore, S.D. Ethnic attitudes toward hospitalization: An illustrative comparison of Anglos and Mexican Americans. *Social Science Quarterly*, 1963, *43*, 341-346.

Memmi, A: *The Colonizer and the colonized*. Boston: Beacon Press, 1965.

Moll, L.C., Rueda, R.S., Reza, R., Herrera, J., and Vasquez, L.P. Mental health services in East Los Angeles: An urban community case study. In M.R. Miranda (ed.), *Psychotherapy with the Spanish speaking: Issues in research and service delivery*. Los Angeles: Spanish Speaking Mental Health Research Center, UCLA, 1976, 21-34.

Moore, J.W. Social class, assimilation and acculturation. In J. Helm (ed.) *Spanish speaking people in the United States*, Proceedings of the 1968 Annual Spring Meeting of the American Ethnological Society, Seattle: American Ethnological Society, University of Washington Press, 1968.

Moore, J.W. *Mexican American*. Englewood Cliffs, N.J.: Prentice-Hall, 1970.(a)

Moore, J.W. Colonialism: The case of the Mexican Americans. *Social Problems*, 1970, *17*, 463-472.(b)

Murguia, E. *Assimilation, colonialism and the Mexican American people*. Austin: Center for Mexican American Studies, University of Texas Press at Austin. Mexican American Monograph Series #1, 1975.

Nagata, J.A. What is a malay? Situational selection of ethnic identity in a plural society. *American Ethnologist*, 1974, *1*, 331-350.

Nall, F.C. and Speilberg, J. Social and cultural factors in the responses of Mexican Americans to medical treatment. *Journal of Health and Social Behavior*, 1967, *8*, 299-308.

Newton, F. The Mexican American emic system mental illness: An exploratory study. *Culture, Medicine and Psychiatry*, in press.

Novak, M. *The Rise of the Unmeltable Ethnics*. New York: MacMillan, 1971.

Opler, M.K. *Culture, psychiatry, and human values: The methods and values of a social psychiatry*. Springfield, Ill.: Charles C. Thomas, 1956.

Padilla, E.R. Hispanics in clinical psychology. In E.L. Olmedo and S. Lopez (eds.), *Hispanic mental health professionals* (Monograph No. 5). Los Angeles:

University of California, Spanish Speaking Mental Health Research Center, 1977.

Padilla, A.M., Carlos, M.L., and Keefe, S.E. Mental health service utilization by Mexican Americans. In M.R. Miranda (ed.) *Psychotherapy with the Spanish speaking: Issues in research and service delivery.* Los Angeles: Spanish Speaking Mental Health Research Center, UCLA. Monograph No. 3, 1976.

Rubel, A.J. *Across the tracks: Mexican Americans in a Texas city.* Austin, Texas: University of Texas Press, 1966.

Ruiz, R.A. Relative frequency of Americans with Spanish surnames in associations of psychology, psychiatry, and sociology. *American Psychologist,* 1971, *26,* 1022-1024.

Saunders, L. *Cultural differences and medical care: The case of the Spanish Speaking People of the Southwest.* New York: Russell Sage Foundation, 1954.

Shannon, L. and Shannon, M. *Minority migrants in the urban community: Mexican American and Negro adjustment to industrial society.* Beverly Hills, Ca.: Sage Publications, 1973.

Smith, M.G. Social and cultural pluralism. *Annals of the New York Academy of Sciences,* 1960, *83,* 763-785.

Smith, M.G. Some developments in the analytic framework of pluralism. In L. Kuper and M.G. Smith (eds.) *Pluralism in Africa.* Berkeley: University of California Press, 1969.

Social Science Research Council Seminar on Acculturation. An exploratory formation. *American Anthropologist.,* 1954, *56,* 973-1000.

Stang, D.J. and Peele, D. The status of minorities in psychology. In E.L. Olmedo and S. Lopez (eds.), *Hispanic mental health professionals* (Monograph No. 5). Los Angeles: University of California, Spanish Speaking Mental Health Research Center, 1977.

Thomas, C.S. and Garrison, V. A general systems view of community mental health. In L. Bellak and H. Barten (eds.), *Progress in community mental health.* Vol. 3. New York: Brunner/Mazel, Inc., 1975.

Torrey, E.F. *The mind game: Witchdoctors and psychiatrists.* New York: Emerson Hall Publishers, 1972.

U.S. Bureau of the Census. *Census of population and housing: 1970.* Census Tracts, Final Report PHC (1) - 191 Santa Barbara, California SMSA. Washington, D.C.: U.S. Government Printing Office, 1972a.

U.S. Bureau of the Census. *Census of Population and Housing: 1970.* Census Tracts, Final Report PHC (1) - 155 Oxnard-Ventura, California SMSA. Washington, D.C.: U.S. Government Printing Office, 1972b.

U.S. Bureau of the Census. *Census of Population: 1970, General, Social, and Economic Characteristics.* Final Report, PC (1) - C6 California. Washington, D.C.: U.S. Government Printing Office, 1972c.

Warner, W.L. and Srole, L. *The social systems of American ethnic groups.* New Haven: Yale University Press, 1945.

Weaver, T. Use of hypothetical situations in a study of Spanish American illness referral systems. *Human Organization,* 1970, *29,* 140-154.

Chapter 4

COMMUNITY MENTAL HEALTH AND MINORITIES
A Multi-Ethnic Approach

Harriet P. Lefley
Evalina W. Bestman

When the United States Congress passed the Community Health Centers Act in 1963, the grand plan was to offer early intervention and to reduce hospitalization by providing easily-acessible, low-cost quality mental health care within the community itself. The delivery system would now be extended to large numbers of clients to whom such services had been generally unavailable, i.e., those who were poor, or from various ethnic or cultural groups. A national network of community mental health centers emerged, based on traditional medical or psychosocial models of treatment, and the doors were opened to clients. Some came a few times, and elected not to return. Others came and stayed, but were not appreciably helped. Many never came at all. It became increasingly apparent that in many centers underutilization was linked to unacceptable or ineffective therapeutic effort, and that one of the critical factors was the experiential and cognitive distance between the typical white, middle-class mental health professional, and the typical catchment area client (Padilla, Ruiz, and Alvarez, 1975; Wolkon, Moriwaki and Williams, 1974).

Had culturally alert behavioral scientists been involved in the early planning phase, they might, of course, have predicted this development. Even in the early sixties, there was a large body of empirical data suggesting that a culture gap between mental health deliverers and consumers could affect each level of the preventive, diagnostic, and therapeutic process. By now, it is quite apparent from the literature that cultures—including ethnic co-cultures within the United States—may differ, not only in adaptive strategies and stress points, but in basic conceptions of the etiology and classification of psychopathy; in modes of behavioral deviance, including differential symptomatology; and in perceptions of appropriate remedies (Draguns, 1973; Lefley, 1974b).

Let us summarize, briefly, some of the problems that arise when ethnic patient meets Anglo healer. These include (among others) linguistic barriers in evaluating psychopathology (Marcos and Alpert, 1976); underrecording or misinterpretation of symptoms (DeHoyos and DeHoyos, 1965); serious diagnostic errors in observing behavior (Simon, Flies, Gurland, Stiller and Sharp, 1973); failure to understand differential response patterns on screening instruments (Gynther, 1972); basic communication difficulties and bias in interviewing (Carkhuff and Pierce, 1967; Williams, 1964); misinterpretation of psychodynamics (Thomas, 1962; Warren, Jackson, Nugaris and Farley, 1973); advice that is counter to cultural mores (Abad, Ramos and Boyce, 1974; Lombillo and Geraghty, 1973); and failure to differentiate between adaptive and maladaptive behavior (Gilbert, 1974). The net result has been differential treatment, utilization, and outcome (Acosta and Sheehan, 1976; Padilla, Ruiz and Alvarez, 1975).

The potential value conflict in psychotherapy aiming at mastery over one's destiny with a client coming from a "high external" culture is one of the more salient problems in cross-cultural interactions. Mazer (1973) has given seven common assumptions of therapists that may be in conflict with those who are culturally different. These include: (a) the assumption that patient goals should aim at achievement of autonomy and assumption of responsibility for one's own actions; (b) the belief that one is capable of change and growth; (c) capability of deferring gratification; (d) the belief that one should self-disclose and regard one's experiences as worthy of investigation; and (e) the therapist not directly disclosing information about him or her. She notes that "psychotherapy, as outlined above, works for people who share these same values—who can feel comfortable in, or at least tolerate, an ambiguous relationship, who believe in change and future; and who value their 'I'. These people, for the most part, are from the educated middle class, and their cultural values mesh well with the psychotherapist's" (p. 114).

In addition to the questions regarding values, one may pose some others relating to the application of the technology so painstakingly learned in clinical training. How does a clinician, for example, deal with an inability to interpret simple linguistic referents (let alone paralinguistic and kinesic cues) in the diagnostic or therapeutic interaction? How does the psychoanalytically oriented therapist differentiate between an appropriate cultural response and neurotic transference (Thomas 1962)? How can a client accept a Freudian interpretation of his or her dreams, when one's own culture offers a systematized belief system for interpreting specific dream symbols (Wingerd, 1973)? How does the Gestalt therapist, with his or her corpus of knowledge and socialization derived from a particular cultural experience, begin to enter the client's phenomenal field? How does the behaviorist assess the functional and dysfunctional characteristics of the client's behavior, its appropriateness or inappropriateness in cultural context, and its contingencies of reinforcement? The fact is that most mental health professionals solve these problems by avoidance. The research indicates that non-white, non-Anglo patients are more likely to receive arbitrary diagnoses based on limited or ambiguous symptoms (DeHoyos and DeHoyos, 1965); are less often accepted for psychotherapy; more often assigned to inexperienced therapists; seen for shorter periods of time; and more often receive either supportive or custodial care, or drugs alone (Gross and Herbert, 1969; Hunt, 1962; Kohut, 1959; Maas, 1967; Singer, 1967; Yamamoto, James, and Palley, 1968).

Concurrent with the emergent findings on these bilateral service barriers—both institutional and epistemological—to lower socioeconomic ethnic clients, was a parallel body of data suggesting that it was precisely such groups, over-represented among the poor, who might need these services the most. Very briefly, evidence from numerous comprehensive studies has indicated that the lowest socioeconomic groups have the highest rates of severe psychiatric disorder (Fried, 1969; Kohn, 1973); that high incidence areas tend to be those with the greatest percentage of poor people, substandard housing, residential instability, and highest crime and delinquency rates (Levy and Rowitz, 1973); and that the interaction of poverty and social discrimination (and perhaps misdiagnosis stemming from these variables) generates astonishing differentials in U.S. mental hospital admission rates, with current (1975) figures, per 100,000 population, as follows: for males, 214.2 for whites versus 444.5 for blacks and other races, and for females, 111.2 for whites versus 212.0 for blacks and other races (Milazzo-Sayre, 1977). For the population as a whole, moreover, epidemiological data indicate that hospitalization for mental illness increases during economic downturns and decreases during economic upturns (Brenner, 1973).

These relationships are not restricted to the United States. In the recent NIMH release of a quarter of century of research findings, it was indicated that more than 50 studies completed in Canada, Europe, and Asia consistently indicated that schizophrenia occurs most frequently at the lowest socioeconomic levels of urban society. Further, although the magnitude of mental disorders in less complex societies seem to be of the same order as that in highly urbanized Western societies, rates differ within societies by social class (Segal, 1975).

It would seem, then, that while there is still considerable dispute concerning the antecedents of mental illness, there is impressive correlative evidence that social-environmental stressors may exacerbate preexisting conditions, trigger mental health crises among the vulnerable, or create a negative ambience affecting child-rearing and family transactions.

Highly concordant with these inferences was the emergence, in the late sixties, of what Schulberg (1977) has termed "a community mental health ideology." While, functionally, this ideology has ranged from a mild community commitment, all the way to utilizing the centers as a political instrument for social equity, the core concepts are very clear. According to Schulberg, the basic components are:

1. *A Population Focus.* Mental health specialists are not only responsible for the care of defined patients but also for their community's unidentified potentially sick members.

2. *Primary Prevention.* The rate of a population's mental disorder can be lowered by counteracting harmful forces in the environment.

3. *Social Treatment Goals.* Treatment's primary goal is not to reconstruct the patient's personality but to help him/her achieve social adjustment in ordinary life situations.

4. *Continuity of Care.* Professional responsibility must be maintained as the patient moves from one program to another in a network of services.

5. *Total Community Involvement.* The mental health specialist, as one of a community's care-giving agents, can extend his/her effectiveness by working with and through other people (p. 3).

Schulberg goes on to cite Baker's (1974) expansion and refinement of community mental health ideology into a new belief system of the early 1970's. Labelled "human service ideology," its basic themes essentially called for comprehensive services through linking and integrating care-giving agencies, optimal accessibility of services, transcending disciplinary and professional boundaries; provider accountability; and focusing on problems in living in terms of the fit between individuals and their environments, rather than on diagnostic labels.

These generic principles, together with preliminary findings of anthropological fieldwork in our catchment area, formed much of the basis of the innovative community mental health program to be described in this chapter. Initiated in 1974, the University of Miami-Jackson Memorial Medical Center Community Mental Health Program (CMHP) began with a conceptual framework that stressed social systems modification and ethnic accountability in its approach to mental health care. This approach derived from an attempt to define "community" in behavioral science terms—as socialization matrix, stressor, and support system for the vulnerable individual—rather than simply as an alternative locale for the distribution of clinical services. In the model developed for the program, the focus was on developing an integrative therapeutic approach to *multiple* communities within a low-income, multi-ethnic catchment area in inner city Miami. This would involve knowledge and assessment of the cultural, socioeconomic, and political configurations of these communities; the range and priorities of their self-defined needs; the stressor and stress points, and alternatively, the adaptive mechanisms and structural supports—in short, the multiplicity of variables related to the mental health of their constituents.

A fundamental element of the model was the concept of *culture broker*, a role described by Weidman (1973) in the health care context as the development of meaningful linkages between the health delivery system and the cultural groups it purports to serve. The term has, of course, been applied in a variety of contexts, ranging from a political buffering role to the modeling function of the marginal individual selected out for mobility (Wolf, 1956). While, historically, this has been a functional role that arose incidentally to meet specific needs posed by modernization, or by the acculturative process, Weidman, one of the major architects of the new community mental health program, suggested the need for a *purposive* role in mediating between clinical and community systems. In her model, the culture broker was neither marginal individual, nor untrained bicultural informant, but a fully trained medical or psychiatric social scientist (preferably an anthropologist), with expertise in a particular culture of which he or she was a member. These individuals would not only mediate and interpret, but would bring a social science perspective to bear on preventive, diagnostic, and treatment modalities for the populations served. In the following program description, a more complete picture is given of the implementation and evolution of this role.

DEVELOPMENTAL HISTORY OF THE PROGRAM

The Health Ecology Project

In 1971, a comprehensive research effort entitled the Health Ecology Project was initiated in our Department of Psychiatry to investigate, in a federally designated poverty area in Miami, the health systems, beliefs and behavior of five ethnic groups who were its major constituents: Bahamians, Cubans, Haitians, Puerto Ricans, and Southern American blacks.[1] In this study of over 500 families, a battery of instruments was administered in each group by indigenous, ethnically-matched research assistants, who maintained longitudinal contact with the families for ongoing, in-depth interviewing. Instruments included a comprehensive sociological questionnaire, symptoms and conditions list, values scale, and a health calendar, maintained daily by sample families. Following the investigation of health beliefs and practices within these 500 families, the fieldworkers spent nine months interviewing folk healers and their patients from each ethnic group.

As part of the research effort, overlay maps had been developed, showing the distribution and accessibility of supportive resources, such as religious, medical, social service, and recreational facilities. The availability of folk healers, botanicas, unorthodox religious systems, and other resources involved in the supportive infrastructure were also delineated. Concomitantly, an ethnic library was established and sets of files were developed for each ethnic group, containing materials from the social science literature, unpublished papers, newspaper articles, demographic data, and other relevant information. These demographic and cultural materials facilitated interpretation of the research findings as they evolved.

Preliminary findings of the Health Ecology Project indicated culturally-patterned differences in the clustering of symptoms; culture-bound syndromes with a large emotional component, unrecognized by the orthodox medical or mental health professions (Lefley, 1979b; Weidman, 1973; 1979); differences in conceptions of bodily functioning (Scott, 1973; 1974); and differential perceptions of causation and remediation of illness. Alternative healing modalities were widely used, often in conjunction with orthodox medical treatment. Orthodox mental health treatment, however, was almost never solicited, although the health calendars and information given during the interviews indicated a high degree of emotional stress.

During this period, the Department of Psychiatry, in conjunction with Jackson Memorial Hospital, was preparing a community mental health center grant proposal, designed to serve a catchment area that incorporated the research population and its human environs. Field data on cultural variations in the distribution, manifestation, and conceptualization of mental health problems (Bestman, Lefley, and Scott, 1976; Lefley, 1979b), together with emergent diagnostic and therapeutic problems among ethnic patients in the hospital system strongly suggested that a community mental health center established along traditional lines would neither be maximally effective nor optimally utilized. Further, while all groups suffered from multiple socioeconomic and environmental stressors, the indications were that, in some cases, culturally specific therapeutic interventions might be required to deal with different ethnic groups living within the same poverty area (see Weidman, 1978, for overview of findings).

The Community Mental Health Program

In March, 1974, the CMHP was funded to serve an inner-city area of 200,000 with a median income of $4,647 and a multiplicity of social problems. The area is predominantly black (over 50 percent) and Spanish-speaking, with the balance primarily poor Anglo elderly. This descriptive statement is based on the tendency of census, hospital, and social indicators statistics to lump diverse populations under these global demographic headings. It was obvious, however, both from the Health Ecology Project findings and the literature as a whole that "Black" and "Spanish-speaking" are by no means adequate as identifying characteristics when it comes to sensitive mental health care. Distinct cultural differences between Afro-Americans and Afro-Caribbean groups, and among Cubans, Puerto Ricans, and other Latinos, suggested the need for a model that would include staff with sufficient linguistic and cultural expertise to meet the needs of clients from diverse populations.

While this paper does not seek to ignore that cultural differences among European or other ethnic groups (Giordano, 1973) and the interaction of social class and ethnicity (Rose and Frank, 1962) may also impinge on mental health treatment, the model developed by the CMHP was specifically tailored to the ethnic communities and assessed needs of Catchment Area IV in Miami. The major characteristics of this catchment area are (a) its ubiquity of social-stressors—poverty, unemployment, crime, poor housing, medical problems, and the like; (b) its multilingual, ethnically diverse composition; and (c) problems associated with ethnicity, e.g., a history of *de jure* racial segregation and discrimination, large immigrant and exile populations, illegal alien status, and differential levels of acculturative stress.

The CMHP model thus began with two primary objectives: (1) To provide highly accessible, culturally appropriate services which would encompass the range of presenting complaints; and (2) to help alleviate environmental stressors by insuring that area residents receive their fair share of adaptive resources.[2]

Staffing Pattern

The integration of a social science perspective with the delivery of services was first manifested in the selection of appropriate staff. The original model was based on the innovative deployment of five teams of mental health workers, one team for each of the ethnic groups studied in the Health Ecology Project. These five teams, then, would serve Bahamian, Black-American, Cuban, Haitian, and Puerto Rican populations, in accord with the predominant ethnic configurations of the catchment area. Extensive mapping of the area indicated that the balance of the population was primarily elderly Anglo-American, and, for this group, a sixth geriatric team was subsequently developed. During 1978, a seventh unit, serving primarily Black elderly, was funded by an Area Wide Agency on Aging grant.

Each team is composed of personnel indigenous to the area and of the same ethnic background and/or cultural extraction as those of the populations served. Each team is directed by a social scientist at the M.A.-Ph.D. level, who is a specialist in the culture and, in almost all cases, of the same ethnic extraction.[3] Directors have come from the following disciplines: anthropology, social psychology, sociology, social work, cultural history, political science, and gerontology. In addition to the four to five neighborhood workers and the team director, each team has a social worker, also of the same ethnic extraction, and the services of part-time psychiatric and psychologist staff, together with other mental health professionals, interns, and volunteers. Again, a unique aspect of this program is that almost all clinical staff, regardless of discipline, is of matching ethnicity. In fact, 90 percent of the entire program staff, including its director, are either Black or Spanish-speaking/surnamed.

In accordance with Weidman's (1978) model, team directors are called culture brokers and, as faculty members of the University of Miami, have a combination of academic, applied social scientist, and service provider functions. In actuality, however, both directors and team members share the culture broker role. These individuals play a bridging, teaching, and training role at the interface of the community and mental health establishment, and within the two systems.

Within the hospital or clinic system, the culture broker's role involves general teaching, consultation and collaboration (Bryant, 1974), and cultural interpretation. In teaching mental health practitioners about a particular culture, the broker focuses not only on those beliefs and practices that may impinge on effective mental health care delivery, but also on adaptive strategies, strengths, and structural supportive elements that may be applied to a preventive model. As a consultant and collaborator in specific cases, the culture broker plays an interpretive and affiliative role in in-house treatment—sometimes, functionally as co-therapist—and an active role in aftercare. Interpretation may involve explaining the "rooted" patient to a crisis worker who is unable to diagnose the observed symptoms within the traditional psychiatric nosology. It may involve teaching a psychiatric resident how to differentiate between legitimate paranoid ideation—i.e., ideas that are considered bizarre in the culture—from ideas of reference or persecution that would be considered in the "normal" range within the conceptual framework of the culture (cf. Mathewson, 1974). It may involve informing an intake worker that certain demands may be perfectly acceptable to a white middle-class patient, e.g., asking a wife to bring her husband in for marital counseling, but would generally not be acceptable in a Spanish-speaking culture (Lombillo and Geraghty, 1973). Conversely, the culture broker facilitates understanding and utilization of services by the ethnic consumer within the context of her belief system and value system. Where diagnosis or treatment conflict with cultural norms or expectations, the broker may take an active role in arranging appropriate interventions. Or, in cases where it seems advisable, he or she may establish linkages between the orthodox mental health care system and a traditional healer.

This role relates to care for individual patients. However, both in the community and the health care system, the culture broker has a larger role: that of social change agent. Within the community, culture brokers and their teams act as catalysts in mobilizing neighborhood resources to deal with a variety of community-defined mental health needs. They organize and direct action-oriented research efforts, always geared to specific programmatic ends. They act as resource specialists, linking consumers with appropriate service agencies. They help the community to take action when such agencies are lacking, inadequate, or insensitive to cultural needs. And they help develop support systems, in both preventive and aftercare terms, for individuals and families in distress.

Within the mental health establishment the culture broker, in addition to the roles previously described, also acts as change agent—as a catalyst in redefining basic conceptions of mental health and illness. For a very long time, psychoanalytically-oriented diagnosis and therapy has dominated the mental health scene. This approach, of course, is universalistic, focuses on intrapsychic functioning, and tries to effect change through transference, abstraction, and insight, rejecting active involvement with the patient's environment. The growth of family and group therapies has enlarged the focus to the patient within one's immediate social field. The role of social scientist in Departments of Psychiatry brings us to the next logical stage: assessment and treatment of the patient in social and cultural context. As we know, the attempted contribution of social scientists has generally met with apathy, resistance, and sometimes outright hostility in the psychiatric establishment (see Weidman, 1971). However, as the culture broker has been able to provide input that results in better patient care and more effective therapist performance (and, in turn, is able to adapt the input through increasing in-house expertise), we have increasingly found a willingness to listen, cooperate, and even reconceptualize on the part of once highly resistant clinicians.

Structure of Components: Team Functions

The comprehensive center contains two basic components—hospital and community based. The Community Mental Health Services (CMHC) of Jackson Memorial Hospital has provided inpatient, crisis intervention, and at times outpatient, partial hospitalization, and child-psychiatric services to Catchment Area IV patients within a centralized hospital system serving all of Dade County. The major role of our teams within the hospital system is to provide continuity of care, particularly for patients from the various ethnic groups where culture brokerage is required to facilitate appropriate diagnosis, treatment, and aftercare arrangements. With mental health professionals, the role also involves consultation, collaboration (cf. Bryant, 1974), cultural and linguistic interpretation (Mathewson, 1974), and general teaching responsibilities. Linkages with the hospital system permit an ongoing reciprocal referral system for patients requiring hospitalization or discharge planning, and facilitate a continuous exchange of transcultural clinical information with a wide range of mental health practitioners.

The CMHP, the community-based section, is the major component receiving most of the NIMH funds, and the one on which this discussion is based. Structurally, the CMHP consists of seven ethnic community teams and their offices in the community; a network of nine team-administered mini-clinic sites offering decentralized preventive, therapeutic, and supportive aftercare services; administrative and research and evaluation sections; and affiliative relationships with special drug and alcohol services and primary health care clinics within the Black and Spanish-speaking communities.

In addition to outpatient and aftercare services, team functions include information, referrals, and social service coordination for a wide range of needs; a neighborhood outreach program involving needs assessment, case-finding, and resource linkages; community-based consultation and education, together with direct services in the home, schools, churches, boarding houses, etc.; development of supportive networks for social isolates; programmatic research including, in addition to needs assessment, ethnographic and demographic profiles and other action-oriented research; and community organization and development. With respect to the latter, the teams act as initiators and coordinators of various projects to bring new resources into their communities or strengthen existing ones; conducting action research to provide supportive data for community-requested programs; link consumer groups with appropriate service agencies; and help residents learn how to utilize these agencies for ameliorating specific neighborhood problems. Concrete examples will be given in forthcoming sections of this paper.

Program Objectives and Implementation

The specific objectives of the CMHP can be summarized as follows:

1. To provide highly accessible and culturally sensitive psychiatric services to individuals in mental health crisis and pre-crisis situations, and to individuals discharged from an inpatient psychiatric facility.

2. To provide a wide range of supportive social services and resources as part of the available treatment capabilities to individuals in the above categories, including those with emotional difficulties or life crisis situations.

3. To help prevent the onset or exacerbation of mental illness through involvement and outreach in the communities of Catchment Area IV—both through case finding and early intervention into individual problem situations, and through intervention directed at changing factors in the environment that contribute to illness.

To implement these objectives, the program set about systematically, first, to conduct a community entry program involving selection and utilization of advisory boards, key informants, and necessary information gathering; second, to organize services responsive to community needs; third, to develop collective action and advocacy programs for the respective communities; and, finally, to conduct an ongoing process evaluation of the linkages between individual and collective efforts and the efficacy of our therapeutic interventions.

Team Entry and Involvement in the Community

Most of the teams (which were staffed and organized at different times) began with preliminary advisory boards of community members who assisted in selecting or approving personnel, and in suggesting the range of needs in the area. The team then proceeded to survey the neighborhoods, through block-mapping and observation, re-assessment of census data to determine ethnic clustering, investigation of the availability and distance of resources, and development of demographic and ethnographic profiles. Team members talked to key informants, to residents, and to people on the street; they established contact with community agencies and informal groups; and they developed linkages with the indigenous community leadership. A variety of social science techniques were used, including participant observation, ethnography, geo-physical mapping, and various types of formal and informal needs assessment surveys, typically based on cluster sampling (depending on ethnic distribution). There are several innovative aspects to this type of multiple perspectives needs assessment. First, survey questionnaires were generally based on empirically-derived issues rather than *a priori* conceptions of mental health problems; their purpose was to set priorities, provide community-requested documentation, or otherwise expand and refine our information on pre-targeted needs. Second, the team's block work and mapping assessed the availability of supportive resources (churches, recreational facilities, local doctors, folk healers, etc.) beyond the range of those commonly surveyed. Third, residence patterns, population characteristics, and cultural specificity were all taken into account, yielding differential need patterns for discrete communities within the same catchment area. These needs, in turn, were meshed with a network of neighborhood facilities providing matching services. Thus, while all units provide essential psychiatric services, one team may allocate a large proportion of its resources to job placement or school enrollment of the children of illegal aliens, while another may concentrate on the multiple health and socialization needs of the elderly.

During the community entry period, a number of discrete research projects were conducted at the request of a community group, e.g., the collection of supportive data to obtain external funding of day care centers, hot lunch programs for senior citizens, and the like. Inevitably, the needs assessment generated immediate case-finding, necessitating mobilization of the teams as referral agents (with functions often including transportation, help with form completion, and interpretation). The first three teams staffed—Cuban, Haitian, and Puerto Rican—immediately established service offices in Community Action Agency (CAA) quarters and began dispensing social services. These high-visibility research and service activities generated a positive response from the community, and laid the groundwork for acceptance of the teams as an effective mental health resource. Concomitantly, the teams were investigating the neighborhoods to determine sites for mini-clinics.

Organization of Services

Using the extensive community information collected as a base, each team proceeded to do the following:

1. Established a location within which to provide psychiatric, social, and, in some cases, medical services

2. Attracted social, economic, health, education, and other resources to these sites or

3. Offered psychiatric services in already established "helping centers" in the communities, such as health centers, community centers, day care programs, school counseling programs, and senior citizens organizations.

Links with other agencies were established. A coordinated system was established in which clinical staff provides direct services to clients, supervision, and training programs for the mental health workers throughout the miniclinic network. Referral relationships were established with South Florida State Hospital and the JMH Psychiatric Institute so treatment resources could be extended to recently discharged patients from Catchment Area IV. The ethnic community teams provide decentralized aftercare services that include, in addition to the traditional medication and counseling, a wide range of supportive and rehabilitative activities. Concomitantly, the Research and Evaluation Unit had developed a coding manual for presenting complaints (supplementing the required "diagnostic labelling" of DSM-II), initiated the Kireskuk and Sherman (1968) method of goal attainment scaling, and began an ongoing feedback process in the form of comprehensive monthly reports to the teams on their activities and caseload characteristics.[4]

Levels of Intervention

In the program schema, there are at least four levels of intervention, with the individual as immediate or ultimate beneficiary. The teams may work with a client in ecological context, within the concentricity of family, neighborhood support systems, and community resource networks. Alternatively, the teams may attack a community-wide problem, with the projection of long-range, but as yet unmeasurable benefits to the individual; or they may work at the neighborhood level remediating problems that impinge on the mental health of groups of individuals.

One of the virtues of this approach is that, up to the present, we have been able to deal with mental health issues at the macrocosmic and microcosmic levels. At the community and neighborhood levels, interventions have involved bringing mobile health screening and treatments units to communities that lacked them; development of numerous special programs and workshops for youth; special programs in the criminal justice system and with ex-offenders; special cultural events focusing on ethnic history, accomplishments, and pride; and the like. Most important has been the CMHP-initiated development of interagency councils in blighted and very needful areas, and the development of a multi-ethnic coalition to press for needed reforms.

Some of the examples given below indicate how the teams have been active in their "catalyst" roles in mobilizing consumers to bring new resources into their communities and to increase the effectiveness and responsiveness of existing agencies.

Collective Actions at the Neighborhood/Community Levels

1. The staff gerontologist, almost single-handedly, created a functioning community organization and service network among a group of elderly residents living in low-income trailer park housing. The gerontologist's conceptual model involved starting, not with an agency service, but with the mobilization of a group of older persons who could be trained to function in an organizational capacity, to identify and develop relevant services, and to become active in changing some of the stressful conditions that impinged on their physical and psychological well-being (Ross, 1978). Through a developmental process involving door-to-door needs assessment among hopeless, impoverished, and distrustful elderly respondents, consecutive feedback of mutual concerns, community organization, and solicitation of rent-free quarters and volunteer services, she was successful in developing an indigenously-administered multi-service center now incorporated by its elderly membership as Northside Neighborhood Family Services, Inc. (NF).[5] Offering multiple health, social, medical, educational, and recreational services, the Neighborhood Family functions as a supportive surrogate family for its members and also maintains a "network system" locating and serving non-ambulatory elderly in the surrounding area. Although few of these people had any experience in community action, they have subsequently become involved in a number of collective efforts to improve their lot. In one collective effort, 26 elderly residents (some in their 80's) petitioned the Commissioners of Dade County, Florida, for HUD sponsored mobile home parks as an alternative to high-rise public housing for the elderly. The rationale was that a collective trailer park would: (a) benefit elderly residents by eliminating arbitrary raises in rents and utility charges by landlords; (b) create a feeling of community and social/psychological interdependence because of the collective ownership and physical setting; and (c) generate more low-rental public housing units for the elderly because of significantly lower construction costs. At this writing, the project is still pending, but its approval appears to be possible.

A noteworthy feature of this action was the willingness of the elderly to organize and press for a project whose implementation probably would not take place within their own lifetimes. A particularly heady effect was the respect and attention obtained from County Commissioners, many of whom had never conceived of older people as capable of political activism, and the resultant resurgence of self-esteem among the elderly petitioners.

Another collective effort—the Reclaim our Neighborhood (RON) demonstration project—grew out of a series of community improvement meetings developed by the NF. With the objective of breaking the maladaptive pattern of apathy and silent withdrawal to destructive behavior, a resident-NF worker began door-to-door contacts to organize residents of a particularly dirty, socially disintegrating, and crime-ridden trailer park. A scant two weeks after the first community meeting, "a miracle had occurred, I could not believe what I saw. There were no stray dogs; the streets were clean. Garbage lids were on tight and no refuse in the streets. Everyone remarked about the amazing change, the difference was startling. There were even new signs up reading 'This is your park. Keep it clean.'"[6]

2. Working in the Allapattah area of Miami, the Cuban team has established two well-functioning mini-clinics, conducted numerous surveys, and become highly involved in community affairs (Sandoval, 1975). Operating in an area with no other agency resources, the team has been active in attracting Community Development Project (CDP) funds into the area. With a client group as a community base, and linkages established with other ethnic interest groups, team efforts have resulted in the allocation of $450,000 to this area for various social projects. Of this amount, $250,00 was earmarked for a centrally located multipurpose service center, which now includes the Cuban mini-clinic as a mental health facility. This action not only brings a critically needed resource into the area, but removes the discrete "mental health" identity from the mini-clinic and phases into a wide range of preventive and ancillary services that are available in the same location. The easy physical accessibility of such services will not only minimize travel time, paper work, and referral problems, but will serve to de-label and de-institutionalize patients by placing them in the context of other people seeking services.

In addition to wide-ranging social and rehabilitative services for clients, the Cuban team has developed a crime prevention program for pre-delinquents in public housing projects, offers extensive services to the elderly, and has been instrumental in developing a bilingual newspaper to serve as a bridge between different ethnic groups residing in its area. Recently the team has become particularly active in a multi-ethnic coalition which unites various interest groups in a push for common community goals.

3. The Puerto Rican Team, working in Wynwood, an area with inadequate educational facilities for Spanish-speaking adults, initiated a project to bring a community school into the area. After organizing and

publicizing a meeting to which 58 community leaders were invited, the team became coordinating agent for election of an *ad hoc* committee and three sub-committees dealing with faculty, program curriculum, and public relations. At present the school is in operation as an Outreach worker of Miami Dade Community Colleges. Five courses are offered, based on consumer-selection, and credits are given for home-county training. This is the first project in which all ethnic groups in a largely Puerto Rican area came together in a collective action to benefit the community as a whole. The project, involving Puerto Rican, Honduran, Dominican, Venezualan, and Peruvian, lays the groundwork for further collective activities among various Latino groups in the Wynwood area.

Both the Cuban and Puerto Rican teams have been instrumental in organizing special Hispanic cultural events. The Puerto Rican team has similarly participated in planning, coordinating, and has ultimately been relocated to a multi-service neighborhood facility. Similarly, they have participated in the planning and execution of inter-agency workshops to establish better linkages among agencies.

4. The Bahamian team developed a summer employment program for low-income Black teenagers (14-16 years old) as part of Project Step. In contrast to other programs, which typically use the teenagers as clean-up and recreation assistants, the focus of the team was on training the youth in a meaningful community experience. In conjunction with another community agency, the team had developed structured program including orientation and training in office procedures, educational films on mental health and social services, recreation, and field experience. The latter involved participation in a community survey (Needs Assessment), leaflet distribution, policing blocks, and using the agency of this group to contact and involve other youth in community activity. The goals of this project were to educate the youth to: (a) become aware of and assess community needs; (b) set goals for the community and become contributing members in effecting goal-attainment; (c) learn responsibility to and for the community; and (d) receive training and certification as interviewers.

The Bahamian team has been particularly active in school consultation and education, and has developed workshops for teenagers with a special focus on insight, motivation, and career development.

5. During the first year of operation, the Haitian team found that 70 percent of its clients were illegal aliens with multiple needs, but questionable eligibility for existing federal, state, or county benefits. The team subsequently became involved in two massive advocacy projects for the Haitian community. The first, a school enrollment project, evolved from the finding that numerous Haitian children were not in school because their parents were illegal aliens and the children lacked student visas. Negotiations ensued with the School Department, the Catholic Services Bureau, a

local Haitian organization, and Legal Services of Greater Miami. The team made contact with Immigration and Naturalization (INS) and with the New York school system, which also has many Haitian students. It was found that student visas and legal status were not required in New York, and that the INS could not point to a ruling barring children from Dade County schools. Following the team's advocacy efforts, admission requirements were changed and the team itself, completing the necessary paper work, has been successful in enrolling 750 Haitian children in school. The process continues with the team handling an average of ten (10) school registration cases per week.

In the second project, the team conducted an advocacy program for social security cards for Haitian illegal aliens. Although the social security office had previously given cards to all applicants, a changed procedure necessitated proof of citizenship or residency status. This ruling created a body of unemployable illegal aliens, ineligible for welfare benefits, with no observable remedies for survival. After negotiation, the team helped over 1,200 Haitians obtain social security cards, and continues to handle about 12 cases per week involving social security and other matters pertaining to immigration. Other collective efforts have involved intensive work with Haitian youth undergoing acculturative stress, particularly in raising self-esteem through ethnic heritage courses and through their involvement in helping services. The Haitian youth group participates in visiting needy people, and in assisting elderly and convalescent Haitian residents. In addition to functioning as a multi-ethnic facility for many aftercare patients, the Haitian team has a particularly useful culture brokerage function. Called to serve as interpreter between Creole speaking clients and agencies such as the court system, public agencies, and the health care system, the team has been instrumental in breaking down barriers due to cultural belief systems as well as to linguistic differences.

Links Between Collective Action and Service

In almost all these examples, group advocacy and community organization has generated availability of direct services to individuals. Moreover, in many team efforts, the involvement of patients in community action has, in and of itself, constituted a highly therapeutic intervention. An effort of the Black-American team, however, is a prototypical example of the program's ability to link individual and collective services with collective action.

This effort began in a public housing project surrounded by dilapidated frame houses, infested with roaches and rats. The team's involvement began with referral of a psychiatric patient, who was visited in his home by a black team member, J.G. Together with direct mental health services offered the patient, J.G. was successful in obtaining for him a large social security check that had been withheld because of inadequate documentation and red tape.

When the patient's neighbors heard that a CMHP neighborhood worker was there to assist him, several approached J.G., saying they had similar problems and needed assistance. Noting the poor environmental conditions—the patient had no hot water, inadequate sanitation, etc.—J.G. reported his findings to the Black team and suggested they do a survey of the neighborhood. The survey subsequently revealed extremely adverse housing conditions, and uncovered 10 cases needing immediate mental health assistance in a small area. Individual problems included widespread depression, mental retardation, illiteracy, physical disabilities, need for public assistance, and inability to obtain documentation required for welfare or other benefits. Overall, housing "unfit for human habitation," vermin, infectious animals, and inadequate sanitation were major environmental problems.

After referrals were initiated for other clients, the team began to negotiate with agencies with matching services to solve the environmental problems. Contacts were established with HUD, Legal Services, and Court Enforcement agencies to inspect all the buildings in the Project. Violations were found and reported, and repairs were initiated. The Fire Department was also contacted to inspect fire hazards. Some of the tenants organized to work with a legal counsel. Subsequent developments have included involvement of the National Tenants Organization to work with residents to alleviate physical conditions in the Project; a news special on local television regarding Project conditions; and contact with the Health Department, with the result that a public health nurse now comes to visit tenants once a week. Additionally, a local television channel became interested in doing a collaborative show with the Black American team, focusing on the relationship between the widespread mental health problems and the poor environmental conditions in the public housing projects.

In sum, the direct services offered one client in a home visit generated a successful individual outcome; this outcome was publicized and indicated to neighbors that CMHP was an effective resource, leading to disclosure of further problems; the Black team utilized its social science expertise to identify further individual cases and environmental problems; agencies with matching resources were contacted and mobilized into action; individuals suffering from depression and hopelessness were offered a channel to resources which permitted them to take action on their own behalf—enabling them to externalize their anger and channel it productively; and, throughout, the Black American mental health team continues to provide a support system for individual and collective change.

Direct Services at the Family/Individual Level

In the terms of our self-imposed mandate, direct services must meet two criteria, wherever relevant; i.e., they must attend to the full range of problems in living presented by the client—not just intrapsychic or interpersonal problems—and they must be culturally appropriate.

Together with offering traditional medication, psychotherapy, family and group therapy, other therapies (dance therapy, drug counseling, etc.) and social/rehabilitative activities, the staff expends considerable effort to obtain financial benefits, job-placement, housing assistance, medical care, and the like. These efforts are extended not only to the client, but to other family members as well. Home visits and ongoing contacts with the family by team workers of the same ethnic extraction have facilitated far more understanding of the client's problems among family members than was formerly the case. This is an often repeated theme among relatives of clients who have received similar services in predominantly Anglo settings.

In addition, the mini-clinic neighborhood setting provides a homogeneous cultural and linguistic milieu for the participating client. The milieu therapy offered, however, is extremely heterogeneous. With its variety of classes and social activities, the mini-clinic functions as a community center and attracts neighborhood participants without identified emotional problems. Since it is not restricted to mental patients, the mini-clinic tends to facilitate the rehabilitative process by providing a truly de-institutionalized setting. In several of the long-established mini-clinics, principally the Cuban and gerontological units, the center provides a "surrogate family" supportive network for the incoming client. In other units, the team may fulfill this function until the center becomes fully operative.

Despite almost universal acceptance of the proposition that social-environmental stressors affect mental health, there has been surprisingly little investigation of the corollary hypothesis that reduction of environmental stress may improve the psychological adjustment of individual patients. While it is assumed, on a common sense basis, that finding a job, better housing, needed medical care and the like would improve coping capabilities, psychodynamic approaches do not, as a rule, address themselves to these issues. Rather, it is generally held that improved levels of intrapsychic functioning will enable a client to deal with or change the external situation.

Since ethical and practical considerations precluded utilizing an experimental paradigm (i.e., randomly assigning clients needing both types of services to aid and no-aid or delayed-aid conditions), the question was approached in another way during the process of evaluating therapeutic outcome of a random sample of 150 clients. The question, very simply, was whether level of success in attaining environmental goals could predict level of success in attaining behavioral goals. Analysis was based on 92 cases that had required both therapeutic and environmental interventions, with eliminination of those few cases where behavioral and environmental outcomes were specifically interdependent.

Environmental goal categories included the following: obtaining financial benefits; job-finding; job training and placement; educational assistance; homemaking aid; day care aid; locating appropriate medical care for self or family members; locating needed documentation; legal assistance and advocacy within criminal justice system; and locating social outlets. Behavioral goals fell into four categories. These were behaviors that indicated: (a) reduction of symptomatology, including diminished bizarre or acting out behavior, improved mood state, self-concept, etc.; (b) improved level of functioning at home or at work; (c) improved interpersonal relationships; and (d) greater efforts by the client to utilize therapeutic resources (keeping appointments, monitoring own medication, participation in group activities, etc.).

Analysis of the data indicated an overall r (90) between environmental and behavioral means of .55 ($p<.001$). To determine whether environmental goal-attainment effectively predicted therapeutic outcome, the group was trichotomized into high, moderate, and low environmental success subgroups. Behavioral means predicted by regression equations were respectively, 63.41, 52.20, and 45.42, as compared with actual means of 63.63, 55.58, and 45.44. (For the total, environmental X = 54.18, $S.D.$ = 9.28; predicted behavioral X = 57.71; actual behavior X = 57.95, $S.D.$ = 11.59.).

The results of this study, which have been reported elsewhere in greater detail (Lefley, 1979), were viewed as lending considerable justification to the amount of time and effort staff has been devoting to the "reality problems" of their clients as a highly legitimate mental health service.

MENTAL HEALTH SERVICES IN CROSS-CULTURAL PERSPECTIVE

It is obviously impossible to provide a cookbook approach to the diagnosis and treatment of mental or emotional disorder in different ethnic populations. This is largely an empirical matter, even for indigenous professionals who are sensitive to the multiplicity of cultural variables that may enter into the therapeutic process. We would like to share here, however, some of the elements that have been considered important and that enter into our case evaluations and treatment orientations. A few of these elements are: (a) existence and level of problems relating to migration, acculturation, and other types of life change; (b) belief systems; (c) sex roles and responsibilities; (d) family structure and role relationships; and (e) value orientations. While it would not be profitable to discuss all of these in depth, we might note some of the factors that we have considered particularly salient with respect to the first element.

Acculturation and Stress: The Social Matrix

Miami is an area of transplanted populations. Southern rural Blacks face accommodation to urban living. Northern Anglo elderly must adjust to loss of family, income, and often to a life of social isolation. Immigration groups face all the problems of uprooting *plus* the trauma of adaption to an alien society. A very brief overview suggests that the groups differ in *type* as well as level of acculturation. For example, Bahamians, representing the oldest wave of immigration, have made a substantial social and political accommodation to the Black-American population. Nevertheless, cultural differences persist, particularly with respect to familial pressures for achievement-orientation. There may also be a generalized problem of identity diffusion. Socialized in the British system, some Bahamians consider their mores, value system, and educational background as superior to that of Black-Americans; others move toward assimilation; while still others opt for a Pan-Caribbean or Black Nationalist identity. The recent independence of the Bahamas has revived the question of identity in "descents" as well as immigrants. The sensitive therapist must note that Island blacks come from a different cultural mainstream than American Blacks; variations in mores, values, psycholinguistic referents, and dimensions of the self-concept should be taken into account in any therapeutic interaction.

Cubans are the predominant ethnic co-culture in Miami, and are now estimated as numbering approximately half the population of the metropolitan area. Miami Cubans are a unique immigrant population. They are relatively well-educated and primarily from non-poverty backgrounds. At first warmly accepted, the Cubans have been subjected to increasing antagonism from old Americans, White and non-White, who resent the economic competition and stress on bilingual skills generated by the Cuban presence. According to our clinicians, the major psychiatric problems facing Cubans have been anxiety evoked by profound changes in life-style, and depression, evoked by loss of country and loss of a clearly defined sense of identity. Role identification, and, in many cases, economic role reversal, have been salient problems. The traditionally close-knit extended family has been subjected to numerous stressors, with women working in significantly greater numbers than before, and Cuban males often forced to take jobs beneath their training or academic credentials. The generation gap is probably the most critical problem, compounded by the cultural gap between grandparents, parents, and English-speaking, Americanized children. Achievement-oriented Cuban parents are in a double bind regarding the role of the schools; while education is desired, the schools act as an acculturative influence and the source of a different value system. Most families suffer from parent-child conflict regarding such issues as independence, openness to experience, and maturational activities such as dating and sexual exploration. It is not surprising that social indicators show an increase in divorce and separation rates, as well as increases in the use of drugs, licit and illicit. It is also not surprising that mental health workers report rises in anxiety, paranoid ideation, and psychosomatic disorders.

Puerto Rican acculturative stress follows a different pattern in bilingual Miami. In contrast to the extensive Cuban population, which is mainly of European extraction, Puerto Ricans are generally from low socioeconomic origins, more racially mixed, more residentially segregated, and more rigidly cast in the traditional family role relationships. Together with the usual effects of uprooting and transplantation, the phenomenon of minority status in a larger Spanish-speaking population tends to increase feelings of social, economic, and political inferiority. In this particular locus, the feelings of Spanish-speaking American citizens *vis-a-vis* more educated and affluent Spanish-speaking non-citizens constitutes a highly specific source of frustration, and emphasizes the point that all Spanish-speaking clients can in no way be lumped together. (See Bestman, Lefley and Scott, 1976 for further discussion of differences in health care behavior among the two Latin groups.)

It is the Haitians, however, who are probably in the greatest mental health crisis. In this case it is not acculturation *per se* (since most have not reached this level of culture change), but rather linguistic, economic, political, and social barriers that constitute the greatest sources of stress. Many Haitians coming to Miami are illegal aliens, from backgrounds of extreme poverty. Most have fled Haiti at great peril and have faced deportation or jail, both on interim island stops, and in the United States when they arrive. Thus, those who ultimately end up as psychiatric patients have undergone so many reality and survival problems, and so much oppression, that the typical diagnosis of "paranoid" becomes highly suspect.

Folk Healers and Mental Health Professionals

The culturally sensitive (and nondefensive) professional may adopt various stances with respect to folk healers. Many reject their science out of hand, viewing them as charlatans, perpetuators of superstition, or workers of malevolent evil. Others consider them valuable assets for learning and referral purposes. Much depends on the belief system as well as on the presenting symptomatology. Possession crisis, or the bizarre behavior that often accompanies religious ritual are certainly best handled by consultation with a Houngan, Espiritista, or Santero. But certain of the so-called culture-bound syndromes, such as *"Ataque,"* or *"Susto"*—regardless of the psychiatric classification—may also require such interventions. Sometimes a psychiatrist will work in tandem with native healers, or use them as resource persons for interpreting behavior. At other times, the psychotherapist himself or herself may actually adopt the role. McCartney, (1975) a Bahamian psychologist, has described for the University of Miami Department of Psychiatry faculty a very speedy cure of depressive neurosis facilitated by simulated Obeah rituals. In Miami's Jackson Memorial Hospital, our former chief of the Crisis Service, a highly trained psychiatrist from Guyana, successfully performed his own specialized ritual to cure a "rooted" patient. Our Bahamian director has also done "exorcisms" to counter or remove evil spirits for patients with strong etiological beliefs. Dr. Mercedes Sandoval, a cultural historian-anthropologist who is director of the Cuban Unit, and a world authority on the Afro-Cuban religion, Santeria, deals with patient-believers within their conceptual frame of reference together with a psychiatrist co-therapist. But what defines a patient's aberrant behavior as truly pathological—requiring psychiatric intervention—or simply as a behavior as truly pathological—requiring psychiatric intervention—or simply as a temporary artifact of a religious belief system? Griffin and Ruiz (1977) reporting on a hospitalized Espiritismo practitioner looked to the patient's family for an explanation. Their criteria for psychopathology were as follows: (a) Possession is suspect when it lasts too long—it is typically a quick and transitory experience; (b) possession becomes abnormal when there is no perceivable stimulus or condition (i.e., a ceremony, thunder, lightning, accidents, etc); (c) it occurs most often in the presence of believers (a secrecy condition); and (d) it can have negative or positive orientation. Positive orientation is *ritual* possession; negative orientation is *sickness* possession. The authors say it is especially important for mental health professionals to understand this dichotomy for appropriate ethnopsychiatric evaluation.

Building a Cultural Knowledge Base

We well recognize that the field is still reaping the unfortunate harvest of years of societal and institutional racism. It will be many years before there is proportionate representation of minority group therapists. Consequently, we must aim toward some kind of education of mainstream therapists in how to deal with clients of differing sociocultural backgrounds.

There are a number of options available to the sensitive therapist for insuring optimal benefits. The following suggestions comprise a preliminary methodology which may be generalized across cases:

1. *Literature Review.* Before initiating treatment, the caregiver should familiarize herself or himself with the available literature on the client's culture. This should include not only sociological and anthropological literature, but the available studies of cultural profile differences on standard psychological/psychiatric instruments. While this may seem a big order, it should be noted that (a) this type of familiarization should be built into any type of academic training, and (b) the results may serve as a body of core knowledge for subsequent clients from this type of generic group.

2. *Ethnic Consultants.* There should be initial and ongoing consultation and review with ethnic consultants. In this connection, two point should be stressed: (a) the consultant need not be a professional—it is far more important that the consultant derive from and understand the client's specific ethnic and sociocultural experience; (b) it would be wise for professionals of matching ethnicity to also have these types of consultants, mitigating the effects of resocialization in the orthodox system and the social distance created by educational and class differences. In this type of interaction, the caregiver should, in addition to requesting input on social and cultural context, check out and validate interpretation of symptoms and behaviors, and seek clues for alternative interpretations.

3. *Cultural Exposure Experience.* Although it is unlikely that most therapists will avail themselves of this option, it would be wise for a caregiver to have some exposure, no matter how brief, to the life style of the ethnic client. This may involve cruising through an ethnic neighborhood, attending a church service, shopping in a ghetto supermarket, or simply observing interactions in groups of people from different cultures in a clinic waiting room.

4. *Utilization Patterns.* Cultural material should be taken into account in interpreting the client's utilization of services; e.g., times of day when "no shows" are most apparent; appointment-keeping patterns (often interpreted as "resistance" when time-orientation values are mismatched); and the relationship of utilization to appointment-spacing, i.e., the greater tendency for appointments to be kept if there is a minimal lag time and they are closely spaced.

5. *Involvement of Significant Others.* In contrast to white, middle-class clients, whose families have some familiarity with the exclusion ethos of psychoanalytically-oriented individual therapy, Spanish-speaking

families generally expect to be included in the therapeutic transaction. Here, several items should be noted: (a) the *mode* of involvement must be culturally appropriate, e.g., in a lower-class Puerto Rican or Chicano family the caregiver cannot ask a wife to bring her husband in for counseling—this should be done through a respected third-party family member (Lombillo and Geraghty, 1973); (b) the *range* of family members must be culturally appropriate. The nuclear parents-siblings arrangement of conventional family therapy is inadequate for the Black and Spanish-speaking extended families, where aunts, uncles, and grandparents may play a significant role in family dynamics and child-rearing.

6. *Belief Systems.* The therapist must be sensitive to alternative conceptions of causation and remediation of illness particularly to supernatural belief systems which involve the notion of malevolent external control. Here, however, a *caveat* should be noted as to superimposing newly acquired knowledge on what may be standard types of neurotic or psychotic symptomology. That is, all patients who verbalize persecution from others and also happen to be Black, Haitian, etc. are not necessarily rooted; they may simply be expressing paranoid ideation in culturally defined ways. The use of ethnic consultants is particularly important in these types of situations.

7. *Adaptive Behavior.* Is the therapeutic goal adaptive in the social and cultural milieu to which the client returns? Will the behaviors that are being shaped enable the client to function at a higher level of social adaptation, or do they have the potential for exacerbating the client's problems in the society in which he or she must live? Are they congruent with the client's belief and value system? Again, these issues should be subjected to ethnic consultation and peer review, because the prescribed treatment plan would be ineffectual if it led to conflict with cultural norms.

8. *Interpretation of Behavior.* The well-trained therapist interprets both verbal and non-verbal behavior in terms of intrapsychic functioning. The culturally sensitive therapist adds another dimension to observations of behavioral cues. Signs of discomfort or unease must be assessed in terms of communicative difficulties or threats against cultural norms, as well as threats to ego-functioning. Since the caregiver is an authority figure, the client may be unable to verbalize anxieties that ensue from conflicting norms, rather than from substantive aspects of the interaction. The pitfalls of erroneous interpretation are particularly salient in these cases. In the example alluded to above, i.e. a caregiver asking a Spanish-speaking wife to bring her husband in for marital counseling, the wife's behavioral discomfort

may indicate fear of transgressing a cultural norm, but may be misinterpreted as adverse feelings toward the husband or fear of self-disclosure.

9. *Using a Checklist*. As an overall methodology, it is suggested that the sensitive therapist use cultural material as a backdrop of knowledge against which to "check-off" items that may or may not be relevant to the therapeutic process. The "indexing and loop" model of the digital computer is probably the best approximation of this process. Input should be checked off against known indicies of cultural differences; if the datum seems to fit, it should be used. If it is contradictory, it should definitely be assessed for resistance and cultural deviance, but alternative explanations should be sought and applied. If the datum is irrelevant, it should be dropped.

In all cases, it should be re-emphasized that ethnic consultants should be used to aid in analyzing and interpreting the "data" of the therapeutic process. Ethnic consultants provide the additional information which ultimately expands the clinician's options for interpretation of symptoms and behaviors, and the selection of appropriate treatment alternatives.

SOME EVALUATIVE FINDINGS

Does a culturally sensitive orientation result in greater acceptability and effectiveness of services? Does a network of neighborhood mini-clinics, with built-in geographical accessibility, generate greater psychological accessibility? From the large number of evaluation studies conducted in the program, a few examples of data relevant to these questions are presented here:

Minority Utilization

A major problem of cultural inaccessibility is reflected in under-utilization of services by minority groups. In terms of N.I.M.H.'s Mental Health Demographic Profile, (1974) and the documented overrepresentation of non-white patients in mental hospital admission rates (Milazzo-Syre, 1977), these are often precisely the groups that require services and to whom outreach services should be addressed. Yet, it has been noted that many CMHCs, even if located in ghettos, serve predominantly White middle-class clientele.

Item: There is an excellent fit of the CMHP caseload characteristics to the distribution of ethnic groups in the catchment area served by our program. These do *not* reflect referrals alone: over 65 percent of our clientele is from outreach. Minority utilization reflects 80 percent of our caseload, representing many individuals who would not normally seek mental health care in a clinical setting.

"No-Show Rates"

In addition to under-utilization, cultural inaccessibility often results in minority group members failing to keep appointments. According to baseline data, broken appointment rates in ambulatory care facilities range from 16 percent to 44 percent (Hertz and Stamps, 1977). At least five research studies indicate that "members of ethnic minorities, especially blacks and Spanish-speaking, are more likely to break appointments" (Hertz and Stamps, 1977, p. 1033). Rates reaching from 40 percent to 56 percent have been reported by various CMHCs.

Item: The CMHP has a no show rate of 9.7 percent for the last three years; it has never gone above 13.4 percent during the three years we have been tabulating the rate.

Drop-Out Rates

We have seen drop-out rates as high as 74 percent for black clients and 75 percent for Mexican-Americans (Wolkon, *et al.,* 1974). Drop-out rates invariably seem to be higher for minority group clients, even though the rate may also be high for Anglos. In the Seattle Project, assessing data on nearly 14,000 CMHC clients, Sue (1977) indicated that the failure-return rate after one contact was over 50 percent for Blacks, Native Americans, and Asian Americans, with a 42 percent rate for Chicanos. This was significantly higher than the 30 percent dropout rate for Whites.

Item: Although it is difficult to develop baselines or compare drop-out rates (which may be related to length of treatment, diagnosis, aftercare status, and other such variables), we believe that our drop-out rate which has ranged from 5.6 percent (1976) to a current (1978) rate of 3 percent, is unusually low. Continuous graphing of the teams, which we maintain for our own programmatic purposes, indicates variability in drop-out rate according to ethnicity (Bahamian and Puerto Rican clients being higher than the others). Nevertheless, at no time has the rate exceeded 12 percent for any ethnic group.

Consumer Satisfaction

In a random sample of 234 clients with a median age of 41 years and mean case activity time of 8.4 months, the following responses were obtained:

a) All clients indicated that they were helped with the problems that brought them to the program: 57 percent "a great deal," 35 percent "a fair amount," and seven percent "a little."

b) Had the program's services not been available, 48 percent of the sample stated that they would have suffered greatly or decompensated. Over 28 percent verbalized prevention of "going crazy," suicidal attempts, or hospitalization.

c) Comparing CMHP services with those of other clinics or agencies, 84.5 percent of clients with prior experience gave a higher rating to CMHP (47.5 percent "superior," and 37 percent "somewhat better").

d) Ninety six percent of the sample said they would return to the CMHP for help if new programs developed.

Effectiveness of Services

a) Using goal-attainment scaling on a systematic basis, as part of the treatment plan and for evaluative purposes, this program does annual therapeutic outcome studies. In the majority of cases, mean goal-attainment scores have been at or above expected levels based on operationally defined behavior objectives (See Lefley, 1979).

b) With a substantial caseload of aftercare patients, effectiveness is also measured with annual recidivism studies. Using Anthony, et al.'s (1972) suggested baseline data (cited also by Bachrach, 1976), the expected rate of rehospitalization for individuals with a history of previous psychiatric hospitalization is 30 percent to 40 percent within the six month period following discharge; after 12 months the rate rises to 40 percent to 50 percent, and three to five years after release the rehospitalization rate is 75 percent. A comprehensive analysis of 447 clients with previous psychiatric hospitalization histories in our program for a range of 8-19 months and a mean of 14 months indicated a 16.5 percent rehospitalization rate. In recidivism studies based on probabilities derived from each client's history (previous time between hospitalizations), it was estimated that of every $1.00 invested in the CMHC, we saved $18.00 in anticipated hospitalization costs.

We have not up to this point attempted in depth evaluation of our preventive efforts, largely due to the multivariate nature of these activities. We realize that a small, time-limited program is unlikely to have an observable effect on incidence and prevalence rate during its relatively short life span, and that it may, in fact, generate an initial rise in such rates through greater exposure and availability of services. The utilization rates previously cited are a case in point. One small project we are designing, however, will compare the adjustment status of Haitian mothers and children who are finally allowed to enroll in public school through the agency of this program, with a control of same or other-nationality aliens who have been unable to complete the process. On a larger basis, we maintain continuous enumeration of new resources brought into the catchment area or new programs generated by advocacy efforts in terms of actual/estimated number of community residents to be served and estimated dollar value. These data will subsequently be correlated with epidemiological and cost data in specified high risk areas.

FOOTNOTES

[1]Principal Investigators of the Health Ecology Project were Hazel E. Weidman, Ph.D., Professor of Social Anthropology, and James N. Sussex, M.D., Professor and Chairman, Department of Psychiatry, University of Miami School of Medicine. The model for the University of Miami-Jackson Memorial Community Mental Health Center was largely developed by these individuals, with Dr. Weidman as the major architect of the anthropological model of ethnic community teams. Dr. Weidman co-directed the Health Ecology Project and is author of several publications (only a few of which are indicated in the References) dealing with its conceptualization and implications. Clarissa Scott, M.A., Field Coordinator of the Health Ecology Project whose writings are also cited, has applied some of the findings in her role as Coordinator of Consultation and Education in the CMHC.

[2]A comprehensive discussion of the evolution of the program during its first year may be found in the complete issue of *Psychiatric Annals*, August 1975.

[3]This has always been true for neighborhood workers, but it has not always been possible for us to find social or behavioral scientists of matching ethnicity to the populations served. Initially, two Anglo anthropologists directed the Haitian and Puerto Rican teams, but were later replaced by Haitian and Puerto Rican behavioral scientists. Despite a long search, we have never been able to hire a Bahamian social scientist as a Unit Director. This team had been led by a political scientist from Anguilla, a Black-American social worker, and a Bahamian clergyman. Because of the geographical location of the team and the ethnic mix in Miami, the majority of this team's caseload is composed of black-Americans, only a portion of whom are of Bahamian descent. The Cuban team, however, has had the same director (a Cuban anthropologist and cultural historian) since the beginning of the program: Dr. Mercedes Sandoval. Dr. Hilda Ross, director of Neighborhood Family I, has also been with the CMHC since its inception.

[4]Special mention should be made here of the invaluable contributions of Clara Dorta, data systems coordinator, to the generation of these reports.

[5]A further description of this program is given in Glasscote, R., Gudeman, J.E., and Miles, D. *Creative mental health services for the elderly*. Washington, D.C.: American Psychiatric Association Joint Information Service, 1978.

[6]Neighborhood Family Services, Inc. Phase I of *Reclaim our Neighborhood*. Unpublished report by Hilda K. Ross, staff gerontologist.

REFERENCES

Abad, V., Ramos, J., and Boyce, E. A model for delivery of mental health services to Spanish-speaking minorities. *American Journal of Orthopsychiatry*, 1974, *44* (4), 548-595.

Acosta, F., and Sheehan, J. Preferences toward Mexican-American and Anglo-American psychotherapists. *Journal of Counseling and Clinical Psychology*, 1976, *44* 272-279.

Anthony, W. A., Buel, G. J., Sharratt, S., and Althoff, M. E. Efficacy of psychiatric rehabilitation. *Psychological Bulletin*, 1972, *78*, 447-456.

Bachrach, L. A note on some recent studies of released mental patients in the community. *American Journal of Psychiatry*, 1976, *133*, 73-75.

Baker, F. From community mental health to human service ideology. *American Journal of Public Health*, 1974, *64*, 576-581.

Banks, W. The differential effects of race and social class in helping. *Journal of Clinical Psychology*, 1972, *28*, 90-92.

Bestman, E. W., and Lefley, H. P. *Treatment of Caribbean patients in Miami*. Paper presented at the First Annual Meeting of the Association of Caribbean Psychologists, Port-au-Prince, Haiti, August, 1976.

Bestman, E. W., Lefley, H. P., and Scott, C. S. *Culturally appropriate interventions: Paradigms and pitfalls*. Paper presented at the 53rd Annual Meeting of the American Orthopsychiatric Association, Atlanta, Georgia, March, 1976.

Brenner, M. H. *Mental illness and the economy*. Cambridge: Harvard University Press, 1973.

Bryant, C. A. *Psychiatric anthropologist in action: From consultant to Collaborator*. Paper presented at the Ninth Annual Meeting of the Southern Anthropological Society, Blacksburg, Virginia, April 4-6, 1974.

Carkhuff, R., and Pierce, R. Differential effects of therapist race and social class upon patient depth of self-exploration in the initial clinical interview. *Journal of Consulting Psychology*, 1967, *31*, 632-634.

De Hoyos, A., and De Hoyos, G. Symptomatology differentials between Negro and white schizophrenics. *International Journal of Social Psychiatry*, 1965, *11*, 245-255.

Draguns, J. G. Comparisons of psychopathology across cultures. *Journal of Cross-Cultural Psychology*, 1973, *4*, 9-47.

Fried, M. Social differences in mental health. In J. Kosa, A. Antonovsky, and I. K. Zola (eds.), *Poverty and health: A sociological analysis*. Cambridge, Mass.: Harvard University Press, 1969.

Gilbert, G. The role of social work in Black liberation. *Black Scholar*, 1974, *6*, 16-23.

Giordano, J. *Ethnicity and mental health*. New York: Institute of Human Relations, 1973.

Giordano, J., and Giordano, G. P. Ethnicity and community mental health. *Community Mental Health Review*, 1976, *1*, (3), 3-14.

Griffith, M. S. The influences of race on the psychotherapeutic relationship. *Psychiatry*, 1977, *40*, 27-40.

Griffith, E. E. H., and Ruiz, P. Cultural factors in the training of psychiatric residents in an Hispanic urban community. *Psychiatric Quarterly*, 1977, *49*, (1), 29-37.

Gross, H., and Herbert, M. The effect of race and sex on variation of diagnosis and disposition in a psychiatric emergency room. *Journal of Nervous and Mental Disease*, 1969, *148*, (6), 638-642.

Gynther, M. D. White norms and black MMPI's: A prescription for discrimination? *Psychological Bulletin*, 1972, *78*, 386-402.

Hertz, P., and Stamps, P. L. Appointment-keeping behavior re-evaluated. *American Journal of Public Health*, 1977, *67*, 1033-1036.

Hunt, R. Occupational status in the disposition of cases in a child guidance clinic. *International Journal of Social Psychology*, 1962, *8*, 199-210.

Kiresuk, T. J., and Sherman, R. E. Goal attainment scaling: A general method for evaluating community mental health programs. *Community Mental Health Journal*, 1968, *4*, 443-453.

Kohn, M. L. Social class and schizophrenia: A critical review and reformulation. *Schizophrenia Bulletin*, 1973, *1*, (Experimental Issue No. 7), 60-79.

Kohut, H. Introspection, empathy, and psychoanalysis. *Journal of the American Psychoanalytic Association*, 1959, *7*, 459-483.

Lefley, H. P. *Ethnic patients and Anglo healers: An overview of the problem in mental health care*. Paper presented at the Ninth Annual Meeting of the Southern Anthropological Society, Blacksburg, Virginia, April 4-6, 1974.

Lefley, H. P. Environmental interventions and therapeutic outcome. *Hospital and Community Psychiatry*, 1979, *30*, 341-344 (a).

Lefley, H. P. Prevalence of potential falling-out cases among the Black, Latin, and non-Latin White populations of the city of Miami. *Social Science and Medicine*, 1979, *13B*, 113-114 (b).

Lefley, H. P., & Bestman, E. W. *Psychotherapy in Caribbean cultures*. Paper presented at the 85th Annual Convention of the American Psychological Association, San Francisco, August 26-30, 1977.

Levy, L., and Rowitz, L. *The ecology of mental disorder*. New York: Behavioral Publications; 1973.

Lombillo, J. R., and Geraghty, M. *Ethnic accountability in mental health programs for Mexican-American communities.* Paper presented at the Annual Meeting of the Society for Applied Anthropology, Tucson, April, 1973.

Maas, J. P. Incidence and treatment variations between Negroes and Caucasians in mental illness. *Community Mental Health Journal.* 1967, *3,* 61-65.

Marcos, L., and Alpert, M. Strategies and risks in psychotherapy with bilingual patients. *American Journal of Psychiatry,* 1976, *133,* 1275-1278.

Mathewson, M. A. *Is crazy Anglo, crazy Haitian? Issues of Ethnic Accountability in Crisis Intervention.* Paper presented at the Ninth Annual Meeting of the Southern Anthropological Society, Blacksburg, Virginia, April 4-6, 1974.

Mazur, V. Family therapy: An approach to the culturally different. *International Journal of Social Psychiatry,* 1973, *19,* 114-119.

McCartney, T. *Neuroses in the sun: Some psychosocial and psychopathological aspects of Bahamian society.* Paper presented at the Scientific Meeting, Jackson Memorial Hospital Institute, Department of Psychiatry, January 24, 1975.

Milazzo-Sayre, L. Admission rates to state and county psychiatric hospitals by age, sex, and race, United States, 1975. *NIMH Mental Health Statistical Note No. 140,* November 1977. DHEW Publication No. (ADM) 78-158.

National Institute of Mental Health. *A model for estimating mental health needs using 1970 Census socioeconomic data.* Rockville, Maryland, 1974.

Padilla, A. M., Ruiz, R. A., and Alvarez, R. Community mental health services for the Spanish-speaking/surnamed population. *American Psychologist,* 1975, *30,* 892-905.

Rabkin, J. G. and Struening, E. L. *Ethnicity, social class and mental illness. Working paper series No. 17.* New York: Institute of Pluralism and Group Identity, 1976.

Rosen, H., and Frank, J. D. Negroes in psychotherapy. *American Journal of Psychiatry,* 1962, *119,* 456-460.

Ross, H. K. The Neighborhood Family. *Aging,* 1978, *Nos. 283-284,* 27-31.

Sandoval, M. C. An emergent Cuban community. *Psychiatric Annals,* 1975, *5,* 45-65.

Schulberg, H. C. Community mental health and human services. *Community Mental Health Review,* 1977, *2,* (6), 1-9.

Scott, C. S. Health and healing practices among five ethnic groups in Miami, Florida. *Public Health Reports,* 1974, *89,* 523-532.

Scott, C. S. *Puerto Rican health concerns: Cultural focus vs. the orthodox medical patterns.* Paper presented at the Annual Meeting of the American Anthropological Association, San Francisco, December 3-6, 1975.

Segal, J. (ed.) *Research in the service of mental health.* Report of the Research Task Force of the National Institute of Mental Health, Washington, D. C. G. P. O. 1975, DHEW Pub. No. (ADM) 75-236.

Simon, R. J., Fleis, J. L., Gurland, B. J., Stiller, P. R., and Sharpe, L. Depression and schizophrenia in hospitalized black and white mental patients. *Archives of General Psychiatry,* 1973, *28,* 509-512.

Singer, B. D. Some implications of differential psychiatric treatment of Negro and White patients. *Social Science and Medicine*, 1967, *1*, 77-83.

Sue, S. Community mental health services to minority groups. *American Psychologist*, 1977, *32*, 616-624.

Thomas, A. Pseudo transference reactions due to cultural stereotyping. *American Journal of Orthopsychiatry*, 1962, *32*, 894-900.

Thomas, A., and Sillen, S. *Racism and psychiatry*. New York: Brunner/Mazel, 1972.

Warren, R. G., Jackson, A. M., Nugaris, J., and Farley, G. K. Differential attitudes of Black and White patients toward treatment in a child guidance clinic. *American Journal of Orthopsychiatry*, 1973, *43*, (3), 384-393.

Weidman, H. H. *Difficulties of synthesis: Conceptual blocks and administrative hang-ups*. Paper presented at the 13th Annual Meeting of the Society for Applied Anthropology, Miami, April 14-18, 1971.

Weidman, H. H. *Implications of the culture broker concept for the delivery of health care*. Paper presented at the Annual Meeting of the Southern Anthropological Society, Wrightsville Beach, North Carolina, March 8-11, 1973.

Weidman, H. H. *Miami Health Ecology Project Report: A statement on ethnicity and health*. Volume I. Unpublished manuscript, University of Miami, 1978.

Weidman, H. H. Falling-out. A diagnostic and treatment problem viewed from a transcultural perspective. *Social Science and Medicine*, 1979, *13B*, 95-112.

Whitehorn, J.C., and Betz, B.J. Further studies of the doctor as a crucial variable in the outcome of treatment with schizophrenic patients. *American Journal of Psychiatry*, 1960, *117*, 215-223.

Williams, J. Jr. Interview-respondent interaction: A study of bias in the information interview. *Sociometry*, 1964, *27*, (3), 338-352.

Wingerd, J. *Ethnocentrism and psychosis: Case study of a Haitian in Miami*. Paper presented at the Meeting of the Caribbean Psychiatric Association, Nassau, Bahamas, July, 1973.

Wolf, E.R. Aspects of group relations in a complex society: Mexico. *American Anthropologist*, 1956, *58*, 1065-1078.

Wolkon, G. H., Moriwaki, S., Mandel, D., Archuleta, J., Bunje, P., and Zimmerman, S. Ethnicity and social class in the delivery of services. *American Journal of Public Health*, 1974, *64*, 709-712.

Wolkon, G.H., Moriwaki, S., and Williams, K.J. Race and social class as factors in the orientation toward psychotherapy. *Journal of Counseling Psychology*, 1973, *20*, 312-316.

Yamamoto, J., Dixon, F., and Bloombaum, M. White therapists and Negro patients. *Journal of National Medical Association*, 1972, *64*, 312-316.

Yamamoto, J., James, Q., and Palley, N. Cultural problems in psychiatric therapy. *Archives of General Psychiatry*, 1968, *19*, 45-49.

Chapter 5

THEMES STRIVING FOR HARMONY
Conventional Mental Health Services and American Indian Traditions

Carolyn L. Attneave

As recently as 1970, American Indians were viewed by the world at large as having no mental health programs or resources (Torrey, 1970). A 1978 report declares that this idea "is misguided at best, conducive to stereotyping and racism at worst" (Beiser and Attneave, 1978, p. 3). This statement is a strong one, but would not only be supported, but pushed much further by tribal leaders and many urban Indian coalitions. The contrast in views is due to ten years of widespread activity that has seen the conventional mental health program developed parallel to, and often in conjunction with, rival of traditional healing concepts and practices.

Jillek (1978), in a recent overview, describes at least five types of healing traditions with strong mental health components that are persistent in various tribal settings throughout the U.S. and Canada. These include a use of dreams among the Iriquois that resembles and yet predates Freudian and Jungian techniques and theories; the use of herbs and psychoactive drugs, which is deeply rooted in most tribes and particularly well documented in the Southwest among the Navajo, Hopi, and Yacqui, and in the Native American Church; the use of regression and re-integration, as well as manipulations of alpha and beta waves that produce sensory deprivation effects among the Northwest Coast and Plains tribes; and a general use of the counsel of training experienced and wise "elders" in all tribes. In all of these traditions, firsthand observers describe how the importance of involving family members and natural "support systems" are taken for granted as part of the therapeutic effort. The generally wholistic view of life is in contrast with scientific medical practice.

Unfortunately, only within the past decade has there been any real effort to identify these traditional systems as potentially integral parts of more formal mental health programs funded by federal and state systems. The later 1970's are bringing the conventional systems of mental health care into focus as both partners and competitors with these earlier traditions. Beiser and Attneave (1978) give a brief summary of the history of one federal effort in this direction. Detailed histories of the development of mental health programs on each federally recognized Indian Reservation are available in a nine volume comprehensive report prepared for the Indian Health Services and made available through Education Research Information Center (ERIC) (Attneave and Beiser, 1974; Beiser and Attneave, 1974; 1977).

HISTORY OF INDIAN HEALTH SERVICES

As Indian tribes were pushed or removed from the Eastern States, and as they were subdued during the settlement of the West, a pattern emerged of exchanging certain basic guarantees and services by the U.S. government for land. In return for residing within a limited area (a reservation), provision of education and health services were invariably mentioned among other rights and privileges.

Initially, Army medical officers were charged with health care of the Indian populations, and continued to provide this, even after the Bureau of Indian Affairs was created to place reservations in civilian status rather than a quasi-prisoner of war atmosphere. Very little information is available about special cases of mental disturbance, and there is little indication of preventative mental health services during this period. In many ways, this sequence of events parallels the situation for most of the U.S., where emphasis was on separating the mentally ill from prisoners and on developing facilities for the care of chronically and severely disturbed persons.

In 1955, health care was transferred to the U.S. Public Health Service, and a special division was created known as the Indian Health Service (IHS). During its first ten years, IHS was too busy establishing basic medical facilities to consider mental health problems, except in crisis situations. Acute and chronic Indian mental patients were transferred to federal institutions, mainly to St. Elizabeth's Hospital in Washington, D.C. Alaska Natives were usually transported to psychiatric facilities in the Northwestern states.

In 1965, however, two factors led to the initiation of formal mental health programs. First, the basic hospital and medical clinic facilities had been established, so that time and energy were available. Second, there were a number of psychiatrists who elected IHS as a means of fulfilling their military obligation after draft deferrment. Several of them were able to include experience with Indian populations as part of their training. Supervising faculty members were very much involved with community based, broadly defined mental health programs. The Psychiatric Residency programs at the University of Washington, University of Colorado, and University of Chicago were outstanding in this regard.

The first program, a pilot project, was authorized when Congressman Ben Rifle, an Oglala Sioux from South Dakota, persuaded Congress to appropriate funds for a demonstration mental health program at Pine Ridge, South Dakota. Much of the local pressure from his constituents arose from their experience with tuberculosis and the Sioux women of the LaKoTa Tuberculosis and Health Association felt strongly that a similar community context for mental health programs was a viable possibility.

Almost simultaneously, the Surgeon General's office recommended a similar program for Alaska, and the Navajo requested services designed to meet their needs. These two additional programs were funded in 1966, without waiting for results from the Pine Ridge demonstrations.

Growth during the first five years was rapid. New areas were opened, new positions were added, and the budget increased. In 1969, the Indian Health Service mental health staff had grown to 26, operating with a budget of $580,000. By 1977, mental health staff numbered 232 and the budget appropriation was $4,200,000. In 1974, 12,987 Indians were seen for outpatient mental health services and 1,872 received inpatient mental health treatment, exclusive of services for alcoholism (Beiser and Attneave, 1977). This figure represents approximately two percent of the total Indian population (about four percent of the reservation population), and better than seven percent of adults 20 and older.

ORGANIZATION OF IHS

The IHS program is administered both centrally and regionally. The national headquarters for mental health programs is located in Albuquerque and, since 1974, has been under the direction of Choctaw psychiatrist, H.B. Townsley. It is staffed by experts in training and service delivery who are available to all parts of the U.S. as consultants and for administrative assistance. The IHS is itself organized in nine "Areas," each of which is, in most cases, composed of several states west of the Mississippi. The exceptions are the Anchorage Area, which serves the single state of Alaska, the Navajo Area which serves that single tribe on the largest U.S. reservation, and the Bemidji Area which serves the states bordering the Great Lakes. A contract agreement with the United South Eastern Tribes permits services to tribes along the eastern seaboard and gulf coast.

Chiefs of mental health programs in these areas have come from a variety of disciplines. Psychiatrists tend to head area programs, but social workers and psychiatric nurses have held these posts. Mental health services are primarily delivered by IHS in conjunction with "Service Units" which are 90 hospitals and out-patient medical clinics spread across 17 states and located primarily on Indian Reservations or close to traditional living places of native peoples in Alaska.

EMERGING URBAN PROGRAMS

Although never restricted to serving only reservation populations, funding for urban and off reservation care was not part of the IHS budget until passage of the Indian Health Care Improvement Act in 1976. Seattle, Portland, San Francisco, Denver, Minneapolis, Oklahoma City, and other urban meccas for American Indians now have "Indian Health Boards," which administer health programs utilizing IHS as well as other sources of funding. Some of these have strong mental health components, while others are more involved with emergency health care and dental programs. Nearly all have treatment programs geared to alcoholism, or liaison with such programs.

IMPACT OF ALCOHOLISM TREATMENT PROGRAMS

Until 1977, when IHS began to phase in responsibility for alcohol treatment, all substance abuse programs were organized independently and utilized IHS staff only as consultants. The alcoholism counselors, largely paraprofessionals, were mainly recruited from the ranks of those who had successfully controlled their own abuse of alcohol, and were funded by the NIAAA and Community Actions Programs, both in urban and rural settings. Most Indian lay groups consider alcohol abuse a high priority as a mental health problem. Therefore, while the stimulation of local leaders by these separately organized programs can only be inferred, one suspects that it had been considerable. It appears that alcohol and drug abuse services evolved as a parallel development with IHS mental health programs, and that Indian as well as professional identification of the common elements involved is one factor leading to the recent decision to bring them administratively under the IHS Mental Health Programs.

THE DEVELOPMENT OF PARAPROFESSIONALS

More dramatic stimulation of the Indian population has been the impact of having available, in each of the areas served by IHS, a cadre of professionals, and paraprofessionals, engaged in the development and delivery of a broad spectrum of mental health services. By the end of 1978, there had been ten years of experience with these services delivered close to home by highly trained staffs, most of whom have interests in the maintenance of tribal cultures. This interest has led not only to a widespread acceptance of mental health programs, but also to a larger than average proportion of consumers of mental health services, when this minority group is compared to populations similarly situated in rural isolation, or to people at the lower end of the socio-economic scale.

In addition to professional services, only recently beginning to be staffed by Indian professionals, much of the acceptance and interest in this type of program has been stimulated by the wide use of paraprofessional native staff. Robert Bergman, one of the first psychiatrists to undertake full time IHS work, and Chief of the national IHS program until 1974, based his own approach on the development of skills of paraprofessionals who first acted as interpreters, and then acquired skills in therapy and program management (Bergman, 1974). This model and its many variations were used throughout the IHS so that the personnel roster shows two paraprofessionals for each professional throughout the service (*IHS Mental Health & Social Services Directory,* 1973).

There is reason to believe that many of these paraprofessionals not only have become major sources of service delivery, but that they have also been a seedbed for the development of professional social workers, psychologists, and psychiatrists as individuals moved from their paraprofessional service categories into academic training programs to acquire credentials and expertise necessary to join professional ranks.

INCREASING NUMBER OF AMERICAN INDIAN PROFESSIONALS

Not only are there steady, though small, numbers rising in this fashion, but they are providing role models and visibility that makes selection of a professional career seem realistic to many American Indian youth and adults who would not have had an opportunity to observe and consider such an option 10 or 15 years ago. There are not a sufficient number of American Indian professionals to provide the services needed or demanded, but they are growing. The American Indian Social Workers Association numbers a little over 100 members. The Network of Indian Psychologists identifies nearly 25 psychologists with Masters or Doctors degrees actively working in the field and an equal number of aspiring students in college and university programs. There are almost a dozen American Indian psychiatrists, enough to completely staff a standing committee of the American Psychiatric Association. There are a growing number of American Indian Masters of Public Health graduates with mental health concentrations, and there is a small number of Indian women who hold the Master's degree in psychiatric nursing. As this cadre grows, the opportunities for employment and the demand for services are increasing even more rapidly, so that even the small normal attrition of those who prefer to practice in non-Indian settings is keenly felt.

Fortunately, however, approximately 50 percent of the total Indian population in the U.S. resides in urban, off-reservation settings. Therefore, those Indians who find themselves "overqualified" for work in the reservation settings, or who prefer a more sophisticated home and work environment, can still be useful to the American Indian population. Their usefulness is recognized in the provisions for training received under the Indian Health Care Improvement Act, which has limited amount of funding for formal training in health related professions, including mental health. Recipients repay the debt on a year for year basis, by serving an Indian population approved by the IHS and the Secretary of HEW.

TYPES OF SERVICES PROVIDED: INPATIENT

Regardless of efforts to remove the stigmatizing stereotype, most persons think first of the hospitalized, chronically, and severely mentally ill when defining mental health services. In 1903, the BIA established a hospital at Canton, South Dakota for all Indians who were mentally disturbed. By 1929, it was overcrowded and consultants recommended that patients could be more adequately cared for closer to their origins. In 1933, 80 patients who could not be returned to their homes were transferred to St. Elizabeth's Hospital in Washington, D.C. Many of them died far away from home without being able to talk to anyone in their own language. In the late 1960's, as IHS began its development of mental health programs, those who still survived were "re-discovered" and attempts were made to return them to local care. Some families reacted as if a ghost had appeared, and for other patients with old records lost, there has been little to aid their reintegration into the community. The best that can be said about this episode might be that many were relieved to die at home in familiar surroundings and hearing their own tongue again.

From 1930 on, the policy of utilizing local state hospitals has been a difficult one. In 1975, a court ruling in South Dakota required that IHS or the tribe pay the state in cash at the rate of a non-poverty stricken citizen. In Arizona, similar provisions have been interpreted by IHS as allowing it to purchase private care at the same or even a lesser rate than the state will charge.

At Gallup Indian Hospital in New Mexico and at Anchorage Native Medical Center in Alaska, special wards for inpatient care were established in the early 1970's. The Alaska ward has been conventionally organized, utilizing chemotherapies, shock treatment, and individual and group therapy. The Gallup ward began with a more experimental approach utilizing milieu therapy, community liaison, extensive use of rehabilitation services, and a rule that there must be a Navajo speaking staff available 24 hours a day.

In both settings, stays of up to a year were possible, but shorter term treatments were preferred. Patients with chronic, intractable problems were reassigned to state hospitals as a last resort. More than 1,800 persons were hospitalized in one or the other of these facilities in 1974.

Brief crisis care is also available, from 24 hours to several days, in the general medical settings of many of the Indian hospitals. Since acutely disturbed patients tend to be disruptive and require care not always available from busy nurses and general physicians, however, there is a trend to develop more inpatient facilities. In Oklahoma and South Dakota, former tuberculosis sanitoria are being utilized. The Rapid City facility, known locally as "Sioux San" is being considered as a Regional facility to accept patients from as far away as Montana, Wisconsin, and Iowa. Phoenix, Arizona is another planned inpatient setting, since it has a large regional medical facility.

Ideally, perhaps, good local relationships with inpatient facilities of community mental health centers and state facilities should obviate the need for special IHS inpatient wards. Gulfs of prejudice exist, however, with both Indian and non-Indian populations expressing reluctance to trust one another. The probability that more appropriate, culturally adapted services can be developed within IHS seems to be the prevailing opinion.

OUTPATIENT SERVICES

A full range of outpatient services has become available as the IHS programs developed. In 1974, 12,897 patients were seen, for a total of 36,433 visits (Beiser and Attneave, 1977). The highest proportions of these are women in their 20's and 30's, followed closely by adolescents of both sexes from age 15 up. Depression and anxiety are by far the most prevalent diagnostic categories for adults, with alcohol related problems also appearing in the leading five categories for patients from age 20 to age 50. Psychologists tend to see more children and individuals with learning problems; social workers to be more involved with those needing adaptations to physical illness; and psychiatrists or nurses tend to see family conflicts in addition to the depression-anxiety cases. There is a tendency, because of legal medical requirements, for the psychiatrist's time to become filled with visits for medications and re-evaluation of chronic patients. The other staff have more opportunity for preventive efforts, consultation with community agencies, and building personal therapeutic relationships.

In-service training programs have developed high levels of skills among many of the staff, especially the Indian personnel who tend to remain for long periods in one setting. Problems of poor morale recur, however, particularly when the non-Indian professionals move or leave IHS after a two year tour of duty, or when federal budgets and appropriations do not keep pace with local needs.

LOCAL TRIBAL INPUT

Each service unit of IHS has some input from a local tribal group and each administrative Area of IHS has a Tribal Advisory Board. The National Indian Health Board, with representation from these local groups, interfaces with the general administration of IHS. Since these advisory groups are not employees of IHS, they have assumed considerable autonomy and often consider other sources of funding, such as Community Action Programs, CETA, and even in some cases direct applications to NIMH or other federal and state agencies. A strong and persistent interest in mental health, as well as medical issues, is characteristic of both local and national Indian Health Boards.

From this mixture of local experience, as both service deliverers and recipients, as well as from a variety of local administrative arrangements, a number of innovative service programs have developed. One of the earliest of these developed its own health program, headed by a social worker. This program contracts with IHS for mental health consultation, but also has developed relationships with a nearby community mental health center and has a comprehensive tribal program of its own.

A central concept of the Warm Springs program has been a continuity of traditional roles and functions (Shore and Nicholls, 1975). One of its tenets has been support of services for all members of the family. Single parent fathers receive housekeeper assistance equally with single parent mothers. A group home not only cares for delinquents and children whose homes are in crisis, but also cares for children who may need medical clinic visits. Foster care, financial and marital counseling, school consultation, and alcoholism programs are made available through the tribal program. Interestingly enough, these services are made available by the tribe to the non-Indians living on the reservation as well, something IHS is forbidden by law to provide. The San Carlos Apache, among others, have used this as a model for developing tribally organized services. The Yakima have carried their ideas one step further and in 1978 secured a community mental health center grant to develop a mental health center to serve themselves and the local Chicano population. The Navajo Tribe and several Alaska Native corporations are also proposing community mental health centers of their own.

A less comprehensive program grew out of the alcohol treatment efforts in Eastern Oklahoma. The Southern Cheyenne-Arapaho tribes have developed a residential facility at Bessie, Oklahoma, where not only the identified alcohol abuser, but the whole family can live and learn to recognize their lives. Centered strongly in the Native American church, this program draws its alumni back periodically for celebrations of traditional as well as Christian holidays.

USE OF MEDICINE MEN AS MENTAL HEALTH SPECIALISTS

In Rosebud, South Dakota, the local tribal community college, Sinte Gleska, provides a nucleus for training and for evaluating the effectiveness of both conventional and traditional mental health efforts. Of particular interest is the effort to revive and strengthen the Tiyospe, a group of up to 20 or 30 families clustered about an elder or medicine man. The 1970's Tiyospe developments include not only traditional healing rituals, but also modern cooperatives for the production and distribution of crops and light manufactured goods, and other efforts to develop stable, secure communities.

Close interpersonal ties are also developed through traditional religious observances and through the use of mental health consultation to the traditional leader-healer. These ties ensure that both preventative and treatment activities are keyed to cultural values as well as to the lifestyle of the families involved. Baseline data on the reservation as a whole are being collected through 1978, using demographic measures and non-reactive methods of observation. As the Tiyospe programs evolve, careful historical records and continued epidemiologic measures will test the viability of that particular model for the Rosebud Sioux. Other Sioux tribes are interested and may well develop similar programs.

Some of the most innovative of early tribal efforts were developed on the Navajo Reservation. One of these, the training of medicine men by the senior traditional healers in cooperation with IHS mental health consultation has been funded by NIMH (Bergman, 1973). Films that include significant segments depicting this program have been the subject of special television reports on BBC and by *Time-Life* as well as in official archives.

The resultant deepening of appreciation of the skills and unique contributions of both conventional and traditional healing expertise is highly desired in other settings, but has not been duplicated in formal training programs. Navajo beliefs have a quality shared by holistic medicine, in feeling that all aspects of life need to be in harmony. Respect for non-Indian medical and professional staff permits use of IHS to decrease symptoms, while the recognition of social factors by IHS permits the use of traditional ceremonies to restore social and spiritual equilibrium. Mutual respect permits joint efforts and promotes consultation in both directions. Whether or not this is possible in other locations is the subject of much discussion (Attneave, 1974; Jillek, 1978; Jillek and Todd, 1974).

THE MODEL DORMITORY

Partly because they are more numerous, and therefore better able to justify special services, and partly because they have a good tribal organization, the Navajo also participated in a preventive mental health program known as the Model Dormitory. Twenty five thousand Navajo children each year must spend time in a residential school due to lack of passable roads and local school facilities. Much research over the years has documented the devastating effects of these experiences on children removed from home and family and herded in semi-military units. A strong statement of this was made in an editorial in the American Pyschiatric Association's Committee on Indian Affairs (Beiser, 1973).

In 1969, a grant to Toyei Boarding School provided funds to reduce the pupil/adult ratio (outside the classroom) from about 200 to 1 to 8 to 1. Adding Navajo adults to the staff provided opportunity for these children in grades 1-3 to have contact with men and women who spoke their language and understood their ways. Weaving, silverworking, story telling, and familiar foods from home became everyday occurrences in the Boarding school environs. The follow-up results comparing these children with a control group at another Navajo Boarding School showed that these children exhibited fewer emotional problems and were better achievers in school (Goldstein, 1974). Unfortunately, the demonstration project has not generated wide support among non-Indian who control funds and policies. However, efforts to replicate this project in a standard fashion are receiving wide tribal support and plans for similar programs were included in the unfunded portions of the Indian Health Care Improvement Act of 1976.

Unlike local public schools, the Indian Boarding Schools are not subject to local controls. They are operated by the Bureau of Indian Affairs, under the Secretary of the Interior, and tend to be unable to respond to mental health consultation from outside agencies in a flexible manner. There is much ambivalence about the value of these schools among adults, many of whom knew no other educational experience. Most efforts at improving these institutions seem to last only for a demonstration period and then fade away, but growing local concern may provide the impetus for future change (Krush, et al., 1966)

CHILD WELFARE PROGRAMS

Where local controls can be mobilized on behalf of children, a number of effective mental health programs have been mounted. Several examples of this come from child welfare and child abuse programs, where the Office of Child Development has provided funding for pilot programs and demonstration efforts. These programs are particularly common in urban settings, although several excellent reservation programs have also been developed. In Minneapolis such a program was developed under the leadership of John Redhorse with the support of the University of Minnesota's special program for Indian social workers. Calling itself, ABENOGEE, the program developed a group home which not only provided services for children in suspected cases of abuse and neglect, but also for their families as well. Mothers received supportive counseling; social services and medical resources were coordinated; extended family were sought out in cases where foster care seemed advisable; and fathers and siblings were includedin the cooperative plans and activities.

A similar program in the San Francisco Bay area has received continuation and expanded funding from a local foundation. On the Makah reservation, the tribal staff operating such a demonstration program not only secured a wide variety of experts for inservice training, but also saw the mental health need for single parents (usually mothers) to have an opportunity to take a "vacation" of a day or two for shopping and recreation in cities 100 or more miles away. The Makah tribe, as well as a number of others, is capitalizing on similarity of White man's interest in saunas and the traditional healing use of sweat baths to include such facilities in its community programs. It would appear that this method is particularly effective in the treatment or reversal of alcohol abuse.

INDIAN CONTROLLED MENTAL HEALTH TRAINING

The Seattle Indian Health Board, a local urban effort, works on a contract basis with IHS for many services, independently secured a grant for training Indian mental health workers, open to all levels of paraprofessional and professional staffs serving the Indian population in the Puget Sound area. These seminars are attended by Indian and non-Indian personnel alike, in about equal numbers. The basic assumption is that, in an urban area, there are many tribes, and no single set of traditions can be utilized to the exclusion of others. It is also apparent that there will be, for some time to come, non-Indians involved in the delivery of mental health services. Therefore, this training program provides an opportunity for developing a core of common themes and experiences that will enable both Indian and non-Indian personnel to gain understanding and skills in cross-cultural mental health, as typified by the local urban Indian and Alaska Native population. Control of the program and the development of texts and curriculum materials remain in the hands of the Indian Health Board. Similar programs can be found in many parts of the U.S. and Canada.

PROBLEMS AND POLICIES

Not all of these programs, in spite of the enthusiasm with which they are undertaken, succeed as well as the examples given. Staff "burn-out" is a common phenomenon. Money is not always available. There is often more demand for services than can be effectively met. It is also true among the Indian communities, as it is among any other political unit, that agreement about priorities for budgets is not always reached easily and smoothly. The trend is toward programs more sensitive to the specific cultural needs of the American Indian population. Perhaps even more importantly, the foundations for Indian staffed and Indian administered programs have been laid. In contrast with other minority populations, who have needed the 60's and early 70's to develop political and social consciousness, the long history of tribal experience with political activities within the reservation system may place this population in an advantageous position. To realize full potential, however, the numbers of Indian professionals must continue to increase, and the efforts of the total professional and general community to develop support and to demolish barriers to full mental health services must continue.

It is perhaps no coincidence that the concerns expressed in the lengthy report of the 1978 President's Commission on Mental Health are echoed in local, regional, and national gatherings of Indian leaders. Wherever one examines the field, the same human problems remain to be solved. American Indian populations are particularly interested in prevention and community oriented services that recognize the interrelation of mental and emotional symptoms with reactions to stress in various sectors of life. Much of what appears new or untried in conventional services seems very old and traditional in Indian perspective. What is hopeful is the emergence of local, tribal, and urban Indian leadership and the skilled professional and paraprofessional Indian personnel who are attempting to plan adequate programs and carry them out.

In the decade of the 1980's, the issues of tribal control and of acceptance of unique blends of conventional and traditional elements in mental health programs will undoubtedly characterize Indian activities in the broad field of mental health. It will be interesting to see if the reactions of the general public and the professions mirror those of one federal bureaucrat who, after spending two days listening to an all Indian group, expressed his bewilderment at the obstacles his agency had placed in their path. "After all," he exclaimed, "what they want would be good for anybody. It just looks different because they developed it themselves."

REFERENCES

Attneave, C.L. Medicine men and psychiatrists in the Indian Health Service. *Psychiatric Annals*, 1974, *4*, 49-55.

Attneave, C.L. and Beiser, M. *Service networks and patterns of utilization mental health services of IHS 1965-73.* A 10 volume contract report (IHS #110-73-342), Rockville, Md., 1974.

Beiser, M. Indian boarding schools: A hazard to mental health. *American Journal of Psychiatry*, 1973, *130*, 491-445.

Beiser, M., and Attneave, C.L. *Overview and recommendations: IHS mental health services 1965-1974. A Summary of IHS. Contract Report* #110-73-342, Rockville, Md., 1974.

Beiser, M., and Attneave, C.L. *Staff and patient characteristics IHS mental health and social services 1974.* Contract report #240-75-001, Rockville, Md. 1977.

Beiser, M., and Attneave, C.L. American Indian mental health: Myth or reality. *White Cloud Journal of American Indian Mental Health*, 1978, *1*, 1-10.

Bergman, Robert L. A school for medicine men. *American Journal of Psychiatry*, 1973, *130*, 663-666.

Bergman, Robert L. Paraprofessionals in Indian mental health programs. *Psychiatric Annals*, 1974, *4*, 76-84.

Goldstein, George S. The model dormitory. *Psychiatric Annals*, 1974, *4*, 85-92.

Jillek, W. and Todd, N. Witch doctors succeed where doctors fail. *Canadian Psychiatric Association Journal*, 1974, *19*, 351-356.

Jillek, W. Native renaissance: The survival and revival of indigenous therapeutic ceremonials among North American Indians. *Transcultural Psychiatric Review*, 1978, *15*, 117-147.

Krush, T., Pajork, J., Sindel, P.S. and Nelle, J. Some thoughts on the formation of personality disorders: Study of an Indian boarding school population. *American Journal of Psychiatry*, 1966, *112*, 868-876.

Shore, J.N. and Nicholls, W. Indian children and tribal group homes: New interpretation of the whipper man. *American Journal of Psychiatry*, 1975, *132*, 445-456.

Torrey, E.F. Mental health services for American Indians and Eskimos. *Community Mental Health Journal*, 1970, *6*, 455-463.

Part II

SELF-IDENTITY AND COMPETENCE

Self-Identity and Competence

Ethnic self-identity has continued to be a major topic of examination in race and ethnic relations. It has special relevance to our theme of community mental health in a pluralistic society, since cultural and community influences shape self-identity and self-esteem. The three chapters in this section focus on the image and self identity of ethnic minority group individuals.

W. Curtis Banks directly challenges the decades of research demonstrating self-hate and negative self-concepts among Blacks. For Banks, previous research has been limited by major methodological and conceptual problems. His argument is that, despite experiences of prejudice, discrimination, and negative stereotyping, Blacks often develop a strong sense of self-esteem through the adoption of values and adaptive strategies in Black communities.

From a similar perspective, Lonnie Snowden believes that a deficit model view of Black Americans has been inappropriately perpetuated in research. With the growing interest among community psychologists in competency and competency training, he points to cultural differences as strengths that should be appreciated, rather than viewed as weaknesses. Snowden advocates the need for a more ecological orientation, involving the match of persons with environments.

Daniel Adelson advances the idea that self-images are related to social conditions. Self-esteem and self-acceptance change as a function of social changes. Thus community change (social reconstruction) and the sense of self-identity and acceptance (self-reconstruction) are intimately related to each other. Increasing the power, participation, and control and fully extending democratic ideals to disenfranchised groups will increase psychological well-being.

Chapter 6

TOWARD A CULTURAL-SOCIAL
LEARNING ANALYSIS OF SELF-CONCEPT
IN BLACKS

W. Curtis Banks

One reason for the central importance attached in psychology to the concept of self is the critical role the sense of identity plays in locating the position of individuals in the social milieu. Within organized societies, this position encompasses not only the sense of belonging to certain definable subgroups, but also provides a basis for guiding people's behavior and predicting the experiences to which they will thereby expose themselves. Many of these experiences are systematically determined by certain aspects of the status position their identity accords them within the social hierarchy. Moreover, the concept of self that individuals have both reflects and contributes to the position of ascendance or subordination that they occupy within the larger social order, and it provides a stable reference for experiences which, while systematic in some respects, are also highly variable across time and contexts.

The purpose of this chapter is to (1) critically examine the traditional view of black self-concept and (2) propose an alternative perspective based upon an adaptation model. Grounded upon a social feedback notion, the traditional view assumes that, because of negative evaluations of Blacks and positive evaluations of Whites in society, Blacks develop self-hatred and prefer to be white. Largely for conceptual reasons, it is proposed that the traditional perspective has serious problems. The approach taken in this chapter is that an adaptation model, whereby Black self-concept is selectively shaped from an array of contingencies, can more appropriately conceptualize self-concept. Blacks are not simply victims of negative forces. Socializing forces in the community of Blacks often buffer the consequences to negative experiences and enhance positive experiences.

SELF CONCEPT AS A FUNCTION OF SOCIAL FEEDBACK

The Traditional Viewpoint

For certain theorists (e.g., Cooley, 1902), self-concept is a construct that represents the summation of the evaluative reactions that others convey to the individual in social interaction. This looking-glass notion of self-concept derives largely from the conviction that the individual within a social vacuum would have no point of reference from which either to distinguish oneself, or to assess the effects of one's own action (except upon oneself and nonreactive objects). Social others provide the criteria by which characteristics of one's own experiences, appearance, and behaviors are measured. One's own characteristics then gain meaning through their association with those of others, their comparison with the characteristics of others, and the reactions they evoke from others. It becomes apparent that one's position within the social milieu is more than an existential accident. For the developing individual, that position determines whether the criteria of reference will generally share one's inherent characteristics or represent a contrast to them; and, in turn, whether those criteria imply a frame of reference with which one's characteristics fit as constructive and positive features of the total order, or as aberrations from the values and norms embodied by the dominant culture and its bio-social referents.

The implications of this general line of reasoning for the way we think of the developing personalities of Black individuals are clear. First, it must become apparent to such persons, as their maturing intellectual and social perceptual skills emerge, that they are identified by their membership in a subgroup defined by racial characteristics. It is also clear that such a subgroup occupies a position within the social hierarchy that is subordinate to the majority (of persons and other subgroups) in status, power, and the attainment of resource holdings (i.e., achievement). Insofar as these indices of social position represent the salient values of the dominant social order, and insofar as such aspects are regarded both as deriving from and contributing to the identifying characteristics that define the subgroup of ''Blacks,'' it appears obvious that a negative evaluative status is given to Blacks in our society. It follows, then, that the looking glass of social comparison with, and evaluative reactions from, others presents a distinctly negative image to Blacks regarding the characteristics that identify them biologically, socially, politically, and economically. It must be considered whether such a conception of the manner in which the self-concepts of Black people evolve has merit in logic and substantive evidence.

Much of the early research and writing with this area readily affirmed the traditional social feedback mode of self-concept, and attempted simply to add to the model. This effort has had mixed success. Some of the earliest work, by Clark and Clark (e.g., 1947) and others, has been interpreted as providing support for this conceptual model. More recently, argument has been set forth, together with supportive evidence, that such early trends represented an historical phenomenon that changed with the awakening of racial pride and political assertion during the 1960's. That is, prior to 1960, Black self-concept was negative. After that time, the "Black is beautiful" movement resulted in positive changes. This hypothesis of the socio-temporal specificity of negative self-concept among Blacks relies both upon the status of the research findings of positive self-concepts after 1960 and the status of the findings of negative self-concepts before. The primary paradigm within which such support was sought, however, yielded little reliable substance.

Clark and Clark, and others had reasoned that if the evaluative status accorded Blacks within American society was negative, Black people must simultaneously come to a recognition of their inferior racial identity and the negative reactions it evokes from others. Compliance with and acceptance of that frame of evaluative reference provided by the dominant (White) society should therefore lead to a rejection by Blacks of those features that comprise their racial identity. Such tendencies were hypothesized to dispose Black children toward positive evaluative preference for the characteristics of identity to which society accords the status of acceptability and toward an evaluative rejection of their own characteristics and identity as Black. The paradigm of preference for White over Black thus provided both a conceptual and methodological framework for the empirical study of negative self-conceptions, and many investigators conducted studies that were regarded as lending support with this paradigm to the hypothesis.

Problems in the Social Feedback Viewpoint

A relatively dominant concurrent trend in conceptualizing and operationalizing the study of the psychology of Black people provided an ultimate stumbling block for that paradigm and the data it generated for over thirty years. The reliance upon a comparative framework within which the characteristics of personality and behavior of Blacks are measured (implicitly or explicitly) against those of Whites led systematically to a test of something other than the appropriate null-hypotheses. While the null-hypothesis of *non-preferential evaluative behavior among Blacks* regarding the preference of Blacks to be White provided the actual test of the prediction of preference for White stimulus characteristics, it was the null-hypothesis of *equal preferential tendencies across Black and White subjects* (i.e., Whites and Blacks do not differ in preferences) that received attention. Within the latter frame, evidence most often seemed overwhelming in its affirmation of the hypotheses, while, empirically, Blacks virtually never displayed what can be regarded as significant white-preferential behavior. In other words, the wrong null-hypothesis (equal preferential tendencies) was being tested.

For example, Moreland (1958) compared the rates at which black and white children identified themselves as being most like a photograph of either a white or black child. Same-race preferential choices were made by 99.5 percent of white children sampled (white-stimulus choices) and 52 percent of black children sampled (black-stimulus choices), an impressive rejection of the null-hypothesis of black-white sameness in own race choice behavior. At the same time, however, black children, having chosen black identity 52 percent of the time, had hardly rejected that identity or preferred an identity as white, the null-hypothesis of non-preferential choice behavior having clearly been sustained rather than rejected in that group. The research demonstrated racial differences in preferences, but not black preference for whites.

In a review of the evidence presented by twenty of the most prominent published studies of evaluative preference, Banks (1976b) showed that only two found the choice behavior of blacks to have rejected the null-hypothesis of change in preferential favor of white stimuli, while four showed rejection of the null-hypothesis in the opposite direction (black-preference) and fourteen had showed the null-hypothesis of non-preference sustained. A similar pattern was found to emerge from a test of the proper null-hypothesis *via* the data from twelve prominent studies of preferential identification, though in that instance Banks reported that none of the investigations (including those of Clark and Clark) had actually shown the predicted white-preferential trend. The overall pattern of findings described by Banks illustrated a phenomenon that failed to obtain in all but six percent of even the most often cited group of empirical investigations, a rate of success clearly to have been expected at chance using the criterion (which Banks employed) of alpha = .05.

Not much can be made of the conceptual significance of either the comparative tendency of blacks not to prefer black racial characteristics, or of the apparent individual differences represented by the fact that at least some of the sampled blacks did choose white stimuli. Williams and Morland (1979), for instance, have attempted to reaffirm both the existence and the social-theoretical importance of white-preference in blacks. Their argument has revolved around the contention that even a "minimal" phenomenon such as this has broad significance for the social context of a racially pluralistic society and the influence that context can have upon the social development of black children. Yet when such assertions of importance are put to the test of demonstrable validity, little can be found to support the notion that white-preference has major significance in blacks or concurs, predicts, or represents any coherent underlying construct of behavior and psychological functioning in that population (see Banks, McQuater, and Ross, 1979).

It has been asserted elsewhere that such a total failure of the paradigm of preference to confirm the negative nature of self-concept among blacks ". . . marks less the methodological inadequacies of past research than the conceptual imprecision of such traditional. . . approaches to black personality" (Banks, 1976b, p. 1185). Nobles (1973), for example, has criticized various traditional approaches to an understanding of the nature of black self-concept, asserting that all have ignored the important antecedents of African culture that form the basis of any proper understanding of black social behavior. In this regard, he has referred to the tribal sense of collective purpose and identity as the archetypical precursor of what he has termed extended self among black individuals in American society. From a somewhat different approach, Banks and his associates have asserted an equally non-traditional formulation of how the racial self-identity of blacks not only results from the relationship they recognize between themselves and the larger society, but serves to identify for them the important features of similar and dissimilar social others, which affect the nature and meaning of self-concept shaping interactions. From either points of view, the appropriate analysis of the manner in which conceptions of self-development and function for black people is one that gives full weight to the role of such processes in locating, for the individual or his or her position in the total social structure, the extended parameters of both space and time that define their collective experience and circumstances of her or him vis a vis other black people, and the highly complex and discriminative manner in which social-evaluative information is mediated by cognitions that determine its impact and preserve and promote self-esteem and social survival.

IMPORTANCE OF COMMUNITY SOCIALIZATION

Certain of the propositions set forth earlier by such theorists as Clark must surely be affirmed by any model. It is apparent that black individuals are exposed to the negative evaluative reactions that allocate to blacks low status, limited political and economic access, and disproportionate formal negative sanctioning. It is also apparent that the *quality* of the social interactions to which one is subject must play some role in shaping a sense of self and its social and evaluative parameters. Personal adaptation would demand that any black be aware of the implications of these realities, while effective survival must demand also that certain insulating mechanisms protect the individual from their most destructive influences. One such mechanism is the community that surrounds the individual and of which he or she is part by virtue of background and identity. In several ways that community serves to buffer the impact of certain social experiences. It provides an intensity of encounters that bring more fully the impact of certain self-shaping experiences to bear upon the individual.

Social-learning theory provides one framework by which we may attempt to conceptualize the operation of such community mechanisms. If we assume from the outset that any behaving organism would survive in its environment in direct proportion to its ability to distinguish the operants of desirable outcomes from those of undesirable ones, it must follow that black individuals would adapt to the social context of society through those strategies by which undesirable outcomes are avoided and desirable ones are optimized. One means of acquiring such strategies is through direct learning experiences. However, the costs of trial and error in a complex environment are so great that, for most higher organisms, the process of intergenerational socialization is important to extend the potential for learning without extending the risk of direct exposure. In this regard, the purpose of socialization is to extend the domain in which learning normally occurs, both in time and space. The potential for the acquisition of productive operants thus may increase through the use of such mechanisms as modeling and communicated predictions and expectancies. In this way, reinforcement events that are distal come to operate upon the individual as proximal events to shape his or her effective functioning. Similarly, social learning provides for an analysis of the manner in which normally proximal reinforcement events are made to operate upon the individual as though they were actually distal. For instance, the cognitive information processing capabilities of the individual are utilized to draw inferences about the meaning of reinforcement events, and to select among them for events that have significance for altering one's real outcomes, versus events that offer little information about one's behaviors or objectives.

In either case, the mechanisms of socialization operate to mediate between the individual and certain experiential events that provide the basis for optimal functioning or undermine proper adaptation. For black people, these mechanisms function to provide the bases by which they learn about positive and negative social consequences in the absence of direct participation in the society, and the bases for discriminating those reinforcement events that have little relevance for their actual functioning. Within our kind of pluralistic society, black people need to extend these domains beyond what even the primary family group can provide. That is, the protective function of such mechanisms is even more critical for people whose position in the social environment involves rejection and exclusion by a powerful majority. Furthermore, the need for distal learning can be expected to relate to the overall proportion of experiential events which are likely to be negative; and such need can be expected to vary inversely with the opportunities accorded the individual for direct experience of positive reinforcement events.

The identity black people acquire in connection with their racial characteristics, moreover, serves to facilitate functioning through extending the limits of potential vicarious experience. To the extent that identification with models promotes learning through observation, identification with a broader group of social others can extend the opportunities for such learning-at-a-distance. Since much of the experience of blacks with the larger society results in negative reinforcement events, the broader domain of vicarious learning insures against direct threat. It further provides an opportunity for the kinds of corrective experiences by which one's social repertoire is pruned of inappropriate or unnecessary responses, without the direct damaging effects of esteem, loss, and so on. Similarly, the limited access society offers blacks to response-reward contingencies limits the acquisition by them of a functional repertoire of social skills. In this regard, models are often the only experiential units through which blacks gain exposure to learning contexts. Extension of the boundaries of identity through which similarity and empathy serve to facilitate vicarious acquisition is therefore critical.

From another point of view, much of the experience of blacks with the social milieu cannot be avoided and must be buffered. In this regard, it is important to recognize that, while early theorists were correct in assessing that negative social reinforcement events are abundant for blacks, the consequences of those experiences would likely be even more devastating than a negative self-concept would convey. Effective adaptation would demand that the individual decipher the meaning of such events, because those that operate as a result of variables other than the individual's own behavior hold little promise of providing survival information. In many instances, of course, such events consist of the behavior of powerful social others. Furthermore, such events, while perhaps not conveying legitimate information about the recipient's behavior or outcomes, may provide critical information about the attitudes, feelings, or intentions of powerful reinforcing agents. Nonetheless, were the effects of such critical information not only to provide signals to the recipient about his or her environment (especially threats therein), but also to undermine his or her esteem and self-determination, the debilitating effects upon his or her motivation and drive to function and survive would be devastating. Yet, we know that many blacks not only survive, but they aspire, they persevere, and they succeed.

SELF-CONCEPT: AN ADAPTION MODEL

Some of our earlier research in this area has begun to suggest a model that may be both theoretically and practically useful for understanding the complex processes that characterize the development and function of black people. Integral within that model is a consideration of the mechanisms that may account for the acquisition of an evaluative concept of self and its maintenance within a cultural context where support is largely absent.

As mentioned earlier, we could imagine that black individuals, like other organisms, have a fundamental need to function in a manner that insures social and personal survival. To this end, the many sources of information in the environment need to be monitored for those which provide insight into effective adaptation. Much of that information is presented in the form of direct reinforcement events, and we may concede, without argument or unnecessary justification, that the character of these events is largely non-supportive and, perhaps, hostile. The task of any individual in such an environment is to monitor the stimulus events that attend one's own behavior, particularly for those that provide contingent information about resource-producing outcomes. At the same time, negative reinforcement can provide the basis for selecting out those actions which have little utility or which evoke contingent resource withdrawal.

In both these regards, the processes that serve to mediate the effects of reinforcement and other stimulus events upon behavior are critical, and operate in a significant way through the vehicle of community. By "limited opportunity" we mean that certain individuals are denied access to task or experiential contexts in which important response repertoires can be acquired and critical resources obtained. In the case of certain institutional domains, such as education, the relationship of skill and resource acquisition is so clear that denial of opportunity threatens survival in a pervasive manner. In any case, the adaptation of the individual is enhanced in direct proportion to the breadth of domain in which such opportunities are provided.

One highly adaptive feature of the sense of self that is extended to embrace a broad community of similar others is its facilitation of learning. The socialization that occurs in the home already provides an insulated mechanism through which knowledge and adaptive coping are acquired without exposure to the threat of failure and sanction. Within a generally hostile society, the extension of the home into the broader community simply insures a wider range of experiences and learning to which an individual may enjoy access, still within a context that may be the only one that provides such opportunities.

Beyond the physical limits of that community, the task of the individual is to apply such strategies of social coping to preserve the esteem one feels toward self and maintain those aspects of his or her behavioral repertoire that have adaptive utility. One of the strongest challenges to that functioning is indeed the negative evaluative sanctions to which a black individual is exposed in the larger out-group community. But the effects need not be manifested in negative self-concepts or wide-spread maladaptive behavior.

One resultant phenomenon is that highly complex cognitive mediating strategies may be used that serve to select out relevant and non-relevant reinforcement experiences. Banks and his associates (1977), conducted a series of investigations to test a model of those processes and the strategies by which they are applied. They found that the information value of reinforcements was judged by blacks to vary as a function of the nature of the source of those events. Negative reinforcements from black social others conveyed a necessity for behavior change with which subjects complied. Such reinforcements also conveyed an evaluative frame with which the subject's task relevant self-esteem was deflated, and the result was a loss in esteem among black individuals. The same reinforcement events were perceived as potentially non-objective and were discredited when their source was a white social other. The resultant effects upon behavior and self-esteem of those events were nil. The point is that negative experiences have different impacts and that black self-concept is determined in a complex manner.

It must be acknowledged, however, that discrediting those who provide negative experiences is frequently difficult. Often, social others whose attitude and belief characteristics can be devaluated by blacks are the same ones who control important resources and distribution. The power thereby associated with social agents whose biases threaten the esteem of blacks also manipulates their survival. In an investigation of this dilemma, Banks, et al. (1977) found that black individuals approached such contexts equipped with adaptive strategies. The need to assuage a powerful agent was satisfied through overt compliance with his evaluative suggestions. Yet the self was protected against esteem-loss or the damaging psychological effects that could attend a self-imposed dissonance. Black subjects approached the context with an extraordinarily high level of initial self-esteem. Strikingly, when that esteem was deflated by their compliance with negative reinforcements from a biased other, the resultant level was equal to that of subjects who had merely maintained a normal level of esteem in a non-threatening situation.

Within their formulation, Banks and his associates (1977) describe three initial elements for the development of cognitive judgements that mediate the effects of social reinforcement:

1. Perception of the contingency of reinforcements that are related to the recipient's progress toward a goal.

2. Perception of the instrumental aim of reinforcements that instinctively match the recipient's progress toward a goal.

3. Perception of various relevant features of the situation and the reinforcing agent as they lend support to alternative hypotheses about the causes of reinforcement events and their consequent information value.

Within the third element, aspects of the sense of community and extended self-play important defining roles. In their research, Banks, *et al.* (1977) found that the racial similarity of the reinforcing agent affected profoundly the recipient's judgements about the information value of its reinforcements and evaluatives, and consequently, the degree of impact of these experiences upon self evaluation and behavior. Interestingly, though the effects of a White agent tended to reflect perceptions by Blacks that certain biased agent characteristics would reduce the probable information value of his or her negative reinforcements, no bias (either positive or negative) seemed to be presumed where Black agents were concerned. Characteristics of social others may not only dictate a community identity that must be attended, but also influence the judgment of the meaning of evaluative behaviors. Furthermore, one central aspect of the experiences of black people with community others may be the balanced pattern of evaluation and social reinforcement that characterizes that in-group interaction. One hypothesis is that the extended self-conception of blackscontributes to attributional judgements of the behavior of black others that are similar to self-attributions. Earlier theory (Banks, 1976a) has already suggested that such a tendency should give rise to a high degree of trust and perceived objectivity in social interactions. Another hypothesis, of course, is that the relatively objective bases of social evaluation and reinforcement within a community contributes to the effective acquisition of goal-attaining behaviors for individuals and consequently to a degree of mutual confidence among those community members which leads them to feel, perceive, and behave toward community others as toward self.

What is most important to consider, in any case, is the suggestion here that two relatively novel conceptual approaches to black self-concept both provide insight into some of the errors that may have attended the application of such global constructs as implied by Cooley, Clark, and others. Nobles (1973) has argued cogently for a formulation of the self-concept construct in blacks from a foundation of African culture in which significant elements of community identity shape and determine the personality of the individual. Similarly, our own research has argued for a more functional analysis of the highly selective social reinforcement experiences which attend membership in the black community, the role of racial identity and community definition in determining the pattern of those events, and the discriminant use of various cognitive-inferential processes that determine the selective impact of those experiences upon the developing individual.

The global assumption that social reinforcements act simply as a whole to shape the behavior and self-conception of blacks is without empirical support. No doubt, many of the social evaluative experiences of blacks in this environment take the form of derogation, and at least some of those experiences, whether within community or non-community contexts, impact upon the developing personality. Yet past conceptions of these phenomena have overlooked the many moderating variables that shape the nature and meaning of social experiences, especially for individuals whose special identity is made salient for themselves and social others within the overall milieu. Even less attention has been directed toward an analysis of the manner in which adaptive cognitive strategies might protect such individuals against the debilitation of esteem-loss, and against the disorganization of their important social learning experiences. As the traditional conceptualizations with this field fall under the weight of empirical critique, the future of theory and research in the area is likely to depend upon such a constructive integration of cultural and social learning concepts.

REFERENCES

Banks, W. C. Some effects of perceived similarity upon the use of reward and punishment. *Journal of Experimental Social Psychology*, 1976, *12*, 131-138(a)

Banks, W. C. White preference in blacks: A paradigm in search of a phenomenon. *Psychological Bulletin*, 1976, *83*, 1179-1186(b).

Banks, W. C., McQuater, G. V., and Ross, J. On the importance of White-preference and the comparative difference of Blacks and others: Reply to Williams and Moreland. *Psychological Bulletin*, 1979, *86*, 33-36.

Banks, W. C., Stitt, K. R., Curtis, H. A. and McQuater, G. V. Perceived objectivity and effects of evaluative reinforcement upon compliance and self-evaluation in Blacks. *Journal of Experimental Social Psychology*, 1977, *13*, 452-463.

Clark, K. and Clark, M. Racial identification and preference in negro children. In T. M. Newcombe and E. C. Hartley (eds.), *Readings in social psychology*. New York: Holt, 1947.

Cooley, C. H. *Human nature and social order*. New York: Scribner, 1902.

Morland, J. K. Racial recognition of nursery school children in Lynchburg, Va. *Social Forces,* 1958, *37,* 132-137.

Nobles, W. W. Psychological research and the Black self-concept: A critical review. *Social Issues,* 1973, *29,* 11-31.

Williams, J. and Morland, J. K. A reply to Banks; "White-preference in Blacks: A paradigm in search of a phenomenon." *Psychological Bulletin,* 1979, *86,* 28-34.

Chapter 7

TOWARD EVALUATION OF BLACK PSYCHO-SOCIAL COMPETENCE

Lonnie R. Snowden

Competence is an idea whose time has come. Potentially, it holds the key to a host of professional and research concerns: focused, accountable prevention; assessment without socially injurious labeling; intervention that accentuates active coping and independence. Equally important in pressing the cause of competency have been demands by ethnic minorities for recognition of their neglected assets and strengths. These groups have confronted us with yet another issue, where the road to a more responsive psychology appears to lead to competence.

The present chapter analyzes the basis for a psychology of competence for Black Americans. Since urging competency based formulation is only an initial step, the chapter reviews concepts and methods for understanding competencies with the goal of identifying particularly valuable approaches. A viewpoint revealed to be advantageous is one having its origins in social ecology. Emphasizing the concept of person-environment fit, the ecological approach to competence is shown to mesh with and clarify an essential concern for sensitivity to cultural relativity. While the present discussion is limited in focus to Blacks, its principles are equally applicable to Hispanics, Asians, and other cultural minorities.

The Deficit Model Re-examined

The literature on the psychology of Black Americans has emphasized their allegedly pervasive deficits. Concern with family life, mental health, and intelligence has dominated Black psychology because of the heavily negative character of conventional formulations. The litany of chaotic family life, extensive psychopathology, and defective intellect has been

179

challenged as missing an authentic representation of the Black experience. Attempts to explain the psychology of Blacks from the inside, oriented to their own values, belief systems, and behavioral styles, have been the result.

Perhaps the critical reorienting feature of the alternative theories and investigations has been the assertion of cultural pluralism. Originating as a critique of "cultural deprivation" explanations of problems, this shift in perspective recognized that to be different from society's mainstream is by no means equivalent to being inferior. The consequences of the shift from deficit to cultural explanations of Black/White psychological differences are beginning to appear in the study of personality (Jones, 1978), the family (Hill, 1972), and intelligence (Williams, 1972).

An example of the confusion of cultural differences with inferiority has been discussed by Baratz and Baratz (1970). Their critique concerns an alleged language deficit among Blacks, that became an important target of programs of compensatory education. From the observation that Black children do not speak standard White English, Baratz and Baratz argue, the inference was drawn that language development in Blacks was inadequate. According to Baratz and Baratz, this reasoning overlooked the status of Black language as a viable, systematic alternative, with a vocabulary and syntax of its own. Thus, Black children do not display retarded language development, but instead have learned an alternative language. Here a cultural difference was ethnocentrically misinterpreted as inferiority, through inappropriate application of the dominant cultural perspective.

Dejoie (1978) presents another illustration of how differences have been interpreted as deficits in the area of achievement orientation. The intrinsic motive to achieve in Black adolescents has been called deficient, and explained as a consequence of insufficient positive feedback (Katz, 1967). Banks, McGauter, and Hubbard (1977) have effectively challenged this interpretation. Their research demonstrated that achievement orientation discrepancies vanished when the subjective importance of the task to Black versus White subjects was held constant. In other words, given spheres of activity of equal personal salience, minority and majority group children showed equal achievement motivation. This finding suggests that the need to achieve, and opportunities for achievement-related pride, identification, and sense of personal control are not necessarily lacking among Blacks, but tend to occur in different realms of endeavor.

Wiggins, Renner, Clore, and Rose (1971), in the context of reviewing the psychology of competence, have further supported this view. While finding the effects of "ghetto-dwelling" to be largely debilitating, they have explicitly recognized the existence of alternative opportunities for competence development and pride.

"The ghetto subculture provides alternative values and dimensions through which self-esteem can be earned and on which real pride can be based. In the context of instrumentality, competence is relative, because it depends on whose values constitute the criteria for success" (p. 413).

The above mentioned examples give evidence of the vulnerability to erroneous judgements of a culturally blind approach. They further suggest the need for a careful appraisal of the actual situation, its constraints, expectations, and values, in considering whether a particular response is competent. The importance of relativity for a culturally valid assessment will be further explored in the later discussions of person-environment fit.

The demand by ethnic minorities for greater recognition of their competencies has not occured in isolation. Many have expressed dissatisfaction with professional psychology's preoccupation with psychopathology, and have wondered about the possibilities of an emphasis on competence. Statements by Zubin (1972) reveal the awakening of clinical psychology to the need for a competence orientation: "Psychopathologists in the past have behaved like bookkeepers who have only red ink available. It is high time the assets of patients were counted as well as their liabilities" (p. 429). A newer helping enterprise, community psychology, has invested in the competence idea its active and dedicated interest. Whether defined as learnable coping skills (Heller and Monahan, 1977), or a repertoire of existing strengths (Rappaport, 1977), competence is claimed as a hallmark of community psychology.

While psychologists have clearly recognized the advantages of an emphasis on assets and strengths, they have been largely unable to provide the concept of competence with adequate theoretical or operational substance. The existing approaches to competence are in most cases vague, highly specialized, or of questionable applicability to problems where cultural relativism must be heeded. Much work remains in bridging the gap between our aspirations toward a competence orientation and the availability of workable theories and procedures.

Cultural Considerations

A prime requirement of any conception is that it be adaptable to alternative cultural frameworks. Culture here is taken to mean "an organized body of rules concerning the ways in which individuals in a population should communicate with one another, think about themselves in their environments, and behave toward objects in their environment" (Levine, 1973, p. 4).

Clearly, cultural pluralism implies that the normative expectations and values of one culture cannot be uncritically applied in understanding the psychology of another culture. The problem, however, can take subtle forms. Not only must overt social practices be culturally conceived, but differences in psychological frames of reference must also be taken into account. Thus, the perception and interpretation of stimulus situations and responses that make up the very organization of human exerience may reflect influential, though easily overlooked, variations. Differences in psychological "structure of meaning" (Marris, 1974) have received the attention of personality psychologists, who have recently begun to document these complexities. Thus, the behavioral definition of common-sense concepts (e.g., conscientiousness) are by no means universal ideas (Bem and Allen, 1974).

The cognitive schema we use to interpret situations and social roles, and which guide us in selecting appropriate or necessary responses, are systems of remarkable variety. This observation is usually invoked to justify an ideographic approach, involving the intensive study of individuals, but, it has cultural implications as well. Recalling the previously cited definition of culture, which stressed characteristic views of self and environment, it seems probable that differences in frame of reference will increase in direct proportion to cultural distance.

As might be expected, cross-cultural psychologists have grappled with defining and disentangling universal versus particular, culture specific modes of functioning. In doing this they have borrowed, along with cultural anthropologists, a psycholinguistic distinction between *emic* and *etic* approaches to investigation. In psycholinguistics, phonemics explore the rules governing sound usage in a particular language, while phonetics explores sound usage rules which are universal (Brislin, Lonner, and Thorndike, 1973).

The distinctions between etic and emic investigatory approaches have been delineated as follows (Brislin, Lonner, and Thorndike, 1973, p. 164):

Emic Approach	*Etic Approach*
Studies behavior from within the system	Studies behavior from a outside the system
Examines only one culture	Examines many cultures, comparing them
Structure discovered by the analyst	Structure created by the analyst
Criteria are relative to internal characteristics	Criteria are considered absolute or universal

As presently conceived, cultural sensitivity can be fairly summarized as encouraging an emic approach to Black competence. It requires a proper competence orientation to reflect what is considered effective performance within the values and definitions comprising Black culture. Some of these will prove, in fact, to be etics, or culturally invariant universals. However, that a specific competency is an etic should be proven, not presumed, by checking its fit with the cultural scheme of Blacks. This process of documenting similarities and differences would not only help Blacks, by identifying culturally fair criteria for judging competence, but would also advance the scientific interests of psychology, by qualifying and confirming generalizations.

As outlined above, the etic approach excludes certain implications that are important to state as disclaimers. The assumption that Black and mainstream cultures are entirely distinct, almost certainly an untenable one, is wholly unnecessary. As noted previously, areas of cultural overlap, with corresponding general competencies, are admissable, and even expected, possibilities. Moreover, nothing in the approach precludes the aquisition of proficiencies associated with a culture different from one's culture of origin. The approach presents no inherent reason why it is either impossible or undesirable to become biculturally competent. The position taken here holds only that culturally distinctive strengths must be taken into account to fully describe the competence repertoires of Blacks.

While the need for cultural sensitivity is unassailable, its achievement lies in the future. One prerequisite that is presently unavailable is a comprehensive, specific understanding of Black culture. Some literary sources are available, but contributions by social scientists have been few. The problem is complicated by the range of geographic, and socio-economic diversity displayed by Blacks. Clearly, Blacks are heterogenous, and any common elements will not be invariant. As Jones (1978) has observed; ''It seems that the tremendous variation in the learning contexts of Black Americans, with their wide ranging ramifications for personality formation, are frequently underestimated. What all Blacks share, and what is likely to be different, and to what degree, remains to be specified'' (p. 251).

Nobles (1975) has begun to develop an analysis of Black culture, originating from the hypothesis that African philosophy is a determinant of Black-American world view. Philosophical tenets reflected in Black ideology, according to Nobles, include cooperation, interpersonal interdependence, and collective responsibility. The translation of this world view into distinctive cultural institutions and specific psychological frames of reference, along with empirical validation of these proposals, are exciting challenges for the future. It will be particularly important in investigating elements of Black culture to adopt new methods, sensitive to the problem of observer misinterpretation. Psychologists may do well to seek methods from other disciplines, such as ethnomethodology (Baily, 1979), that takes personal frame of reference as an object of study. The possibilities of role-construct theory (Kelly, 1955), that allows the subject's own organization of experience to emerge, should also be explored.

Competence

As with many notions having a strong common-sense tradition, every-one knows what competence means, but no one can rigorously define it. Goldfried and D'Zurilla (1969) state, "There would probably be general agreement among various investigators that the concept of competence refers to effective functioning within one's environment. This definition, however, does not represent much advancement beyond Socrate's view of competent individuals: 'those who manage well the circumstances which they encounter daily and who possess a judgement which is accurate in meeting occasions as they arise and rarely miss the expedient course of action'" (p. 155).

Interest in developing an affirmative definition of mental health, to replace its conception as an absence of psychopathology, has brought the task of defining competence to the forefront. Following a review of the area, Jahoda (1958) identified six types of criteria of positive mental health: attitudes towards the self, self-actualization, a synthesizing or integrative personality function, autonomy, perception of reality, environmental mastery. Five of te six criteria refer to personality constructs, reflecting the heavy influence on formulations exerted by the major theories of personality. The humanist-posited tendency to actualize one's potentialities (Maslow, 1954) and psychodynamic notions of identity (Erikson, 1968) and ego strength enjoy perhaps the widest acceptance. While differences of opinion clearly exist, there are a few contraditions among personality conceptions, and indeed they share several fundamental characteristics. All imply a restricted number of abstract qualities, which are located within the individual.

Despite their theoretical richness, concepts like ego strength and self-actualization seem poorly suited to conceiving of Black competencies. Problems created by their abstractness and individual orientation probably overshadow any potential benefits. One problem has been described by Dejoie (1978): "The vagueness and abstractness of the trait constructs from personality theory often allow them to be conceptualized in terms of cultural values which generally tend to be traditional, middle class, and EuroAmerican in orientation" (p. 6). In the language of cross-cultural psychology, these constructs imply etics, without evaluating whether they are really Euro-American emics. This problem was illustrated in the previous discussion concerning the relativity of achievement motivation. Because of the global nature of the achievement motivation contract, it can be unwittingly cast into specific forms that are inappropriate when considering Blacks. The result is an apparent deficit in a general property, achievement motivation, when the actual deficit is one of interest in pursuing a particular activity.

Establishing that a presumed competency is appropriate for a particular culture is an important empirical problem. Here again, global traits are poor candidates. Trait indicators forsake specific knowledge, skills, and attitudes, as discussed by Sundberg, Snowden, and Reynolds (1978), in favor of long-standing behavioral dispositions. Their functional validation involves making predictions from appraisals of trait status to specific behavioral criteria. The hazards and difficulties in predicting from traits to behavior have been widely discussed (e.g. Mischel, 1968). Requisite knowledge, skills, and attitudes are likely to be better predictors of culturally significant achievements than are measurements of global traits.

Defining competencies in more concrete, specific terms would seem to provide a means of avoiding such problems. However, in substituting specific behaviors for broader theoretical conceptions, the theorist sacrifices the elegance and parsimony of the latter. Indeed, the number of specific behaviors that are potential competencies is limitless. A prime advantage of abstract conceptions is their power to reduce many specific instances to a few general ideas.

When evaluated against the cultural relativity standard, however, this diversification of potential competencies is revealed actually to be quite advantageous. As anthropologists have often discovered, cultural requirements for adaptation are remarkably diverse. Imposing *a priori* restrictions on the range of adaptive performances runs the risk of excluding those behaviors as competencies that seem trivial in the culture of the investigator, but are functional coping skills in the culture being investigated. To avoid this error, potential competencies should be drawn from as broad a range of possibilities as can be managed.

An alternative to the personality focus of the previously considered approaches is to consider the individual's social adjustment. A pragmatic concern, the need to evaluate the community functioning of retarded people and formerly institutionalized mental patients, has guided much of the work in this area. Psychologists are increasingly persuaded that capitalizing on survival skills and adaptive competencies is more productive than trying to reverse whatever deficits these groups may exhibit (Sunberg, Snowden, and Reynolds, 1978). Social adjustment approaches are designed around the concept of role, which is taken to mean particular, socially prescribed patterns of behavior. Social adjustment scales evaluate role performance in what are judged to be important areas of functioning: worker, household manager, parent, participant in community organizations (Sunberg, Snowden, and Reynolds, 1978).

While a detailed review of social adjustment measures is unnecessary for present purposes, their characteristics are particularly important to consider. The current group of social adjustment measures can be faulted as insensitive to cultural relativity. The behaviors that constitute role definitions are drawn from stereotypic mainstream life. Underlying current social adjustment indicators is a single standard of successful performance which reflects a majority point of view. As with many existing approaches to competence, the danger of these measures is a potential confounding of nonconformity and incompetence.

Despite this shortcoming, the orientation of social adjustment measures includes several ideas of potential value. Chief among these is the idea that competence is a *transaction*, defined as an effective coping response to a culturally imposed expectation. This recognition of the role of social expectations serves to broaden the scope of competence. So conceived, competence becomes a phenomenon of both people and situations, the appraisal of which allows for explicity considering cultural requirements and culturally based interpretations of behavior. Adopting this perspective also weakens the tendency to accept reflexively the interpretations of a situation that form the understanding of the dominant culture.

Consider, for example, a Black youngster who has been asked in school to learn the names and positions of presidential cabinet members. From the perspective of the school, this task involves mastering culturally worthwhile material by application of skills in recognition, retention, and recall. For the youngster, on the other hand, the situation as perceived may involve fending off a relatively unimportant task, while avoiding a pejorative appraisal of his or her intellectual merit. In situations that seem appropriate and important, however, the aforementioned skills may be applied. Thus, the youngster may be proficient at learning the titles, authors, and lyrics of top ten records, or memorizing names and positions of members of a basketball team. What would be characterized as incompetence in school would result, therefore, not from a skill deficit, but either from disinterest in the immediate task, or even a failure to identify which among available skills are appropriate to solving the problem at hand.

The contribution of a transactional analysis to our understanding of such problems is its explicit formulation of the demands of the social environment. By understanding what the environment requires, we are more likely to evaluate both individual and social frames of reference to pin-point areas of troubling discord.

The specific, relative conception of competence thus far presented emphasizes several characteristic features of the ecological explanation of effective behavior. The applicable ecological principle is that of person-environment fit, which has been clearly explained by Holahan (1977): "Specifically, psychological adjustment may be defined as the state in which an individual's needs and proclivities for action are congruent with the demands and opportunities of the particular settings in which he or she operates." Competence from this perspective becomes that relationship between person and social setting which serves best to satisfy the interests of both.

Bowles (1978), in interpreting a case from consultation practice, has illustrated the utility of thinking in terms of person-environment fit. The subject of her report is a 12 year old Black girl, referred by her sixth grade teacher who complained that the girl was stubborn, aggressive, bossy with peers, and uncooperative. Inquiry into her home life revealed that the girl's mother was incapacitated by alcoholism and incapable of assuming child-care responsibilities. Consequently, the burden of child rearing fell to the girl in question, who was indeed caring for two younger siblings. Bowles was struck that the qualities forming the basis of the complaint constitute an effective response to the challenging situation at home. Thus, what was important for success at home, direct, assertive leadership, was incompatible with the more conformity-oriented role expectations of the school.

The relativity premise of ecology is further elaborated in its contribution to the principles of methodological validity. "Ecological validity" has emerged as a consideration in the validation of indicators of psychological concepts (e.g., tests). Bronfenbrenner (1977) defines it as requiring that "the environment experienced by the subjects in a scientific investigation has the properties it is supposed or assumed to have by the investigator" (p. 516). As with the emic approach of cross-cultural psychologists, ecological validity involves explicitly questioning the match between the frame of reference of investigators and that of the local culture. In the case of competence, this translates into determining that the skills, knowledge, and attitudes considered competencies by an investigator are useful in the life situations actually experienced by the subject. Empirical sampling of situations in the person's actual life space is an important corollary of this requirement.

Several unique advantages originate from the ecological perspective on competence. Failures of adaptation can be recognized as conflict, and not the exclusive product of personal inadequacies. A newly introduced option for conflict resolution is to change the expectation and options afforded by the social setting; no longer does the individual bear the sole responsibility to change. Another new possibility is to identify alternative roles or settings that capitalize on the individual's existing competencies. Traditionally, such alternative settings have been largely used as an accommodation to personal deficits, such as "special classroom" placement. Here, they would be designed as genuine opportunities for people to use their assets to meet the legitimate needs of an ongoing organization.

Since cultural conflict may be viewed as a particular form of person-environment incongruence, these are particularly salient benefits. When a Black person successfully adapts to Black institutions or cultural forms, then his or her competencies may function maladaptively under the different rules governing the institutions of mainstream society. The approach to competence being presented avoids the implication that either the culture or the home or the attributes of the person are to blame for any manifest discord.

An example of person-environment mismatch produced by contrasting cultural patterns has been suggested in the writing of Henderson and Washington (1975). Noting racial differences in patterns of child-rearing, they have hypothesized that the Black community invests effective responsibility for control of children's behavior in an extensive network of adults. One source of support for this expectation is Noble's hypothesis of heightened collective identification and cooperation among Blacks. Because of this extended parenting, children's behavior receives proper monitoring and more immediate sanctions than is the norm in American society. Children may be expected to develop more active exploratory tendencies and assertive styles, since respected external agencies can be counted on to reliably check excesses.

The school,however, exercises less direct and legitimate control, while expecting a relatively docile, immobile pattern of behavior. The cultural conflict is clearly drawn. Henderson and Washington suggest that parents should be collaboratively engaged in the system of school and classroom governance in order to reintroduce the community pattern of monitoring and authority.

Toward Evaluating Black Competencies

An approach to competence, then, will be most faithful to a Black point of view when it taps adaptively salient skills, attitudes and knowledge in significant social environments, as perceived by members of the culture. The search for competencies should examine the transactions of individuals, instead of focusing on inferred processes and traits of personality. Attempts to characterize the institutionalized rules, values and roles comprising the social side of the transaction must carefully avoid imposing what closer scrutiny will reveal to be oversimplified versions of mainstream cultural forms.

One of the existing approaches to competency incorporates features approaching these requirements. The behavioral analytic model presented by Goldfried and D'Zurilla (1969) is an attempt to define competence both concretely and in light of the adaptive tasks of a particular social system. The method is behavioral in its preference for concretely defined competencies, and analytic in its systematic probing of the situation with which the individual must cope. The behavioral-analytic model has been applied at a large university to provide a basis for evaluating the competency of first year students. An innovative aspect, called criterion analysis, is briefly described below.

The first criterion step, situational analysis, involves a comprehensive ecological survey of relevant tasks and contexts. Undertaken specifically was the collection of a large and representative sample of situations that proved problematic for the university students under study. The sources of this information were student's self-observations, observations by resident advisors, interviews with faculty and staff, and a survey of the folders of persons who applied for help at the psychological counseling facility. These sources provided an initial pool of over 600 specific challenging situations from academic, interpersonal, and other salient spheres of life. The pool was later refined by clarifying ambiguities, adjusting the inclusion of detail, and elimination of redundant, trivial, or unusual situation descriptions.

The second stage, response enumeration, involved identifying a set of potential responses to each problem situation. The situations were presented to college-bound high school seniors in one study and to entering college freshmen in another study, who were instructed to indicate how they would respond. The situations that attracted responses spanning a wide range of effectiveness were retained because of their potential for discriminating differing levels of competent behavior.

The final stage of criterion analysis calls for an evaluation of potential responses. To capture the criteria and values operative in the setting, the ratings were performed by dormitory counselors, faculty, and other "significant others" in the environment. Thus, the standards for evaluation were not theoretical, or mainstream ideals, but rather the judgements of a sample of individuals from the ecosystem.

Clearly, the instrument resulting from this procedure would be inappropriate for evaluating Black competence. It is specific to the culture of one particular university, and this cultural specificity is precisely the method's virtue. By applying similar techniques within a particular Black community, an instrument with equal cultural sensitivity and relevance would be devised. The spirit of criterion analysis is determining the requirements for success at a task through empirical evaluation. Looking at actual experience, instead of imposing preconceptions, is a means of reducing the danger that culturally inappropriate biases will occur.

The outline of another procedure currently in the early stages of development has been provided by Dejoie (1978). This method is concerned with analyzing person-situation interactions to ascertain the individual's actual repertoire of attitudes, skills, and knowledge. Performing such an analysis is envisioned as not only delineating environments and matching them with abilities, but also as identifying culture specific, or emic competency concepts.

The procedure can be summarized as follows. First, the individual's salient environments are identified. Next, respondents and significant others would maintain logs for describing within each environment: "critical incidents, behaviors either outstandingly effective or ineffective with respect to attaining payoffs in the environments with a minimum of negative consequences." (Dejoie, p. 15). Recorded in these logs would be a significant behavior, relevant situational factors, the effectiveness of the behavior, and reasons for judging it to have been effective. Furthermore, collecting such data provides an empirical basis for determining interrelationships among behaviors. The structure of these interrelationships suggests constructs. Thus, theoretical development could proceed from observed similarities among competencies, instead of relying upon theoretically generated preconceptions.

Common to these methods are those features that allow for an unbiased representation of Black competencies. These features are: 1. Defining important situations and tasks from the respondent's point of view; 2. Restricting potential competencies as little as possible; 3. Judging the value of a response by its impact, as perceived by relevant participants in the culture.

Conclusion

A culturally based and competency oriented formulation of Black Americans is certainly overdue. The tasks, in fact, are closely intertwined, inasmuch as cultural values, rules, and expectations, on the one hand, and individual psychosocial assets, on the other, stand in complementary relationship. Development of our understanding of Black competence not only will respect the legitimate claims to pride of the Black community, but will force psychologists to better clarify the interaction between the individual and the social environment.

REFERENCES

Bailey, K. D. *Methods of social research.* New York: Free Press, 1978.

Banks, W. C., McQuater, G. V., and Hubbard, J. L. Task liking and intrinsic achievement orientation in black adolescents. *Journal of Black Psychology,* 1977, *3,* 61-71.

Baratz, S., and Baratz, J. E. Early childhood intervention: The social science base of institutional racism. *Harvard Educational Review,* 1970, *40,* 29-50.

Bem, D., and Allen, A. On predicting some of the people some of the time: The search for cross-situational consistencies in behavior. *Psychological Review,* 1974, *81,* 506-520.

Bowles, H. C. *The child, the community and the inner-city elementary school: Implications for the consultant role.* Paper presented at the meeting of the Western Psychological Association, San Francisco, California, April, 1978.

Breen, P., Donlon, T., and Whitaker, U. *The learning and assessment of interpersonal skills: Guidelines for administrators and faculty.* (CAEL Working Paper No. 4), Princeton, N.J.: Educational Testing Service, 1975.

Brislin, R. W., Lonner, W. J., and Thorndike, R. M. *Cross-cultural research methods.* New York: John Wiley, 1973.

Bronfenbrenner, U. Toward an experimental ecology of human development, *American Psychologist,* 1977, *32,* 513-531.

Dejoie, M. M. *Towards an assessment of competence in Black adolescents.* Unpublished manuscript, 1978.

Erikson, E. H. *Identity, youth and crisis.* New York: W. W. Norton, 1968.

Flanagan, J. C. The critical incident technique. *Psychological Bulletin,* 1954, *51,* 327-358.

Ginsberg, H. *The myth of the deprived child: Poor children's intellect and education.* Englewood Cliffs, N.J., Prentice-Hall, 1972.

Goldried, M. R., and D'Zurilla, T. J. A behavioral-analytic model for assessing competence. In C. D. Spielberger (ed.) *Current topics in clinical and community psychology,* Vol. 1, New York: Academic Press, 1969.

Heller, K. and Monahan, J. *Psychology and community change,* Homewood, Ill.: Dorsey, 1977.

Henderson, F. and Washington, A. G. Cultural differences and the education of black children. *Journal of Negro Education,* 1975, *44,* 353-360.

Hill, R. B. *The strengths of black families.* New York: Emerson Hall, 1972.

Holahan, C. J. Community psychology: a tale of three cities. *Professional Psychology,* 1977, *8,* 25-31.

Jahoda, M. *Current concepts of positive mental health.* New York: Basic Books, 1958.

Jones, E. E. Black-White personality differences: Another look. *Journal of Personality Assessments.* 1978, *42,* 244-252.

Katz, I. The socialization of academic motivation in minority group children. In S. Levin (ed.), *Nebraska symposium on motivation*. Lincoln, University of Nebraska Press, 1967.

Kelly, G. S. *The psychology of personal constructs*. New York: Norton, 1955.

Levine, R. A. *Culture, behavior and personality*. Chicago: Aldine, 1973.

Marris, P. *Loss and change*. New York: Pantheon Books, 1974.

Maslow, A. H. *Motivation and personality*. New York: Harper and Row, 1954.

Mischel, W. *Personality and assessment*. New York: Wiley, 1968.

Nobles, W. W. *The black family and its children: The survival of humanness*. Paper presented at the meeting of the National Council for Black Child Development, Atlanta, June 1975.

Rappaport, J. *Community psychology: Values, research, and action*. New York: Holt Rinehart, Winston, 1977.

Sunberg, N. D., Snowden, L. R., and Reynolds, W. M. Toward assessment of personal competence and incompetence in life situations. *Annual Review of Psychology*, 1978, *29*, 179-221.

Wiggins, J. S., Renner, K. E., Clore, G., and Rose, R. *The psychology of personality*. Reading, Mass.: Addison-Wesley, 1971.

Williams, R. L. *The Bitch-100: A culture specific test*. Unpublished Manuscript, St. Louis University, 1972.

Zubin, J. Discussion of symposium on newer approaches to personality assessment. *Journal of Personality Assessment*, 1960, *61*, 231-238.

Chapter 8

SELF RECONSTRUCTION AND SOCIAL RECONSTRUCTION AS TWO ASPECTS OF THE SAME PROCESS
A Community Psychology Perspective

Daniel Adelson

In discussing cultural pluralism and community mental health, I would like to provide an integrative framework for purposes of analysis, research, and action. The title of this chapter states the basic elements of this framework. It involves the relationship between the self (i.e., self-identity, self-valuation, etc.) and society (i.e., social valuation, social belonging, etc.). The framework is based on research and conceptual syntheses carried out over some period of time by Adelson (1953; 1957; 1965; 1970a; 1970b; 1972; 1974), among others. It finds its roots in the philosophy and theorizing of the pragmatists—William James, John Dewey, Horace Kallen, and, most specifically, George H. Mead, to whom we owe the title, and draws in its multileveled approach on the work of other seminal figures (see Adelson, 1972). Its roots may also be found in the history of the past several decades and in developments in community mental health and in psychology over the same period of time. Let us review some of these.

The American Dilemma and the Brown Decision

It is now over a quarter of a century since the 1954 U.S. Supreme Court, in its *Brown vs. Board of Education* decision, initiated a movement towards the further resolution of "The American Dilemma." (Gunnar Myrdal entitled his classic 1944 work on Black-White relations "The American Dilemma" to indicate the dilemma faced by Americans as they consider the American ideas of equality and freedom and the reality of racial inequities.) With the *Brown* decision, which had a profound and fundamental effect on human relations in America, the Supreme Court, in essence, laid the groundwork for basic changes in majority-minority relations and attitudes and for democratizing and humanizing the way individuals in the United States relate to and accept one another, and, it may be suggested, the way ethnic and other minority groups relate to and accept themselves. This major step toward the fulfillment of human right was also a step for the mental health of the nation.

The *Brown* decision represented a milestone for social science because the Court, in arriving at its judgement, had the benefit of evidence gathered by social scientists. The leader of this group was Kenneth Clark who, with his wife Mamie (Clark and Clark, 1947), had shown that majority group devaluation of minority group characteristics, in this instance, skin color, may result in preference among some Black children (when they were asked to choose between a white or a brown doll) for the white doll, though these children identified with the brown doll—a preference it may be noted that diminished with age. Self-devaluation by minority members, however, was not a new phenomenon for social scientists. Kurt Lewin, among others, had addressed it in his discussions of self-hatred among the Jews, and of raising minority children. W. E. Dubois had, before him, been concerned with expressing the warmth and beauty of color.

The 1960s and 1970s

After the *Brown* decision, the 1960s and 1970s saw pieces of legislation and principles, e.g., affirmative action and maximum feasible participation of the poor that provided a further legal base for self-development and for seeking justice in line with American ideals. It could be argued that this legislation initiated a period of struggle for human rights of every man and woman, not only ethnic minorities. With the beginning of the 1970s, gray groups, gay groups, and women organized to seek their rights. The American Dilemma is, after all, the Human dilemma—needing resolution again and again in terms of interpersonal and intrapersonal conflicts and the social-economic-political structures within which they are embedded. This unanimous *Brown* decision, if explicitly a judgement about the need for desegregation, was implicitly a reaffirmation of our American—in this instance universal—ideals, values, and human rights.

Community Mental Health and Community Psychology

These historical events have been the revolution on the larger scene. On the other side of the wall—within the mental health system as such, the world of hospitals, wards and clinics, patients, and clients—two other revo-

lutions were taking place in the early 1950's. The advent of the tranquil-
izing drugs made it possible to treat many formerly unmanageable and
even chronic patients in the community. The crystallization of the "therapeutic community" which was pioneered by Maxwell Jones (1968),
recognized the individual's needs for a voice in his or her fate and for a
sense of community.

With the turn of the decade came the Joint Commission report (1961),
Action for Mental Health. This report, however, focused on mental illness and
not mental health, contained only one three-word reference to desegregation, and made no reference to ethnic or minority groups, or even to
poverty. Between 1961 and 1978, the year of the Report of the President's
Commission on Mental Health, came not only the Community Mental
Health Center Act, but the War on Poverty, affirmative action, the withdrawal from Vietnam, Watergate and its resolution, and the fight for rights
of various minority groups with historical figures such as Martin Luther
King and Cesar Chavez leading their own peoples in the struggle for
justice.

Community Psychology arrived in 1965, the middle of these three
decades at a Conference (Swampscott) to discuss graduate training of
psychologists in community mental health—a conference that, staging its
own quiet revolution, focused on the need for a new area of psychology—
community psychology. There is, however, no escaping one's origins, and
community mental health has remained a major concern of many community psychologists, many of whom, educated primarily as clinicians,
find the community mental health system easier to adapt to in terms of their
backgrounds and the system's needs and opportunities. Nevertheless, the
decision to establish community psychology independent from community
psychiatry and community mental health was no idle choice. It meant a
break from the medical model and the pathology model. It also meant a
turning to possibilities and potentialities for theory and practice represented by other areas of community thinking and of psychological and
other social science disciplines.

There is one conception that resulted from Swampscott which merits
attention in this context, namely that of *participant-conceptualizer*. The full
significance of this concept remains to be explored and developed. But
those who often lead the way are, indeed, the participant conceptualizers,
leaders of ethnic groups, leaders of gray and gay groups, leaders of
women's groups in various areas who draw out of their own participation
and encounters to enlarge understanding and to provide leadership for
individual growth and social change. The community psychologist has
much to learn from them as he or she observes, studies, and moves towards
conceptualization and integration of these observations and encounters
with his or her knowledge and skills as a psychologist within a framework

for analysis, research, and action. I have proposed such a framework in terms of the individual's encounter with history (Adelson, 1974).

I see many of the principles and foci of the chapters in this volume falling within this framework. The framework is based on principles of participation and control. Even as it is concerned with the self and a competent self with a sense of identity, it is also concerned with the larger system factors and with need for system reconstruction in relation to self-growth. To understand system factors in the larger community, epidemiologic studies are often needed. It is centrally concerned with history—history as seen by participants of different generations, classes, roles, and statuses and their sensibilities (to use Robert Chin's concept). The framework is also concerned with the various systems to which individuals have to relate so often in direct encounters such as school, work, health, and religion as well as family, as people interrelate their strivings for growth with community conditions and opportunities for growth as is necessary within a process model. I am developing an eight level model for facilitation of such self and social reconstruction—or put differently—the individual's encounter with history (Adelson, 1974).

SELF-RECONSTRUCTION AND SOCIAL RECONSTRUCTION AS TWO ASPECTS OF THE SAME PROCESS

To George H. Mead (1934) we owe the seminal analysis his students put together in *Mind, Self and Society* on the basis of his class lectures, pointing out the functional relationship between mind, self, and social interaction. If, with Angyal (1941), we agree that human begins have two basic needs or strivings—the striving for autonomy, for increasing sense of control over environment and fate, and the striving for homonomy or belongingness—the evidence is impressive that the set of conditions in those systems to which we "belong" have a profound effect on both our mental and physical health and the possibilities of our development. Whether we look at Levy's work (1943) on overprotected and overrejected children, Zimbardo's work (1971) on guards and prisoners, or the work of sociologists on social class, on ecological areas of the city, on social disorganization, on mental hospitals or other institutions, we find testimony as to the negative effects of various social conditions on the mental and physical health of human beings and on their sense of self-esteem and self-acceptance.

The question becomes, "Can we find the opposite, that is, examples of individuals changing conditions and social relations to have a new sense of self-identity and self-acceptance?" One interpretation of history is that, all through the ages, human beings have striven to change conditions to provide a way for their own greater growth. From Moses to Ghandi to Harriet Tubman to Martin Luther King, we may follow man and woman's progress towards the goals of liberty, equality, and fraternity (Adelson, 1974), which, at the level of psychological needs, can be translated into needs for autonomy in the context of homonomy, with the strivings and the struggles representing a resolution of the tension between these two aspects (i.e., autonomy and homonomy) of humankind's psychological nature.

The Bill of Rights and the evolution of rights over time relate to these basic needs of human beings. The right to vote, freedom of religion, press, and assembly, and other rights, which have been stated not only in our Bill of Rights, but in other amendments to the Constitution and elsewhere in the body of law, touch every person. Participation in the actual government, however, has tended to be indirect, and there has, for most citizens, been little participation in changing the institutions in which they participate everyday, such as the family, the school, the work setting, and the religious institution. These have essentially existed as given. The impact of "future shock", however, which, like all futures, is now everywhere around us, the impact of social science findings, increased insight into the human condition, and increased education for larger numbers of individuals, and, above all, the impact of families, schools, and work settings that are no longer able to meet the needs of individuals who had previously turned to them for fostering, comfort, and growth, have caused individuals to question, change, seek alternatives, and reconstruct.

Ethnic groups in America, so long deprived and discriminated against, have led this movement. Included also now are women, gay groups, gray libbers, and various other groups who have come to the realization that it is possible for them to shape their futures as well as be shaped by their past and current conditions. In this shaping, they have changed and are changing themselves—taking on new roles with significant impact on their self-images and self-esteem. In doing so they have found the value of participation and involvement, and they also have challenged the professionals who work with them from their power positions, from afar and from behind their desks. These individuals have also recognized what the professional has to offer in terms of knowledge, skills, and understanding.

As we examine the individual's participation in history—its encounter with various social institutions, and struggles to change them—we come to recognize that this process has two aspects: Self and social. Through this examination, we come to understand the significance of Mead's statement to the effect that self and social reconstruction are two aspects of the same process.

The concept of self-reconstruction and social reconstruction as two aspects of the same process stresses the fact that, with the community psychology, we move towards concern with a more active human being participating in a transactional relationship with the systems around as a key to health.

This conception of community psychology brings to the fore the idea of development or process, from individual, to group, to community, cultural, and historical development and the need to understand stages of process or development and their interrelations at these different levels. With Freud, Erikson, Piaget, Bennis and Shepard, Kohlberg, and others, we have seen the evolution of process models in psychology with respect to stages in human, cognitive, group, and moral development. This conception also brings to the surface the idea of "system" and the need to apply and explore system concepts and theory as these relate to health, education, and growth. Psychologists, to be sure, have been among the key contributors in the development and application of system views, whether we look, to the gestalt psychologists for theoretical under pinnings in perception and cognition or to the organizational psychologists for practical application (Katz and Kahn, 1978).

The idea of culture (Adelson, 1972; Castenada and Ramirez, 1974) also comes to the fore, in terms of what lasts over historical time, what individuals build and make for themselves, and what gives them a sense of unique identity and, therefore, of meaning and power. Whether at the level of shared symbols, at the level of art (emotion captured in form), or at the level of science (for purposes of understanding, prediction, and control), it is culture which provides a base for meaning and continuity. Through language and art forms, the possibility of expressing that uniqueness, individuality, and authenticity is made possible and of bridging gaps which hinder communication.

COMMUNITY PSYCHOLOGY AS THE INDIVIDUAL'S ENCOUNTER WITH HISTORY

In suggesting that community psychology may be defined as the individual's "encounter with history" I am defining community in three ways: (1) community as "shared destiny" from groups with shared interests or destinies that may be fairly encompassing as, for example, ethnic and religious groups, to groups that share one or two interests, such as health professionals, or psychologists, or prenatal parents—each of which groups has a longer or shorter history of its own; (2) community as "system of systems" either family, school, neighborhood, or work setting (hospital or ward, for example), each also with a longer or shorter history of its own; and (3) community as a "particular place in space and time," where individuals are in various kinds of direct and indirect relations with each other. The task of the community psychologist within these conceptions and definitions is to facilitate and explore the transactional relations at "a specific time and place" between community as "shared destiny" and community as a "system of systems," for example, the relationships of a particular ethnic group with a history of its own to the different systems of the community—each of which also has a history of its own. This definition helps translate the historical process to the "here and now," even as it draws on the past to provide a base for making changes for the future. It attempts to move beyond the one-to-one or one-to-group relationship that is often examined in a vacuum isolated from historical context, and tries to make "history" something individuals can participate in actively in relation to their own membership and reference groups and their own problems over historical time. Human beings are social. Their reference and membership groups provide sustenance and courage even under the most stressful conditions (Adelson, 1962; 1964). Associated with higher morale even under the extreme conditions of the concentration camp was an interpretation of history that did not leave the experience in the void whether this related to leftist interpretations or to Zionism (Adelson, 1962; Bettelheim, 1947). The historical perspective seems, indeed, to provide a guide for the future, a stay in difficult moments. It bears strongly on the two basic needs or strivings of man—homonomy and autonomy (Angyal, 1941). Through a sense of history, humankind, the symbol user, is able to identify with individuals and groups in the past and the future—to find courage in this identification, belongingness, a view of difficult moments overcome, and positive and joyous moments experienced.

The historical perspective may also be necessary for resolution of the underlying alienation that marks our times—as through history a better understanding of the forces that have led to alienation is gained and through various communal arrangements and experiences alienation is resolved.

A Psychohistorical Framework for Growth Facilitation

Given these three definitions of community psychology, a broad model is needed, which, as noted above, will provide a framework for the facilitation of human encounter with history at the psychological level, at the level of the here and now, in relation to significant membership and reference groups and in transactional relation with the social systems within which the individual lives and works.

I have begun to develop such a framework, which draws on various aspects of the psychological literature, as well as my own research. It is a dynamic in the other aspects. Thus it is both a process and systems oriented framework (Adelson, 1974).

It has eight levels, all of which are interdynamically interrelated. They lend themselves in particular to four focal aspects: the I-thou relationship (levels 1 and 2); the action-research and/or analysis of self and system (3 and 4); the cognitive-emotional interaction (5 and 6); process with respect to authority (power, control) and with respect to peers (self and other acceptance) (7 and 8). It incorporates, in psychodynamic interrelationships, many of the concerns of this volume from culture to history, from self to system change, and it also draws on prior research from various areas of psychology.[1] In that sense, it is a reconstructive framework, open-ended, awaiting the challenge without which there is no responsive growth.

As we move into the 1980s, it might be said that if, in the 1950's, we were still mainly within a traditional psychoanalytic model focused on the self and, in the 1960's, we shifted the focus to social and community systems, calling for community change, and almost ready to discard the analysis of the self, then, in the 1970's, we have come more and more to realize the transactional relationship between the self and social systems, between self-growth and development and community reconstruction and development. As we deepen our understanding of this relationship, we shall move closer to that harmonious orchestration of cultures and ethnic groups of which Horace Kallen, the philosopher of cultural pluralism, spoke.

FOOTNOTE

[1]Graduate students have used the framework for consideration in assertiveness training (Shan Steinmark); the women's movement (Robin Deutsch); the gay movement (Harold Booth); and the organization of a Filipino community in San Francisco (Jovina Navarro).

REFERENCES

Adelson, D. *Group cohesiveness and value conflict under extreme conditions.* Unpublished study, 1953.

Adelson, D. *Attitudes toward first names: An investigation of the relation between self-acceptance, self-identity, and group and individual attitudes.* Doctoral dissertation, Columbia University, 1957.

Adelson, D. Some aspects of value conflict under extreme conditions. *Psychiatry,* 1962, *25,* 273-279.

Adelson, D. Attitudes toward first names. *International Journal of Social Psychiatry,* 1964, Special Convention Issue No. 1.

Adelson, D. *A note on suggested differences between community psychiatry and community mental health.* Position statement for Boston Conference on the training of Psychologists in Community Mental Health, May, 1965.

Adelson, D. A Concept of comprehensive community mental health. In D. Adelson and B. L. Kalis (Eds.), *Community psychology and mental health: Perspectives and challenges.* San Francisco: Chandler, 1970. (a)

Adelson, D. Self-valuation, social valuation, and self-identity: A framework for research in social and community psychology. In D. Adelson and B. L. Kalis (Eds.), *Community psychology and mental health: Perspectives and challenges.* San Francisco: Chandler, 1970. (b)

Adelson, D. Towards a conception of community psychology: The implications of cultural pluralism. In D. Adelson (Ed.), *Man as the measure: The crossroads.* New York: Behavioral Publications, 1972.

Adelson, D. Community psychology as man's encounter with history. *Journal of Community Psychology.* 1974, *2,* 402-405.

Angyal, A. *Foundations for a science of personality.* Cambridge, Mass.: Harvard University Press, 1941.

Bettleheim, B. Individual and mass behavior in extreme situations. In T. M. Newcomb and E. L. Hartley (Eds.), *Readings in Social Psychology,* New York: Holt, Rinehart, and Winston, 1947.

Castenada, A., and Ramirez, M. *Cultural democracy, bicognitive development, and education.* New York: Academic Press, 1974.

Clark, K. B., and Clark, M. Racial identification and preference in Negro children. In T.M. Newcomb and E. L. Hartley (Eds.), *Readings in Social Psychology.* New York: Holt, Rinehart & Winston, 1947.

Joint Commission on Mental Illness and Health. *Action for mental health.* New York: John Wiley & Sons, 1961.

Jones, M. *Beyond the therapeutic community.* New Haven, Conn.: Yale University Press, 1968.

Katz, I., and Kahn, R. L. *The social psychology of organizations.* New York: John Wiley & Sons, 1978.

Levy, D. M. *Maternal overprotection.* New York: Columbia University Press, 1943.

Mead, G. H. *Mind, self, and society.* Chicago: University of Chicago Press, 1934.

Myrdal, G. *An American dilemma: The Negro problem and modern democracy.* New York: Harper, 1944.

Zimbardo, P. The power and pathology of imprisonment. *Congressional Record,* 1971, Serial no. 15.

Part III

FUTURE ROLES IN A PLURALISTIC SOCIETY

Future Roles in a Pluralistic Society

The four chapters in this final section are concerned with broad issues concerning future roles for community psychologists in a pluralistic society. While many of these issues have been discussed in previous chapters, the authors in this section adopt strong positions with respect to directions for community psychology and mental health efforts.

In his chapter, Eligio Padilla angrily criticizes the deficit model views of minority groups. Past research and theory have inaccurately portrayed the intellectual, family, and mental health characteristics of ethnic minority groups. These inaccurate views, in Padilla's opinion, stem from a history of racial bias and misunderstanding in society. Padilla advocates the involvement of community psychologists as social change agents in political, institutional, and community arenas in the promotion of mental health.

Social change and improved research strategies in communities cannot progress without the development of adequate conceptual schemes or theories. Robert Chin, in a search for "Paradigm Lost," tries to specify characteristics of a theory of change that is relevant for communities in general and for ethnic minority communities in particular. His interest is in the development of a theory that can be used as basis for analyzing and intervening in various ethnic communities, through the discussion of Chinese Americans as a case in point. Central to Chin's paradigm is the necessity for community psychologists to understand the "sensibilities" or cognitive outlooks of communities.

Thom Moore, Donna Nagata, and Renee Whatley are also concerned with social intervention in a culturally pluralistic society. After defining the roles for the social interventionist, they indicate the kind of skills and the type of training that are necessary. An important ingredient for the interventionist is a value orientation of cultural pluralism and an understanding of cultures and ethnic backgrounds.

In the final chapter of Section Three, Bernard Kramer raises some thought-provoking problems regarding the development of mental health programs. In attempting to respond to ethnic minority groups, programs have been created to better match or fit the cultures and backgrounds of minority groups. Kramer raises the possibility that programs giving local communities more control over policies and meeting the unique demands of specific communities may, in the long run, contribute to segregation and dualism, rather than to intergration and pluralism. In principle, it should be possible to have person-environment matches for different groups of persons that do not segregate. Kramer cautions us that, in practice, dualism may be the unintended side effect.

Chapter 9

PSYCHOLOGISTS AS ADVERSARIES AND ALLIES OF THE CHICANO COMMUNITY

Eligio R. Padilla

It had rained continuously the day I arrived in Seattle to look for an apartment prior to beginning graduate school. The weather did little to relieve the gloom I felt in being in a strange environment, separated from my wife and our newborn daughters. My family would not join me for what seemed an interminable period of more than two months, when our girls received medical clearance to travel. To compound matters, my initial efforts as a graduate student were "nothing to write home about." I often daydreamed of escaping from my loneliness and the University of Washington, and returning to my loved ones in New Mexico. But there were no avenues of escape: I didn't even have enough money to get to Walla Walla. Fortunately, I began to adapt to the rigors of graduate study, and when my family finally arrived, all traces of depression evaporated.

It was also raining four years later on the day I left Seattle with a Ph.D. in my pocket—and all the rights, privileges and honors thereto pertaining. I was looking out the window of the airplane, comfortable in the fact that I was above rather than below those rain-laden clouds, when I became aware of a feeling I hadn't experienced in years and which initially I could not identify. Slowly I became conscious of a sense of depression which gradually enveloped me. At first, I believed it to be a psychophysiological reaction to the overenthusiastic celebrating which followed my final dissertation defense. The feeling persisted, however, and actually grew more intense. I had heard that graduate students sometimes experience depression upon the discovery that their major goal has been accomplished, with a resulting sense of emptiness that only a new major goal can fill. In my case, it wasn't that finally obtaining the Ph.D. had left me without any long-term goals. On the contrary, as a newly appointed assistant professor in the Department of Psychiatry at UCLA, the academic challenge was even more formidable. Moreover, the personal challenge of trying to be a good husband and father had increased exponentially with the birth of our second pair of identical twin daughters. I clearly could not attribute my state of mind to the lack of long-term goals.

I finally found the source of my discontent by taking a critical look at myself and at my profession. I found it ironic that, except for a class in the first semester of the first year of graduate school, I had not had the opportunity to seriously consider the forces that have shaped psychology or the directions the profession might take in order to move toward the humanitarian goals it espouses. As a student, I had been preoccupied with the myriad demands of graduate school: reading books, writing papers, collecting data, filling out applications, learning the art of psychotherapy and focusing with great intensity on very narrow aspects of the science. I could not attempt to synthesize the many disparate elements of my experience into a meaningful whole. It has been a long, painful process because I have discovered inadequacies in myself and in my discipline that previously were not so blatantly apparent.

Limitations to the Psychologist's Role

While at UCLA, I found it gratifying to be a catalytic force in helping a few individuals feel better and function more effectively, and to train others to provide such a service. I discovered, however, that I could not accept waiting passively for clients who seek relief from their distress. I could not accept having an impact on so few. I wanted to do something about the social conditions that contributed to their need to see someone like me. I realized that I was exceeding the limits of my training in making a commitment to the concept of social change. How does a person trained as a clinical psychologist go about facilitating major social change so that all Americans, especially those previously excluded, can begin to reap their share of the material and psychological benefits of living in this society? While struggling with this monstrous problem, I was advised by a few senior colleagues that social change as a guiding principle is inappropriate, unscientific, and unprofessional for a psychologist and that such mundane activities were better left to social workers and politicians. However, it occurred to the behaviorist in me that, regarding the issue of social change, one could not *not* respond. As Rappaport (1977) accurately observes, the passive acceptance of the status quo is equally political as active intervention. Nevertheless, my colleagues had piqued my curiosity about the extent to which psychologists have been politically active. What I learned, I found quite disturbing.

Psychologists as Political Activists

Kamin (1974) and others have documented that psychologists have, in fact, never been immune from political and social pressures and have often enthusiastically participated in the political process. Rather than apolitical, objective observers, whose interpretations of individual and social behavior are unaffected by the political and social controversies that rage beyond the walls of academe, a historical review reveals that psychologists have typically acted as maintainers and rationalizers of the status quo, i.e., agents of social control (Rappaport, 1977). During World War I, Robert Yerkes, Professor of Psychology at Harvard University and President of the American Psychological Association, suggested that psychology could contribute to the war effort through the intelligence testing of recruits. The idea was accepted, and more than 2,000,000 American soldiers were tested. After the War, the National Research Council established a committee whose job it was to take the national debate on immigration "out of politics," and to place it on "a scientific basis" (Kamin, 1974). Its first product was a book by Carl Brigham (1923) entitled *A Study of American Intelligence.* Brigham showed that immigrants drafted into the Army who had been in the country 16 to 20 years before being tested were as intelligent as native-born Americans, while immigrants who had been in the United States less than five years tested as "feebleminded." The first group of immigrants were mostly from Great Britain, Scandinavia, and Germany, while the more recent arrivals were from southern and southeastern Europe. The decline in intelligence among immigrants, Brigham asserted, coincided precisely with the decrease in the amount of "Nordic blood" and the increase in the amount of "Alpine" and "Mediterranean blood" in the flow of immigrants. So-called objective science was used as propaganda to justify the passage of the National Origins Quota Act of 1924. This law not only restricted the total number of immigrants, but also assigned quotas to the number of immigrants from each European country. The earlier Census of 1890 was used to further curtail the immigration of the "biologically inferior" from southern Europe. Following the "triumph" of psychologists who helped resolve the debate over immigration on a "scientific basis," the development of intelligence and achievement testing as a national institution was assured.

From its initial contact with minority groups in this country, aspects of psychology have generated data and theories to rationalize dehumanizing, oppressive practices directed at these groups by the larger society. The interests of psychologists and minority groups have often been in conflict. For the sake of discussion, I want to adopt an adversary position between psychology and Chicanos and to critically discuss the development of various substantive areas of psychological research.

Psychology Versus Chicanos on the Subject of Intelligence

Kamin (1974) argues convincingly that the assumed objectivity of many psychologists and their detachment from political and social bias is a self-serving myth. A review of psychological research *aimed* at Chicanos, blacks, and American Indians suggests that much of what has been conducted by psychologists has indeed been politically oppressive, morally corrupt, and devoid of genuine concern for their fellow human beings. Even the brilliant Lewis Terman, one of the most highly respected psychologists in American history, was biased by a force apparently stronger than scientific objectivity. After testing a *pair* of Indian and Mexican children, Terman (1916) wrote:

> Their dullness seems to be racial, or at least inherent in the family stocks from which they come. The fact that one meets this type with such frequency among Indians, Mexicans and Negroes suggests quite forcibly that the whole question of racial differences in mental traits will have to be taken up anew...here will be discovered enormously significant racial differences...which cannot be wiped out by any scheme of mental culture.
>   Children of this group should be segregated in special classes... they cannot master abstractions, but they can often be made efficient workers...There is no possibility at present of convincing society that they should not be allowed to produce...they constitute a grave problem because of their unusually prolific breeding. (p. 112)

Given such clear direction by such an eminent scientist (to the point of providing conclusions), psychologists rushed to take up anew the whole question of racial differences in intelligence. Enormously significant differences were found when Chicanos (Garretson, 1928; Garth, 1923; Haught, 1931; and Young, 1922), American Indians (Jamieson and Sandiford, 1928; Telford, 1932), and Blacks (Brigham, 1923; Yerkes, 1921) were compared to members of the majority. In reviewing this quasi-scientific line of investigation, the papers are so similar as to suggest that a basic formula was developed, with a line left blank to designate the particular group that was to be proven inferior by the study. Despite the efforts of George I. Sanchez (1932a; b), whose scholarship and scientific integrity stand in sharp contrast to that of his contemporaries, psychologists often persisted, throughout the 1930's, in their belief that Chicanos, American Indians, and Blacks were, by nature, less intellectually capable.

Two distinct movements led to the decline of Terman's genetic doctrine. First, the rise of behaviorism in the 1920's laid the groundwork for an argument based on environmental differences. Secondly, the rise of Hitler, who was to use genetic arguments to rationalize genocide, led many horrified American social scientists to reject theories based on race and to embrace cultural and environmental differences as causal factors (Kamin, 1974). According to the doctrine of cultural deprivation, Chicanos, American Indians, and Blacks perform poorly on IQ tests, not because of heredity, but because of cultural deficits. Cultural deprivation theories of one form or another were predominant in American psychology until 1969 when Arthur Jensen challenged the status quo by reviving Terman's contention that "...the whole question of racial differences in mental traits will have to be taken up anew" (p. 110). While the debate between cultural deprivation theorists and Jensen and his followers grew quite heated, there were points upon which opposing forces could agree. One school of thought blames the individual's genes; the other one's environment or culture. Nevertheless, both are consistent in the belief that the target groups are, for whatever reason, undeniably inferior. This consensus, as Rappaport (1977) astutely notes, made both portions functionally equivalent and equally oppressive.

Psychology Versus Chicano Families

The importance of the family in personality development is widely accepted throughout the social sciences. It is also, however, generally recognized that there is no one-to-one relationship between family structure and individual personality development. Loving, well-functioning parents may hae unstable, disturbed children; unstable, disturbed parents may have well-functioning children. There is, of course, a positive correlation, but it is scientifically hazardous to overgeneralize. This conclusion is especially pertinent to the study of minority families, which have been subjected to less sytematic study, but far more sweeping generalizations (Thomas and Sillen, 1972).

The most noteworthy example of this type of vast overgeneralization is the Moynihan Report, *The Negro Family: The Case for National Action,* issued by the U.S. Department of Labor in 1965. Moynihan described the black family as a "tangle of pathology," which is "approaching complete breakdown when compared with the white family...which has achieved a high degree of stability and is maintaining that stability" (p. 76). Thomas and Sillen (1972) effectively summarize many of the false premises that underlie Moynihan's analysis. They challenge anyone to adequately identify *the* White family. It should be obvious there is no homogeneous White family. Libraries are filled with studies on regional, generational, and urban-rural differences among White families. They also criticize Moynihan's implications in making the so-called White family the ideal to which all other groups must aspire. They then ask if White families possess the characteristics of stability which are used to show Black families in utter chaos. Moynihan used divorce and children born out of wedlock as his major indices of instability. These statistics show that American families in general are not flourishing and that, in fact, the rate of increase in these statistical categories is greater for White than Black families (Ryan, 1965). Poor families—White, Black and all shades in between—are more likely to manifest the characteristics of family disintegration. Poverty—more than race, ethnicity, culture, values, attitudes, etc.—is primarily implicated in the deterioration of the quality of family life.

Among members of the Black family, it is the Black woman who is subjected to particular criticism and abuse. She supposedly creates the "tangle of pathology" by first of all emasculating her husband. Moreover, the matriarch causes a profound confusion of sex roles among her off-spring. Females overidentify with the stereotypic masculine characteristics of the matriarch to eventually become castrating matriarchs themselves. Males overidentify with the stereotypic female characteristics and become fixated at the Oedipal stage because of the domineering mother and absence of the father. Later on, the males must adopt hypermasculine patterns of behavior in order to compensate for their basic effeminacy. Billingsley (1968) and Thomas and Sillen (1972) do a masterful job of criticizing this notion, which comes elegantly wrapped in a package of psychoanalytic speculation, related to empirical fact only by mere happenstance.

Why is an overview of the theories of the structure and function of Black families presented in this paper? As in the case of IQ tests, theories about family life within one minority group can be applied, with little modification, to other minority groups with the results equally dehumanizing. Consider theories about Chicano family life. "Spanish American children were seldom permitted to show much initiative or express boldly their own ideas. They were as rigorously trained for dependent behavior as the average Anglo American child is schooled for independence" (Kluckhohn and Strodtbeck, 1961). These distinguished social scientists state that an inadequate paternal role model (as opposed to the matriarchy of the Black family) is the "source of serious difficulties in the father-son relationship. One may even speculate that it is one of the reasons for the hostility and aggression (sadism even) which is noted in the behavior of many Spanish American men...some patently aggressive behavior can always be observed in Spanish American communities...(such as) homicides...(and) cruel treatment of animals" (p. 127).

Because of the "unquestioned and absolute supremacy of the father and the absolute and necessary self-sacrifice of the mother" (p. 411), Diaz-Guerrero (1955) concluded that the Mexican family offers fertile ground for the development of neuroses among its children. Highly probable conflicts for male Chicanos include: "...(1) problems of submission, conflict, and rebellion in the area of authority; (2) preoccupation and anxiety regarding sexual potency; (3) conflict and ambivalence regarding his double role; (4) difficulties in superseding the maternal stage: dependent-feminine individuals; (5) problems before and during marriage: mother's love interfered with the love of another women; (6) the Oedipus complex, as Freud describes it: almost every aspect of the ideal setting for its development is provided by the premises of the culture and the role playing'' (p. 415). On the other hand, young female Chicanos are equally likely to develop neuroses, but for less complicated reasons: ''...the main area of stress should fall around her variable success in living up to the stiff requirements that the cultural premises demand. Her inability to live up to them should show itself in self-belittlement and depressive trends'' (Diaz-Guerrero, 1955, p. 416).

Kiev (1968) argued against exclusively blaming the father for the inevitable neuroses of Chicanos: ''The narcissistic attitude of Mexican mothers toward their infants, coupled with their tendency to identify with their children as sibling rivals, leads· them to overindulge and infantilize their children, which ultimately prevents successful differentiation of ego and id, and critically affects the child's psychosexual and psychosocial development...ambivalence toward children is seen in the infrequent use made of child-care facilities despite the high incidence of child mortality, the frequent giving away of children and often brutal treatment of children...'' (p. 224).

The objections raised by Thomas and Sillen (1972) regarding this type of psychoanalytic speculation holds with equal force in this case. In a review of the literature on Chicano families, Penalosa (1968) concluded his paper by succinctly stating: ''Mexican American family structure has not been subjected to any systematic analysis. It may be said without any exaggeration that neither the empirical data nor adequate theoretical framework is yet available for the carrying out of this task'' (p. 688). Yet the speculating, theorizing, and stereotyping continue unabated among many social scientists, which raises questions about their scientific objectivity and sensitivity. It is to this disturbing possibility that we turn next.

Psychology Versus Science

Until very recently, many psychologists in California, interested in assessment, were content to rely solely on IQ tests to settle questions of mental retardation among Chicano students. As a consequence, approximately 13 percent of the Chicano student enrollment qualified for placement in classes for the educationally mentally retarded. The sole criterion in the operational definition of mental retardation was a low IQ score, despite the fact that the American Association for Mental Deficiency had for years advocated the development and use of measures of adaptive behavior as a second criterion (Heber, 1962). Psychologists failed to respond to their scientific and professional responsibility of developing measures of adaptive behavior. Fortunately for Chicano and Black students, Dr. Jame Mercer (1973), a sociologist at the University of California, Riverside, took on the admittedly formidable task of developing and norming measures of adaptive behavior. Mercer also developed scales designed to measure the locations of the child's family in the sociocultural space of American society. Given these scales, it was then possible to develop pluralistic norms in which a child's performance is compared with the performance of children who come from similar sociocultural backgrounds. Thanks to Mercer, the percentage of Chicanos who qualify for placement in classes for the educationally mentally retarded has been reduced to less than one percent, or what is expected in the general population when both criteria are used. One wonders how many Chicanos and Blacks would not have been stigmatized with the label of mental retardation if the issue had been addressed using more valid and appropriate scientific expertise and professional practice.

The point here is that some psychologists persist in acting as if their operational definitions are synonymous with the more abstract concepts to which they refer. Thus, IQ has become thoroughly confounded with the abstract notion of intelligence, so that differences in IQ between Anglos and Chicanos are transformed into differences in intelligence between Anglos and Chicanos. Some psychologists fail to appropriately recognize that a change in an operational definition may produce a dramatic change in the results. As a result of the change in the operational definition of mental retardation, the number of Chicano children labeled as such plummeted almost overnight. Responsibility for the incorrect labeling of an outrageous number of children will, of course, be diffused, but the fact remains that, as psychologists, we cannot look beyond our profession to begin the task of aiding minority groups.

Another example of the tendency to make tremendous inferential leaps from narrowly drawn operational definitions is the contention that minority individuals in this country and individuals from other countries do not have as great a need for achievement as do their Anglo American peers. McClelland's (1961) technique has been used to generate scores of studies to support this widely-held belief. Ramirez and Price-Williams (1976) studied ethnic and sex differences in achievement motivation utilizing McClelland's technique, a projective test of TAT-like cards. Following the standard scoring procedure, they obtained the predictable results: Anglo children scored higher than Chicano and Black children. They then looked at a subset of the projective test consisting of pictures showing interactions between adults and children. Their hypothesis was that socialization of Chicano and Black children leads to a closer identity with the family and that their children would have greater achievement motivation to cooperate for the attainment of common goals. The result relevant to this discussion was that changing the operational definition to scores based on cards showing parent-child interaction led to Chicanos having a significantly greater need for achievement than Anglos. Ramirez and Price-Williams (1976) concluded that McClelland's notions are based on a Western view of human behavior that is individually motivated, consonant with a socialization process that encourages children to view themselves as individuals distinct from their families, culture, history, and environment.

American Indian tribes have also been evaluated for the need to achieve with the typical results interpreted to suggest that they also are deficient in their need to achieve. Observations that children of certain tribes will not raise their hands to answer questions in class unless they are sure that all their peers can answer have been suggested as being behavioral manifestations of this alleged deficit. However, a fundamental question remains unanswered: What is it that one (or a group, tribe, or nation) is or should be trying to achieve? It would seem that the ultimate test is whether or not the need for achievement, as defined by that society, is adaptive in the long run for that particular group. Through a highly refined sense of cooperation, in which the "we're number one!" complex is virtually unknown, several of these tribes have managed to thrive for thousands of years in a land which others have thought uninhabitable. Their need to achieve harmony and peace with their fellows and with their environment, measured not by projective tests, but by the success of their values, attitudes, and lifestyle, is a need the rest of American society should emulate, rather than denigrate.

Another myth or stereotype popularly expressed by some is the belief that Chicanos cannot delay gratification. Empirical support for this generalization comes from research where children are asked to choose between immediate acceptance of a smaller reward and a larger reward to be given days or weeks later. For example, in one condition of a study conducted by Price-Williams and Ramirez (1974), children were asked to choose between getting $10 immediately or waiting a month to receive $30. As usual in these studies, statistically significant differences between Chicanos and Anglos were obtained. Because of the statistically significant differences, *readers* often fail to make the psychologically significant observation that a majority of Chicano children (77 percent) were also willing to wait a month for the additional money. That is, while there are between group differences on a particular attribute, both groups may largely possess the attribute. At a conceptual level, it is ironic that Chicanos are seen as being unable to delay gratification when in actuality Chicanos, because of their depressed economic state as a group, are more likely to be forced to delay gratification or to forget about gratification entirely.

The examples above illustrate the need to avoid the possible misinterpretation of research findings that may occur in the minds of readers toward culturally different people. Gergin (Gergin, 1973) also makes the additional point that the concepts psychologists find especially interesting are always culture-bound in their meaning:

> ...self-esteem could be termed egotism, need for approval could be translated as need for social integration; cognitive differentiation as hair-splitting; creativity as deviance; and internal control as egocentricity...if our values were otherwise, conformity could be viewed as pro-solidarity behavior...(p. 312).

Another aspect of psychologists to build their theories and interpret their findings on the basis of unrepresentative samples and an excess of questionable assumptions. For example, the literature on the Chicano family largely supports the belief that the *macho* is an absolute tyrant who rules the household with an iron fist. *El jefe* may allegedly abuse his wife and children with equanimity or do anything else that enters his presumed neurotic, sadistic, sexually-confused, and underdeveloped mind. Rather than following the pattern of accepting those assumptions as the starting point of their research, Hawkes and Taylor (1975) decided to test the basic assumption that Chicano families are dominated by a patriarchal power structure. Moreover, they decided to test the assumption in the most traditional, unacculturated population where the power structure is likely to be most explicit. They interviewed seventy-six migrant families randomly selected from 12 migrant camps in California. The couples were asked who made the decisions and who took the agreed-upon action in many areas of family life. The results show that equalitarianism (joint decision-making and action-taking by the husband and wife) was the dominant pattern in about two-thirds of the migrant families, with the remainder equally divided between male and female dominance. Hawkes and Taylor (1975) close their discussion with the following comment: "We suggest that many of the traditional stereotypes of groups such as ethnic minorities noted in the literature and in public assumptions need more adequate verification. It is possible that more sophisticated methods of research may negate many of our previous assumptions" (p. 811). I do not at all agree with their suggestion that traditional stereotypes need more adequate verification. I also do not believe that more sophisticated methods of research are always necessary. In most cases the basic requirements of science (e.g., representative samples) will suffice. There is, however, as Hawkes and Taylor imply, a need for more sophisticated researchers who can critically evaluate previous assumptions. Certainly, there should be more sophisticated approaches in studying minority groups.

The current state of the clinical lore and the social science literature is such that I usually see only caricatures of Chicanos, if they are at all recognizable. Utilizing concepts adapted from psychoanalytic and cultural deprivation theories, social scientists have compiled an imposing list of deficits, flaws of character, and cultural handicaps. Chicanos are viewed as emotional, explosive, oral, alcoholic, sadistic, promiscuous, sexually exploitative, and basically effeminate. On the other hand, Chicanos are thought to be simple, infantile, smothering, rejecting, ambivalent, and depressive. Both males and females are seen as neurotic, dependent, present-time oriented, unable to delay gratification, complacent, lacking in the need to achieve, superstitious, and unintellectual. The implications for Chicanos as students, consumers of social, legal, health, and mental health services and simply as people are quite obvious. The schools can in no way be held responsible if Chicano students are not properly educated. Social, health, and mental health systems and professionals should be less concerned about the quality of services made available to these undeserving, ungrateful people. The implication to some is that Chicanos are a hopeless, miserable lot, whose childrearing practices and culture condemn them to second-class citizenship. Believers in this "cult of cultural inferiority" (Clark, 1965) are as absolute in their condemnation of Chicanos and other minority groups as were the proponents of the biological supremacy of "Nordic Blood."

Some readers will undoubtedly object to this less than sympathetic description of psychology and related disciplines and professions. I am admittedly taking a harsh view. To some it may seem exaggerated and heavy-handed, and may arouse feelings of annoyance or anger. Such feelings would themselves be of value in illustrating the relative strength of Chicanos in their continuing struggle for a better world. My caricature of the scientist-practitioner will have little consequence beyond arousing among a few individuals transient feelings of irritation or anger. On the other hand, the caricatures of Chicanos produced in such great abundance by many social scientists will continue to be used to rationalize discrimination against Chicanos in the various institutions of our society.

Two relatively recent developments have occurred which threaten the status quo in psychology *vis-a-vis* Chicanos. In the past decade, a critical mass of Chicano psychologist and social scientists has been achieved. The emergence of ethnically and culturally different people in the field has been facilitated by liberal psychologists who accurately identify the need to broaden standards of admission. A philosophically more conservative argument has also been made to justify recruitment efforts. Nearly thirty years ago, Frank Beach (1950) made the observation that psychological theories are based on extremely narrow phylogenetic and empirical grounds, describing psychology as the study of the white rat and the college sophomore. The evolution of psychology from a very narrow empirical foundation is likely to accelerate as the presence of minority scholars increases. Thus, the argument for increased minority participation in psychology goes beyond broadening standards for admission. It rests on the need to *raise* the standards by which psychology is practiced as an experimental, descriptive and applied science. Following the tradition established by George I. Sanchez nearly 50 years ago, Chicano psychologists and their allies are making progress toward these goals.

Chicano psychologists are a vigorous and growing group, but their number remains relatively small (Olmedo, 1977; Padilla, 1977). Fortunately, the development of community psychology has created the potential for a working alliance with a larger group of psychologists whose values and goals appear to be in harmony with those of the Chicano community. In what should constitute required reading for graduate students and faculty, Julian Rappaport (1977) has brilliantly developed the rationale for a new paradigm in psychology, one which could have a revolutionary effect on the discipline. According to Rappaport, community psychologists value cultural diversity and relativity, and work toward identifying and changing aspects of the social structure which degrade people. Because of the stated values and goals of community psychology, great expectations have been raised among those who persist in their belief that psychology may yet be a liberating rather than an oppressive force in the community. Raised expectations regarding what community psychology can accomplish in turn raise the criteria by which the discipline will be evaluated. Simply improving upon past performance will not suffice; the historical record is so dismal as to serve as an invalid basis of comparison. Whether or not community psychologists succeed in reaching the goals they themselves have so clearly defined remains to be seen. However pleasing to the ear, there are many reasons for Chicanos to be cautious about the rhetoric emanating from community psychology, a few of which will be considered below.

Community Psychology Versus Chicanos?

Psychologists' periodic, allegedly humanitarian forays into the Chicano community have been characterized by research that is detrimental rather than beneficial to the group, and by service programs which promote innovation without change (Graziano, 1969). Psychologists' influence on social policy and the resources made available to them to conduct their research and service programs have been related to their willingness to justify the prevailing social order. Rappaport suggests that psychologists in the community have promoted social control in the guise of social science. On the other hand, community psychologists who value cultural diversity and relativity, who identify with the people rather than institutions, and who work for social change, will have relatively few financial and professional resources with which to sustain their efforts. Their struggle must be viewed as a lifelong commitment with no guarantee that their efforts will reach fruition. Overcoming the inertia of their peers who are comfortable and prefer to maintain the status quo and the resistance of those who are opposed to social change will prove to be too much for some community psychologists. These allies who encounter problems may quit in frustration and go through the motions of working for the people. Even without the loss of those who decide the struggle is not theirs after all, community psychology, like other disciplines, will hopefully not become institutionalized, with all the excess conceptual, professional, and organizational baggage that accompany the process. There is also a possibility that community psychology, in its frustration and aging, will become preoccupied with research, grants, journals, experts, credentials, book publication, etc., at the expense of the principles and the people for whom it was originally established.

It should be obvious that community psychologists will have considerably less influence on social policy than psychologists whose interests reflect those of the wealthy and powerful in our country. Psychologists are highly unlikely candidates to lead the reform of our entire society, but, as Rappaport suggests, their activities can be based on a value system and a scientific paradigm consistent with the aims of such reform. Much of psychology's contribution will take place in the routine of psychologists' daily activities. Mental health centers, schools, and the legal system present opportunities for the implementation of a new perspective and a corresponding decline in the mislabeling, misdiagnosis, and mistreatment of Chicanos and other culturally different people.

Nowhere are the opportunities for reform greater for psychologists than in their own discipline. Community psychologists can become allies of the Chicano community without even having to leave their usual place of employment. They can do so by educating their colleagues and convincing them to use appropriate means of studying and contributing to minority groups. Rappaport (1977) summarizes the basic conflict as follows:

> In American psychology the traditional paradigms adopt an implicit faith that the single standard of white, middle-class society is, on an absolute basis, superior to all others. At the same time, because rank-ordering is built into these psychological paradigms, some will always be on the top and others in the middle and still others on the bottom...

The basic contradiction in such a system render its professed aims of equal opportunity to life, liberty, and happiness virtually impossible.... In education, in mental health, in employment, in living environments, and in the legal system, equal access to psychological and material resources is incompatible with a distribution of resources on the basis of rank-ordering people against a single standard of competence (p. 22).

FOOTNOTES

[1]Written in fond remembrance of Professor Nathaniel Wagner, a true friend and ally.

REFERENCES

Beach, F. A. The snark was a boojum. *American Psychologist*, 1950, *5*, 115-124.

Billingsley, A. *Black families in white America*. Englewood Cliffs, N.J.: Prentice-Hall, 1968.

Brigham, C. C. *A study of American intelligence*. Princeton: Princeton University Press, 1923.

Clark, K. B. *Dark ghetto*. New York: Harper & Row, 1965.

Diaz-Guerrero, R. Neurosis and the Mexican family structure. *American Journal of Psychiatry*, 1955, *112*, 411-417.

Garretson, O. K. A study of causes of retardation among Mexican children and mixed and full blood Indian children. *Psychological Review*, 1928, *30*, 388-401.

Garth, T. R. A comparison of the intelligence of Mexican and mixed and full-blood Indian children. *Psychological Review*, 1923, *30*, 388-401.

Gergin, K. J. Social psychology as history. *Journal of Personality and Social Psychology*, 1973, *26*, 309-320.

Graziano, A. M. Clinical innovation and the mental health power structure: A social case history. *American Psychologist*, 1969, *24*, 10-18.

Haught, B. F. The language difficulty of Spanish American children. *Journal of Applied Psychology*, 1931, *15*, 92-95.

Hawkes, G. R., and Taylor, M. Power structure in Mexican and Mexican American farm labor families. *Journal of Marriage and the Family*, 1975, *3*, 807-811.

Heber, R. F. A manual on terminology and classification in mental retardation. *American Journal of Mental Deficiency*, 1962 (Monograph Supplement 64).

Jamieson, E. and Sandiford, P. The mental capacity of Southern Ontario Indians. *Journal of Educational Psychology*, 1928, *19*, 536-551.

Kamin, L. J. *The science and politics of I.Q.* Potomac, Md.: Erlbaum, 1974.

Kiev, A. *Curanderismo: Mexican American folk psychiatry*. New York: Free Press, 1968.

Kluckhohn, F. R., and Strodtbeck, F. L. *Variations in value orientations*. Evanston, Illinois: Row, Peterson and Company, 1961.

Kuhn, T. S. *The structure of scientific revolutions.* Chicago: Chicago University Press (2d ed.), 1970.

McClelland, D. C. *The achieving society.* Princeton: Van Nostrand, 1961.

Mercer, J. R. *Labeling the mentally retarded: Clinical and social system Perspectives on mental retardation.* Berkeley and Los Angeles: University of California Press, 1973.

Moynihan, D. P. *The Negro family: The case for national action.* Washington, D.C. U.S. Government Printing Office, 1965.

Olmedo, E. L. Patterns of Hispanic representation among doctoral level scientists and graduate students in the United States. In E. L. Olmedo and S. Lopez (eds.) *Hispanic mental health professionals* (Monograph 5). Los Angeles: University of California, Spanish Speaking Mental Health Research Center, 1977.

Padilla, E. R. Hispanics in clinical psychology: 1970-1976. In E. L. Olmedo and S. Lopez (eds.) *Hispanic mental health professionals* (Monograph 5). Los Angeles: University of California, Spanish Speaking Mental Health Research Center, 1977.

Penalosa, F. Mexican family roles. *Journal of Marriage and the Family,* 1968, *30,* 680-689.

Price-Williams, D. R., and Ramirez, M. Ethnic differences in delay of gratification. *The Journal of Social Psychology,* 1974, *93,* 23-30.

Ramirez, M., and Price-Williams, D. R. Achievement motivation in children of three ethnic groups in the United States. *Journal of Cross-Cultural Psychology,* 1976, *7,* 49-60.

Rappaport, J. *Community psychology,* New York: Holt, Rinehart & Winston, 1977.

Ryan, W. *Blaming the victim.* New York: Random House, 1971.

Sanchez, G. I. Group differences and Spanish-speaking children: A critical review. *Journal of Applied Psychology,* 1932, *16,* 549-558.

Sanchez, G. I. Scores of Spanish-speaking children on repeated tests. *Pedagogical Seminary and Journal of Genetic Psychology,* 1932 (March), 223-231.

Terman, L. M. *The measurement of intelligence.* Boston: Houghton Mifflin Company, 1916.

Telford, C. W. Test performance of full and mixed-blood North Dakota Indians. *Journal of Comparative Psychology,* 1932, *14,* 123-145.

Thomas, A., and Sillen, S. *Racism and psychiatry.* Seacausus, New Jersey: The Citadel Press, 1972.

Yerkes, R. M. (ed.) *Psychology examining in the United States army.* Washington, D.C., 1921.

Young, K. Mental differences in certain immigrant groups. *University of Oregon Publications,* 1922, 1(11).

Chapter 10

CONCEPTUAL PARADIGM FOR A RACIAL-ETHNIC COMMUNITY
The Case of the Chinese-American Community

Robert Chin

As indicated by Montero (1977), research and theory on racial and cultural minority groups are at an infancy stage, at least in terms of being sensitive to the problems and needs of these groups and of designing innovative theories and approaches for understanding ethnic communities. The need for sensitivity and innovation, a theme that has been consistently expressed, can no longer be dismissed as "another one of those demands that ethnic minorities make because of distrust over the social sciences." Indeed, while this paper seeks to present and to advocate a model for analyzing and intervening in racial and ethnic communities, a case can be made for the model's relevance to any community. I offer here the tools for analysis by a community worker, to create a framework for an inter-disciplinary approach. I present for this purpose a paradigm.

Paradigms are patterns or models to be used for analysis. The specifics are not to detract from the tools being shaped by the use of a model. Paradigms evolve and change; they are created to be replaced by more useful ones. The scope of this paper is to formulate a paradigm from the case of the Chinese-American community, with the idea that the paradigm is used to prepare a tool kit and a work agenda for the future. We seek, through this model, Paradigm Lost.

Three conceptual schema can be used in developing a paradigm for intervening an ethnic-racial community. The first identifies contemporaneous facts and interdependent variables of a cross-section of a community or situation. In the social sciences, this is probably the most commonly used framework, laying out concepts and variables for understanding what and how events occur. Nevertheless, as noted by Kelly (1979), focus upon the "here and now" in relating causal agents and effects is narrow and limiting. In contrast to the first conceptual scheme, the second type, which is becoming increasingly used in the social sciences, focuses on organic growth and development over time; an observer or researcher longitudinally records how events come about and how they undergo change due to their own forces, or to impacts from their environment. The third type, which I call the Theory of Changing, centers on how events are changeable through intervention. It is this scheme that is adopted in this paper.

In order to be most useful, the Theory of Changing must combine practicality, logic, values, and social science methodology. The following characteristics should be considered in the theory:

1. The Theory must provide levers or handles for influencing direction, tempo, and quality of change for improvement. Variables that explain and are causal may be the least alterable. It must help to identify variables that are accessible to control.

2. It must be based on an interactive inter-systems model, taking into account the roles of a change agent and client system. It must understand each system's values, perceptions, and rights of self-determination. It must, therefore, be manipulable and avoid violating the client system's values, whenever possible. Heller and Monahan (1977) recommend that change agents or social regulators fully consider community mores, sentiments, and practices before taking action and that any action be guided by these considerations.

3. It must take cost into account. Prohibitive costs would rule out highly controllable and value-resonant variables. The high costs may be for the change agent, the client system, or, because of the method, the technique or strategy for changing the client system.

4. It must provide a reliable basis for diagnosing the strengths and weaknesses of the forces determining conditions facing the client system and the change agent system.

5. The Theory must account for the phases of intervention so the change agent can develop estimates for timing termination of his or her relationship with the client system. It would identify starting points, gradients of the forces, oscillations and dialectics, and internalization or institutionalization of the change. Developmental processes are important.

6. It must be able to be communicated effectively, with a minimum of distortion, to the client system.

7. It must be able to be aware of, and take assessment of, its own appropriateness for different client systems.

8. It must produce generalized learning by the client enabling him or her to cope with similar issues. Learning to learn should be a part of the theory.

9. It must be able to make statements that are testable through some disciplined inquiry or explicit methodology.

10. It must be capable of creating data matching its concepts, so cumulative data can be gathered across many settings.

11. It must not be counter to established knowledge in the fields of psychology, sociology, or other disciplines, or to the practices of the established social service professions, without explicit explanation and justification.

These requirements for a theory of intervention, integrating practicality, values, and research methodology, have not been sufficiently developed into a comprehensive whole. Community psychology is more at the stage of recognizing the complexities of planned social change, rather than of formulating a comprehensive theory of community intervention. For example, in his analysis of techniques for social intervention, Rappaport (1977) states:

> Theoretically, such techniques should follow from conceptions about the level of society at which one is intervening. Conceptions of "how things work" at a given level of analysis should dictate strategies of intervention. The problem is often thought of as technological: "what change techniques, based on what conceptions, delivered how, when, where, and by whom, are appropriate and effective in changing what social systems, with what characteristics, given a particular level of analysis?" (p. 158)

Given the complexities of formulating a theory of intervention and the current lack of a comprehensive theory of this kind, it is not difficult to understand the constant pleas in community psychology for high quality conceptualizations, theories, and empirical research (Bloom, 1978). Without adequate conceptual tools and formulations, community psychologists may be reduced to theoretical orphans who engage in practices, programs, and services like ideological true-believers. Analysis and intervention in ethnic minority communities may pose special problems because of the urgency and press of mental health needs and the cultural and historical patterns that may differ considerably from more mainstream American community life.

The purpose of this paper is to demonstrate how some of the 11 characteristics outlined in the proposed paradigm for social change are important to consider in analyzing a community, in this case, the Chinese American community's strengths, problems, and approaches to assistance. The intent is not so much to justify the entire paradigm and its application; rather, I want to select key characteristics that are important and yet, often ignored in a "here-and-now" analysis of causal factors and effects.

THE CHINESE AMERICAN COMMUNITY

Sensibility

In order to derive social policies for ethnic minorities, it is necessary to understand the processes, dynamics, and structures within ethnic communities. This assertion is obviously true. The point of contention is over the nature of understanding. Many ethnic minorities claim that social scientists frequently do not fully understand ethnic minority communities because of biases, inadequate conceptualizations, or poor research strategies (Brazziel, 1973). I do not want to add criticism without providing suggestions for new tools that can be used to derive policies. Central to my view is that the psychological "sensibility" of the community and its individuals be understood.

Sensibility is used here as a world outlook, a perceptual stance, a cognitive map with strong affective and evaluative components. Attitudes and values are included. Sensibility is humanistic and inclusive and allows conceptualizing a community as a population with common direct or indirect experiences. Sensibilities are the grounds upon which sensitivity, reactions, and interpretations of particular events are found. For example, racism might be included as a part of the total sensibility of a group or event, even though individuals within the group are not direct victims of racism. Thus people and communities have certain sensibilities (e.g., outlooks, values, cognitive styles, etc.) that must be appreciated by community psychologists. In order to understand the sensibilities of a particular community, history, developmental processes, values, goals, interactive systems, needs, role relationships—characteristics in the proposed paradigm—must be examined. Without knowledge of a community's sensibilities, intervention efforts are likely to be resisted, misunderstood, and ineffective. Let us now examine the Chinese American community and its complex systems and derivative sensibilities. Five systems are discussed. They are: (1) traditional and contemporary service-giving functions and agencies; (2) stratifications and sub-groupings, and intergenerational relations of Chinese-Americans; (3) events of history; (4) institutional racism and ethnic identity; and (5) knowledge building activities and practices of the service deliverers, as these practices affect sensibilities. These five systems are treated in their broad scope as sources of the sensibilities of Chinese-Americans. They interact with each other to produce consequences, and, it should be noted, the five systems can be examined on the dimension of time: Past, present, and future. My point is that the five systems interacting with each other and having their own developmental histories with implications for the present and future produce a complex array of possibilities.

Development of Chinese Service-Giving Functions

Chinese organizations in the United States evolved in three stages, from original community structures, including the family and family organizations, to church and missionary agencies, and then to social services provided by the new professionals. The original tension in services was between the traditional organizations and the church. Later, the professional social service worker, often having the same motivation as the earlier church workers, provided new services and with them, new community tensions. Let us examine this evolution.

The first Chinese organizations in the United States, dating from the beginning of the 20th century, provided services surrounding the deaths of immigrants. United States cemeteries were rigidly segregated. Rituals during and after burial, which, in Chinese tradition were public ceremonies, required community organization. There developed a function of removing the bones of the deceased after a period of U.S. burial for reinterment in the family plot in the ancestral village in China. This could best be performed by an institution or clan association. These services were binding forces in the community prior to 1940. Since then, U.S. regulations have been relaxed and the shipping of bones to China has not been necessary.

Another set of functions of these Chinese organizations was to establish rules for community governance. For example, they would advise how far apart a new laundry or restaurant must be from another, to ensure against unfair competition. Disputes between businesses, and between clans, would be heard and judged by the community-wide benevolent association. Family and internal clan disputes came before the clan organization. Cruel treatment of a wife could be appealed to the clan association of her original family. These counseling and legal functions were handled, thereby, within clans and communities, not by outsiders.

The next development in early social services was the introduction of Christian church work in Chinese communities. These provided an intermediate form of agencies, organized under home mission societies, that offered competitive assistance to the Chinese structures. They attempted to evangelize the Chinese, but had the effect of a service agency. Protestant denominations established mission churches in Chinatowns, and "Sunday schools" began in neighborhood churches to teach English and the Bible. These later became national churches with distinguished records of developing leadership of the American-born Chinese for social services. They were centers of social liberation for women and for family orientation, immigration assistance, and socialization. They also brought to the community new attitudes, motivations, and behavior about problems, including help-seeking and help-giving roles.

The establishment of formal social service and community agencies coincided with the founding of the New Society in China, and with the increasing numbers of new immigrants to major U.S. cities. Many immigrants were joining families or individuals already settled in cities, due to the U.S. immigration policy giving preference to reuniting families. Even when this was not the reason, new immigrants tended to cluster in cities where there were existing Chinese communities.

Chinese community organizations established in the U.S. in the first half of the 20th Century started to lose importance. The magnitude of problems overwhelmed the capability of the traditional organizations. New kinds of services were needed. There was a loss of vitality and usefulness in organization leadership; they were not able to incorporate the American-born generations into leadership positions, and they did not attract new immigrants in large enough numbers to replenish membership. An additional factor was that the traditional organizations were proud of their historic role in Chinese political affairs. They had supported the revolution overthrowing the Manchu dynasty in 1911 and the war against Japanese aggression in the 1930's and 1940's. They became identified with the Nationalist government and its Kuomintang Party, while the new immigrants were refugees from China and from communism.

Another contributing factor to the breakdown of the Chinese community organization was that the traditional infra-structure of the Chinese communities had been closely connected with gambling and protection schemes. In the period up to the 1940's, the powerful, secret societies, Tongs, vied for control over these marginal and illegal activities. Civic authorities interfered upon the outbreak of violence. There were sporadic police campaigns in many cities to "clean up Chinatown." Gambling and other such activities played, ironically, a dual role. While they provided recreational and psychological support, they concurrently created social pathologies and distress for families and individuals and undermined the quality of American lives. Symbiosis was often achieved with the police and civic and political groups to sustain these activities, which unfortunately served to deplete community money and talent. This symbiosis played a major part in shaping Chinatown community structures.

It is clear that these organizations and practices served then (and to some extent in the present) as havens for new immigrants from the uncertainty of American society. They served the older Chinese-Americans as outlets for civic and political identification, and the newer, non-English speaking migrants were not connected or attracted to these structures, especially those who had lived and worked in Hong Kong for any significant time, because they were culturally separate.

Community organization of power changed as the range of activities covered by this power narrowed to symbolic manipulation of a few social functions. The change was accompanied by increased residence in enclaves within the city, but outside the area of Chinatown, and by major shifts in the composition of the Chinese populations within cities.

As an index of the transition experienced in Chinese communities in America, there is an increasing clamor of voices claiming to represent "the community." The old organizations still are considered important community structures by major civic authorities, the press, and those taking a historical view. But a very crucial debate was taking place: Who speaks for Chinatown? Determining who speaks for the community becomes one of the central tasks of the community psychologist seeking to achieve community representation in programs, boards, and sponsorships. This need is heightened by the tendency of other groups to see a racial-ethnic community as a whole, autonomous unit. Outsiders are reluctant to differentiate community forces and groups, wishing not to intervene into community politics and dynamics. There is also a general policy to "let the native leaders rule over their own people." In these circumstances, buccaneering individuals may become leaders; they are then sometimes destroyed through attributions about their motives by their constituencies.

The resulting sensibility about community organizations and social service agencies reinforced a Chinese cultural attitude that questions the motivations of service-givers. Communities have experienced the reciprocity norm, which teaches that they are not getting service for nothing. Givers must want something in return. Communities anticipate self-interest in these individuals, under the table deals, direct buccaneering, or, in recent times, ego- or power-tripping. This is slowly being replaced by a growing notion that government "owes" something to its people. Communities are beginning to share a righteous indignation over the inadequacy of services or help.

As new agencies for social service, mental health, legal aid, etc. are being developed, they are staffed by professional workers and young adults most often from outside the community. These newcomers see themselves as in closer touch with "the community" than the earlier professionals and church workers. They are a new professional establishment operating as caretakers and do not necessarily see the old Chinese social institutions as allies. Frequent conflict of concept and approaches to rendering service occur between and among these two factions. The new group of professionals startle the Chinese organizational leadership by their salaries and their approach to rendering service by observed and assumed need, rather than by association within the community. They also have different methods of treatment and freer access to assistance. In the future, professionals must discover their clients' understanding of service agencies and develop roles and styles that are closer to those known and used by the Chinese organizations they are supplanting. For example, professionals must appreciate that the traditional Chinese approach is to use a go-between to obtain services from a service agency. Chinese expect to give this intermediary something in return; relationships become personalized. Modifications to allow for the rights, assumptions, and dependencies of agencies with those in the community are critical to the development of future social policy.

The professional, service-rendering agencies will increase in number and scope. Some questions to confront in planning for the future, and for the training of new professionals, are: At what stages of a developmental sequence of an innovative agency or service will change occur from its intended purposes, and at what stages will pioneering staff exhibit "burn out" and institutionalized slow down? Will the service giving functions result in a new sensibility of relationships among individuals and the community?

These questions, and many others concerning service programs and community intervention, cannot be fully addressed without reference to the history and dynamics of the Chinese American community. I have argued that intervention techniques must operate within a context. Social change agents must use this context and develop the appropriate sensibility in order to identify variables that are accessible to control, to understand role relationships, cost factors, timing of intervention, etc., in communities.

Stratifications, Subgroups, and Intergenerational Relations

As mentioned previously, non-Chinese groups tend to view Chinese, or the Chinese American community, as a homogeneous group or entity. In actuality, Chinese Americans are composed of diverse subgroups, divided in many different ways. The consequences of heterogeneity are apparent. Intervention efforts for one subgroup may not affect other subgroups; defining community needs is a complex task; and different factions may be in direct competition for services and funds. To understand the significance and magnitude of the heterogeneity, it is necessary to examine the stratifications.

Most original settlers in the continental United States, those who arrived prior to 1940, were primarily from the Toishan district and the Szeyip, a rural area of south China's province of Kwangtung. Other Cantonese from the Sam Yip dialect area around the capital city of Canton, Kwangchou, provided a smaller number of migrants, who did not occupy a major position in the Chinese-American community. Later, there was an influx of refugees from communist China which, however, did not significantly alter the composition of the Chinese community. Nevertheless, since many had lived in Hong Kong for a lengthy period, they arrived with new language and orientations. If Chinese from Taiwan and the current wave of ethnic Chinese from IndoChina are included, then one important stratification in the immigrant community is derived from origins. Cultural and national traditions, values, language, and conditions of immigration are likely to divide immigrant Chinese. A second source of heterogeneity is the length of time in America. There are four basic subgroupings, although the proportions of each subgrouping and their numbers have shifted over time. The subgroups are: (1) old timers of at least two generations born and socialized in U.S.; (2) first generation born and raised of immigrant parents; (3) migrant students and professionals who stayed; and (4) recent immigrants and refugees, or those reconstituting families. Differences in the period of U.S. residency have direct implications for level of acculturation, generational differences between parents and children, magnitude of culture conflict, and English language skills.

The third important stratification is socioeconomic. Because of the high visibility and achievements of a group of Chinese Americans in educational and occupational endeavors, important socioeconomic differences among Chinese Americans are masked. The individual incomes of Chinese Americans probably exhibit greater variability than those of Whites (Urban Associates, 1974). Statistical indices of income and underemployment show a large number of Chinese on the bottom of the income measures. Due to barriers of language, ghettoized occupations, and the dramatic increase in immigrants, there will be an increasing core of the poor. To argue the effects of socioeconomic differences is unnecessary in view of the widely accepted importance of these differences in mental health, life styles, values, etc. (President's Commission on Mental Health, 1978). The issue here is one of recognition—namely, that the diversity among Chinese should be appreciated by social scientists, change agents, and the public.

There are some further considerations to make. First, in 1940, Chinese Americans numbered a bare 100,000. In 1970, the number was over 430,000. Projections indicate that by 1980, there will be between 800,000 and 900,000 Chinese in the United States (Owan, 1975). This tremendous growth necessitates constant changes in intervention techniques and flexibility in social policies to accommodate recent events. Second, exposure to different sub-groups among the Chinese and to non-Chinese communities has created an interesting phenomenon, in which orderly growth and change within families are undermined. For example, immigrant wives may become quickly disenchanted with traditional female roles, after contact with more acculturated and "liberated" Chinese Americans. More assimilated Chinese Americans may begin the search for their ethnic "roots." Thus, exposure to a diverse range of Chinese models accelerates changes in personal identities. Conflicts between individualism and group membership loyalties that are normally seen in Chinese families may occur more rapidly because of the strong emphasis on individualism in American society.

Events of History

The major international and historical events contributing to discernable American attitudes and to the community's sensibility are composed of three variables: (1) American foreign policy; (2) internal events in China; and (3) the Christian missionary movement. These events shaped the destiny of the Chinese in America in terms of political attitudes and of Chinese attitudes toward the role of government and central administration. The events also shaped the views of the Chinese in America toward community action; they affected political power of various community groups and generational lines within communities.

Although a historical account is beyond the scope of this paper, it should be noted that attitudes of Americans toward China and the Chinese show an oscillation between respect and contempt, benevolence, hostility, and admiration. In the 1840's, when the first significant numbers of Chinese entered the United States, Chinese were fairly respected for their willingness to work and to assume much needed services such as cooks, laundry workers, and railroad workers. Within a few decades, they were viewed contemptuously as unfair labor and cheap competition in a depressed national economy. Anti-Chinese sentiments peaked in the 1880s with the passage of the Chinese Exclusion Act, which served to restrict further immigration of Chinese. From 1910 to the 1940s, a more benevolent, though still hostile, attitude developed. The Christian missionary movement was responsible for this feeling of benevolence, since the church's goal was to foster the salvation of the Chinese. The effect of the church and the Christian movement can be seen among Chinese now in the United States. Although Hsu (1971) has argued that Chinese have traditionally been more involved in filial piety and ancestral worship than in orthodox Christian religion, many early Chinese were Christians when they emigrated. Furthermore, the educational system in Hong Kong fostered religious affiliation because of the higher quality of religious schools there. Many of the immigrants are Christians. Thus Christianity has had an impact upon the Chinese American community.

The attitude of benevolence because of the Christian movement and a feeling of admiration because of China's relationship with the United States against Japan during the second World War were evident, up until the late 1940's. The communist takeover of mainland China in 1949 probably revived hostility toward Chinese in the United States. For many years, Chinese Americans who spoke favorably of the Peoples Republic of China or who had close ties with family members there were viewed with suspicion as communist sympathizers. The relocation of the Nationalist Chinese to the island of Taiwan also created conflicts in that Chinese Americans were further divided into political, personal, or economic loyalties to the Peoples Republic of China, Taiwan, or neither country (this last option was particularly adopted by many American born Chinese whose main concern was for Chinese in the United States rather than international loyalties).

Beginning in 1970, with the visit of President Nixon and the Shanghai Communique, American policy began to shift toward official recognition of the Peoples Republic of China. Initial American sentiments were ones of wonderment and admiration at the major changes seen in the country. Social ills such as gross poverty, disease, and crime, previously seen in China, have been reduced. The government has provided successfully for physical security against wars and bandits and has largely eliminated famine which had periodically struck rural areas.

These historical events are important for a number of reasons. First, they help to shape American attitudes toward Chinese and Chinese Americans (Sue and Kitano, 1973). The favorability of views toward Chinese Americans seems to be directly related to the favorability of views toward overseas Chinese. Second, historical events and American attitudes shape the behavioral patterns of Chinese Americans. For example, overt expressions of sympathy toward the Peoples Republic of China were suppressed by many Chinese Americans, until official U.S. policy was more accepting of China. Third, Chinese American attitudes concerning the role of government and community action have been affected. Prior to the 1960s, especially when China lacked a strong central government that could respond to people's needs, involvement in political affairs was minimal. The Christian church and its social service functions served the people to some extent. With the recognition of the role of community involvement and the response of the government in the Peoples Republic of China, many Chinese in the United States have also developed more initiative in community action and in seeking governmental programs. Finally, the major historical events with their effects on the contemporary Chinese American community have promoted even greater diversity and heterogeneity, a phenomenon previously discussed. To understand the Chinese American community and its sensibilities, these historical factors need to be examined.

Institutional Racism and Ethnic Identity

Historically, Chinese have encountered a great deal of discrimination. In California during the mid 1800s, special taxes were collected on Chinese laundries and on Chinese queues (braided hair). Chinese were unable to testify against Whites in court and, in 1882, Congress passed the Chinese Immigration Act, America's first bill to restrict immigration on the basis of race. The immigration policy and regulations had a direct impact on the size, family structure and, more crucially, the attitudes of Chinese toward their own presence in American society. Early anti-Chinese sentiments in California became national policy in racist legislative actions at a time when national immigration policies were based on quotas assigned to a country from which the emigrant applied. It was not until a decade and half after World War II that the Chinese were placed on the same basis as other countries for quotas. These past immigration laws, coming as they did from outside the community, created a population, in part, artificially determined. For example, immigrant men, who were used for cheap labor, could not bring in their wives or other females. Although a small number of women did, legally or illegally, enter the United States, they often became unwilling prostitutes for the Chinese laborers. Thus families could not be reunited; the normal succession of generations could not develop; and clan, district (depending upon area of origin in China), or tong (secret society) organizations became prominent in meeting the social, recreational, and economic-business needs of the early Chinese. The influence of these organizations can be seen in the many larger chinatowns throughout the United States.

The history of discrimination against the Chinese, coupled with the Civil Rights movement in the 1960's has sharpened the sensibility of many Chinese Americans as a minority group with similar experiences to those of Blacks, American Indians, and Hispanics in terms of prejudice, inaccurate or overgeneralized sterotypes, discrimination, etc. Indeed, many of the college students of the late 1960s attempted to organize Chinese communities against racism and to provide services for those in need. These events have also brought about issues concerning ethnic or racial identity as Chinese, Americans, Chinese Americans, Asian Americans, and non-White ethnics. The original sojourner sensibilities gave way to those of the marginalist, integrationalist, racial minority-pluralist, multiculturalist, or multistock Americanist. Indeed, it is not uncommon to find Chinese Americans who project different identities. These alternatives have been and will be shaped by the historical events. The U.S. restoration of relations to all of China, and the implied modifications of the social and political climate in China will strengthen the Chinese aspects of the racial-ethnic identity. Intermarriage leading to "disappearance" of the Chinese as a community will be balanced by new waves of immigrants.

Knowledge Building and Practices of Service Deliverers

Most of the discussion in this paper has been over historical events and the influence of these events in the dynamics of the Chinese American community. To fully understand the sensibilities of Chinese Americans, social scientists, in their quest for knowledge and intervention techniques, must move beyond narrow discipline orientations and appreciate developmental sequences.

The future of the Chinese American community will be affected by the range of factors in the proposed paradigm, with national and international events an important determinant. Immigration will play a substantial role in affecting the population base and social scientists and change agents will continue to be confronted with increasing diversity, different needs, and different sensibilities in the Chinese American community. Research and knowledge building must consider not only the past events, but also the international developments that affect the present and the future.

Modifications in service delivery practices should also consider Chinese American sensibilities. The traditional reluctance to use public service facilities is due in part to the long history of inadequate services provided by the government (both in China and the United States) for Chinese and in part to the use of Chinese American organizations. Now that the government has provided more adequate services and long-standing Chinese American associations have been unable to meet the changing needs, one can reasonably expect greater participation and demand for social services. In the process of offering services, nevertheless, rigid regulations and guidelines of the service delivery system and of funding agencies can hinder maximum utilization and effectiveness of such services. For example, many community mental health centers operate on a catchment area concept, in which a center serves a particular geographic community. Because of the special linguistic or cultural needs of some Chinese Americans, regulations must be flexible enough to allow clients to seek another center when the one in their catchment area cannot meet clients' needs.

Concluding Comments

In this paper, I have argued that social change, intervention, and knowledge can be enhanced if a more adequate paradigm for these activities is adopted. The paradigm proposed in this paper was intended to provide some tools and guidelines. One key concept was the notion of sensibility, which, although ill-defined at present, can serve as a beginning point for analyzing subjective experiences. While the main focus was on the Chinese American community, its history and dynamics, the notion of sensibility can be applied to other groups and communities.

References

Bloom, B. L. Community psychology: Midstream and middream. *American Journal of Community Psychology,* 1978, *6,* 205-217.

Brazziel, W. F. White research in black communities: When solutions become a part of the problem. *Journal of Social Issues, 1973, 29,* 41-44.

Heller, K., and Monahan, J. *Psychology and community change.* Homewood, Ill.: Dorsey, 1977.

Hsu, F. L. K. Psychosocial homeostasis and jen: Conceptual tools for advancing psychological anthropology. *American Anthropologist,* 1971, *73,* 23-44.

Kelly, J. G. 'Tain't what you do, it's the way that you do it. *American Journal of Community Psychology,* 1979, *7,* 244-261.

Montero, D. Research among racial and cultural minorities: An overview. *Journal of Social Issues,* 1977, *33,* 1-10.

Owan, T. Asian Americans: *A case of benighted neglect.* Paper presented at the National Conference of Social Welfare, San Francisco, May, 1975.

President's Commission on Mental Health. *Report to the President.* Washington, D.C.: U.S. Government Printing Office, 1978.

Rappaport, J. *Community psychology: Values, research, and action.* San Francisco: Holt, Rinehart and Winston, 1977.

Sue, S., and Kitano, H. Stereotypes as a measure of success. *Journal of Social Issues,* 1973, *29,* 83-98.

Urban Associates. *A study of selected socioeconomic characteristics based on the 1970 census. Vol. 2: Asian Americans.* Washington, D.C.: U.S. Government Printing Office, 1974.

Chapter 11

TRAINING COMMUNITY PSYCHOLOGISTS AND OTHER SOCIAL INTERVENTIONISTS
A Cultural Pluralistic Perspective

Thom Moore, Donna Nagata, Renee Whatley

As the concepts, functions and roles of applied psychology (primarily clinical psychology) tend to expand from diagnoses and individual treatment to the study of families, groups, organizations, and social systems, contemporary training programs must develop ideologies and curricula to reflect the new trends. In the last fifteen years, community psychology has experienced a degree of acceptance and respect in established applied psychology training programs. For instance, Barton, Andrulis, Grove, and Aponti (1976) report that course content relevant to community psychology and community mental health increased from less than 20 percent in 1962 to 69 percent in 1976 in training and internship programs. In addition, 50 psychology departments reported coverage of community psychology and community mental health topics in courses in 1970, while 141 reported coverage in 1976. The emergence and acceptance of community psychology has stimulated considerable thought regarding training issues (Heller and Monahan, 1977; Iscoe and Spielberger, 1970; Spielberger and Bloom, 1977; Rappaport, 1977). These developments indicate that community psychology has gained a foothold in curricula across the country. It also suggests that serious thought is given to training.

Social intervention, an endeavor to change or intervene, is influenced by factors of feasibility (resources), and paradigm choice. Change, as advocated here, is not a mere re-ordering of elements in a system (whether that system be a personality system, school, or community), rather the social interventionist is concerned with an absolute and relative change of greater and more lasting impact, a second-order change as described by

Watzlawick, Weakland, and Fisch (1974). For example, an exceedingly subtle, but problematic solution concerns the relationship and diagnostic formulations of acculturated therpists working with unacculturated clients. Notions of racism toward a specific cultural group are probably more crystallized and pervasive than any other attitudinal set in this society, and it is complicated by the condition of limited economic resources. Unfortunately cultural styles are viewed as an index of whether an individual or group should share in the resources of a society. The impact of such indices on the helping situation can be characterized as "no-help." It is well documented that people with limited economic resources are less likely to be accepted for outpatient treatment (Rogow, 1970; Schofield, 1964; Srole, et al., 1962), more likely to be diagnosed as schizophrenic and hospitalized (Hollingshead and Redlich, 1958), receive custodial care or drug therapy, have low probability of discharge, and have severe readjustment problems when released to the community setting and a high probability of rehospitalization (Meyers and Bean, 1968).

This paper is concerned with the role of the social interventionist in promoting and maintaining a pluralistic society. The term "social interventionist" is used here in place of "community psychologist" to include any trained professional who participates in society, either at the individual, group, community, or institutional level. Academic researchers, psychotherapists, program evaluators, and community organizers who value interventions will be considered under this category. Cultural pluralism is discussed as the ideological framework from which social interventionists should derive their methods and techniques. It is proposed that pluralism as a process, as opposed to an end-state, is applicable at multiple levels, thus raising significant questions regarding training.

THE INADEQUACY OF ASSIMILATION

Although an extensive discussion of pluralism and cultural pluralism has preceded this chapter (see introduction), it is worth restating that pluralism is an ideology that supports the rights of groups of things to be different within a common society. Cultural pluralism specifically suggests that cultural groups in a given "larger society" should be allowed, even encouraged, to retain their unique identity, along with their membership in that larger social framework.

Furthermore, recall that cultural pluralism represents an ideology, not a theory, since it is not openly acknowledged in this country. To fully understand what a pluralistic viewpoint can offer to the interventionist, it will be useful to examine the mode in which cultural diversity has been dealt with. The following brief discussion of assimilation will provide this background.

America is a country of immigrants. Peoples from all over the world have come to live here, some by choice, others not. Historically, and to this day, the predominant conceptualization of how this diversity was to be handled is called assimilation. Assimilation proposes that cultural, ethnic, and racial minorities minimize their differences and maximize their manifestations of characteristics of the established, normative society. Triandis (1976) refers to assimilation as a "policy of making each cultural group adopt the culture of the mainstream" (p. 1). Assimilation, then, opts for the existence of a mass culture as opposed to a plurality of cultures and has frequently been called the "Melting Pot" theory.

While assimilation has prevailed as the foundation on which the country's policies and practices have been based, evidence suggests it has not been entirely successful. Kopan (1974), in reviewing the historical and current context of assimilation, says: "The fact is that, in every generation throughout the history of the American Republic, the merging of varying streams of population, differentiated from one another in origin, religion, and outlook, has seemed to lie just ahead—a generation yet to come per-haps" (p. 49). . . . "the melting pot. . . simply failed to melt" (p. 53). Kopan cites factors such as prejudice, pride, politics, and a search for "cultural roots" that contributed to the failure of assimilation. Kopan's (1974) observations are similar with those of Gordon's (1964) who suggests that, while assimilation may have taken place within political, economic, and educational institutions for some, sub-societies of minority cultures have been maintained in the pluralistic institutions of religion, family, and recreation. These latter areas are described by Gordon as representing more "ethnically closed" network patterns.

On a more psychological level, assimilation can be viewed as prob-lematic. First, any mass culture robs individual subgroups of their uniqueness. Second, since mass culture has commonly been defined by "Whiteness, middle-classness, and maleness," cultures involving non-White people, lower socio-economic standing, and females are denied their importance in society and are asked to assimilate to standards which are virtually impossible to attain. The toll of this eventual "nonfit" between certain cultures and the normative standard is well illustrated by Ueda's (1974) description of the negative effects of assimilation on Japanese-Americans. Although Japanese-Americans are often pointed to as the "model minority group" or as being a "fully assimilated ethnic group," closer examination reveals that neither label holds true—"the ironic fact is that the Japanese has 'made it' only inasmuch as he/she has been able to fabricate an artificial and ingeniously contrived definition of self that con-forms with philistine values in American society and that conceals the social turmoil and psychic suffering of the life he [sic] has led in this country" (p. 72). A major problem with the assimilation model is that it does not offer any practical mechanisms by which cultures are to come together and melt. Power, economics, physical, and individual differences all present realistic barriers. These easily observable differences, along with other less obvious ones, such as cultural pride and cultural networks, depict resources not for a mass culture, but for something else. If the bulk of assimilation effects are viewed as negative, and its hope for realization slim, what is an alternative?

CULTURAL PLURALISM — AN ALTERNATIVE

The pluralistic approach to multiple cultures in the same society can be seen as more constructive than the assimilative approach on several levels. It has direct implications for individuals, ethnic communities, and institutions, as well as for professionals. Presented here are just a few of the possibilities pluralism offers.

On an individual level, pluralism has a clear role in promoting acceptance of individual differences and how these differences are to be interpreted. Cultural preferences would be viewed not as deficits, but as assets. As Valentine (1971) points out, cultural variability with respect to certain skills (e.g., educational) should not be viewed as either deficit, or even as simply cultural difference (Baratz and Baratz, 1970), but rather as evidence of biculturality, an asset. Thus, there do not exist numbers of non-majority marginal individuals who lack skills in coping with the mass culture. What exists are numbers of individuals who experience two cultures. Triandis (1976), advances that the existence and experiencing of multiple cultures is something toward which pluralism should strive, and uses the words "additive multi-culturalism" to describe this end. A culturally pluralistic society, then, would foster this atmosphere of positive, not negative, differences. Research (Clark and Clark, 1947; Rosenberg and Simon, 1971; Kardiner and Ovesey, 1951; Hare, 1965) supports this important link between societal standards and self-esteem, not only for groups, but also for individuals.

On a group level, pluralism could conceivably allow various cultural groups to feel free to display their differences and share them without fear of rejection. Previously quelled expressions of interest in one's cultural group may begin to emerge and the possibilities for increases in both inter- and intra-cultural group communication and support. Groups could then learn and exchange each other's differences and similarities.

Pluralism would also have positive implications for institutions such as schools. Students who had previously been labeled disadvantaged and blamed for their difference might then be viewed as possessing positive characteristics never before tapped. "Blaming the victim" (Ryan, 1976) strategies would be more difficult to carry out if cultural pluralism were indeed a *functional* philosophy in the schools.

For many organizations and institutions, policy decisions are both necessary and desirable. The input of all cultural groups involved would have direct effect on policy making. Taking into account this diverse cultural input would make it more difficult to develop policies that are sensitive only to a single cultural group. Rather than being restricted to a general and normative outcome, decision makers could begin to engage creative alternatives utilizing a mixture of input. As Naroll, Benjamin, Fohl, Fried, Hildreth, and Schaefer (1971) have mentioned, the great civilizations of the past have been characterized by a harnessing of heterogeneity rather than ignoring or dissolving it.

The above points are just a few of the potentially positive influences of pluralism for society. But it must also be realized that the value-laden nature of cultural pluralism presents areas of concern that are less clearly defined. Berkson (1920) pointed out the potential problems involved and raises an important ethical and political issue: while cultural pluralism may be democratic for groups, how democratic is it for the individual? This chapter does not advocate a pluralism that would deny the individual of his or her right to independence from a group. What *is* advocated is that the social interventionist be aware of and open to diversities within, as well as between, cultural groups.

Consequently, the social interventionist must understand and take seriously the description "social." That is, there must be an appreciation of the power of the human will and its influence on structuring the social environment. Here, there is a need to acknowledge an underlying tension that exists between individual independence and interdependence, because existing social structures reflect our attempts at satisfying these tensions. Implied also is that the source of these tensions is the availability and use of psychological and physical resources. Social change refers to how we go about reducing such tensions, creating systems and changing.

In the process of social change, however, the destination is vague, elusive, and often unknown. One can hardly do better than to contemplate a paraphrase of the earlier quote of Rein: "Values. . .constitute the network which helps us organize. . .And they are crucial for any creative work; for without them we have no question to ask" (p.14). The creative works of people have resulted in various ways of looking at similar problems, they account for cultures, and cultures are the symbolic presentation of our values. Thus the social interventionist should be trained to maximize pluralism.

TRAINING CONCERNS

Just what can be expected from programs designed to train social interventionists with a cultural pluralistic orientation? One of the first ground rules a program must establish is that culture should not be treated as an invariant predeterminant of behavior. While it is recognized that behavioral predictions are possible based on cultural membership, this is not to suggest that each individual will perform according to the cultural rules. Argyle (1969), in discussing the personality structure of members of two cultures, says that the difference within either population will be greater than any difference between them. Thus, the recognition that cultural pluralism is an ideology that appreciates differences.

TRAINING RATIONALE

There are numerous aspects of our discipline to which its form and structure must be continually attuned, i.e., the acknowledgement that the discipline develop a knowledge base that is subjected to periodic evaluation (Reiff, 1970; Sarason, 1972). More recently, Trickett and Lustman (1977), reporting on the Austin Conference, observed that knowledge in our profession enjoys a dual role of "coequal status": (a) knowledge for understanding; and (b) knowledge for effective action. It is this dual role that tends to frustrate the implementation of training programs; having *one* program to do both things requires creative, insightful, strong, and committed people. Training programs for social interventionists have to face the fact that there is a shortage of knowledge in the form of research activities that yield methodology, specific analytical procedures, or effective interventions. Consequently, to be effective as a science and to progress, there must be a development of expertise characterized by concepts, research skills, empirical data, and meaningful change in techniques and strategies.

Presently, community psychology and other social intervention training programs have no choice but to adopt the spirit, reminiscent of the Boulder training model, to prepare individuals who will seek knowledge through research and become involved in the application of the knowledge. The advantage of this position is that knowledge is treated as functional beyond its intrinsic value of understanding, and the significance of adding application is to enhance its validity and reliability. As interesting discoveries and successful interventions into the human condition are experienced, the relationship between knowledge and application will become apparent. For clinical psychology, the Boulder training model has been attacked (represented by the professional training school) because of the practical difficulties individuals have experienced in assuming a role involving two time consuming activities. This is not sufficient reason to ignore the crucial role of such a training model.

NEED FOR THE KNOWLEDGE OF CULTURES

With cultural pluralism being the significant concept to the social interventionist, the Boulder training model becomes imperative. The interventionist must know how to gather information; therefore methodology is likely to be more important than content. A methodology is the tool used to discover and compare cultural differences, and these differences are a dynamic force in the society at large.

Being unaware of cultural differences is likely to result, for the social interventionist, in the same problems anthropologists experienced before they realized that cultural data was subject to differential interpretation (emic and etic).

As advocates for a specific culture, the social interventionists' interpretations will potentially have a significant impact on the lives of others. Several writers (Baratz and Baratz, 1970; Greenfield, 1973; Rist, 1970; Ryan, 1976; and Valentine, 1971) have spoken to the effect of developing theories about individuals, organizations, and cultures from an outsider's perspective. Greenfield directly speaks to interpretations as they are applied to theorizing about organizations (particularly schools). He says:

> In abandoning received theories about organizations in general and about schools in particular, we will have to look to a new kind of research—one that builds theory from the data rather than one that selects data to confirm theories developed apart from the data. This requirement directs us to theory built from observation in specific organizations; it directs us as well to understanding the actions, purposes and experiences of organizational members in terms that make sense of them.

Baratz and Baratz (1970) criticize social scientists for adopting models that ignore the significant role culture plays in the socialization process. These models have led the social scientists to think, for example, of Black Americans in a manner which is detrimental to them. The essence of Baratz and Baratz's argument has been succinctly stated as follows:

> Social science has refused to look beyond the surface similarities between Negro and white behavior and, therefore, has dismissed the idea of subtle yet enduring differences. In the absence of ethno-

historical perspective, when differences appear in behavior, intelligence or cognition, they are explained as evidence of genetic defects or as evidence of the negative effects of slavery, poverty and discrimination (p. 32).

As a further example, they cite the current position of language acquisition, which is assumed to be a measure of intelligence. However, the only language accepted as the norm is standard English, and any other linguistic form is judged as inferior and demanding less intelligence to master. It logically follows that children speaking non-standard English are less intelligent. The policy consequences of this model have been early childhood education like Headstart which further reinforces the notion of genetic or environmental inferiority. Often, these programs fail because they ignore the current functioning, attitudes, norms, values, beliefs, and expectations of the sub-culture. Baratz and Baratz propose that we adopt a technique of describing different normative configurations in our society, rather than looking for deviation from normative behavior.

Valentine (1971), an anthropologist, has made a case for biculturation: that is, people can be simultaneously enculturated and socialized in two different ways of life—a contemporary form of their traditional (Afro-American, Native American, Mexican American, Asian American) lifeways and mainstream Euro-American culture. One of his major points in support of social interventionists adopting a bicultural orientation is that the dominant cultural explanation (etic) of the behavior of minority children has resulted in these children being identified as deficient. He cites a case study in which he was told by a psychiatrist "that what goes on in the home or community is totally irrelevant to the problems of diagnosis and disposition: medical diagnosis and therapy are determined strictly within the clinical setting without consideration of extraneous data from the outside world." Valentine discovered that his subject (client) looked entirely different in his home culture than the image the institutional specialists had of him. He suggests that a professional acquainted with both the dominant and the racial or ethnic minority culture would deliver more appropriate service.

It is clear then that when the etic oriented interpretations of behavior are manifested as cited in the above examples, a single standard of culture will be promoted above the standard of cultural pluralism. Even more disturbing, the preferred cultural standard becomes oppressive by rejecting differences. The social interventionist must learn that different behaviors corresponding to cultural styles do not represent a collapse of the society. Further, he or she is to become knowledgeable about particular cultures and work for their acceptance by the general population. Greenfield (1973) describes organizations as social inventions and, in discussing change (intervention) in a school setting, he says "... that we must begin to understand more thoroughly and deeply the varieties of experience people have in organizations we call schools, and we must not limit the experiences studied to those of particular groups." In essence this same notion of understanding applies to the social interventionist if she or he intends to be effective.

The idea that effective treatment requires an understanding of the client's environment and experience does not originate solely with the cultural pluralistic notions espoused herein. Others (Sager, 1972; Jones and Seagull, 1977; Wilson, 1971) have expressed similar concerns throughout the literature, based simply on principles of adequate helping techniques. In a recent paper, Jones and Seagull (1977) make several suggestions for traditional therapists working with culturally different clients, and we would contend that the same suggestions are relevant to any intervention-change effort. Paraphrased, Jones and Seagull assert that the therapists should (a) seriously indulge in an introspective analysis of their own irrational feelings and stereotypical notions regarding the cultural group of which their client is a member, (b) openly acknowledge the difference within the helping situation, (c) expose themselves to literature about the culture of the client, and (d) accept their own fallibility with "...wry humor and some grade." Our conceptualization endorses those suggestions and extends them to include the utilization of knowledge obtained through a variety of sources (i.e., consultant-type resource persons, significant others, literature reviews), to ascertain the culture-specific norms that guide and shape the client's behavior, to reconceptualize individual strengths based on those norms, and to consider, as possible diagnostic hypotheses, issues of culture-clash and cultural dis-continuities as contributing elements to presenting problems. Whether the solution to the problem is addressed individually or institutionally, in a helper, protest, or revolutionary mode, it would be essential to determine:

a. What is the cultural meaning of seeking help from "outsiders" for each individual cultural group,

b. What elements in the service delivery support, contradict, or denigrate specific values or beliefs of the groups it is the system's mandate to serve.

Another role, in addition to the previously discussed helper roles, a social interventionist might take is that of an advocate. An advocacy role is based on a protest. An advocate essentially represents the interests of individuals or collectives of whatever size and seeks to assure their needs be met (Davidson and Rapp, 1976). An adequate understanding of the cultural boundaries of the client or client group, as well as that of the target person or organization is essential to the representativeness of the advocacy effort and its efficiency. In any advocacy effort, an initial determination of needs is essential. That the nature of the need and the form of the proposed solution may vary as a function of cultural variables seems obvious. Yet advocates often tend to shape strategies and tactics based solely on dimensions of the problem. A specific example may serve to illustrate the potential value of the perspective in shaping tactics. Radzialowski (1974), in his discussion of Polish-Americans, discloses the nature of the relationship between land (home) ownership and self-esteem for that culture. He explains the fact that 70-80 percent of Polish-Amerians own their own homes because:

> They brought with them from the village of the Polish Plain not only the land hunger of peasants from an area suffering from overpopulation and land shortage but also the precapitalist notion that land is the most important component of status. A man was entitled to take his place as a full fledged member of the community only when he was a householder...The words "on rent" are still said today in a very contemptuous way (p. 134).

Given this cultural definition of home ownership, for instance, it would be inappropriate to advocate the alleviation of a housing shortage in a predominantly Polish neighborhood simply through the building of apartment complexes, since (although it may resolve the problem objectively defined as the unavailability of sufficient living space) the strength of the unintended consequences may make the effort counter productive.

It is not our intention to suggest that every intervention effort must be guided by cultural variables. A diversity of cultures, however, makes uniform solutions ineffective and change agents must give cultural variables serious consideration in program design and implementation.

The question of sufficient knowledge of culture-specific norms leads us to consider an additional role for the social interventionist: namely, the necessity to form linkages with those people who are specialists in cultural norms and to routinely utilize their storehouse of knowledge. Prime candidates for such resource people are cultural anthropologists and urban sociologists who devote a substantial portion of their time observing distinct cultural/ethnic groups, determining normative behavior patterns, as well as hypothesizing the functions of those behaviors within the delimited cultural setting. It would be unrealistic to expect that all helpers know all things about all peoples, but it would not be unrealistic to expect that all helpers seek available information from reliable sources to make an accurate assessment of when, where, and how cultural variables influence client identified, problematic behaviors.

CURRICULUM SPECIFICS

Once agreed that a culturally pluralistic society is valued and that social interventionists will work to that end, the training program must provide theory, research, and methods for the student. The criterion for training is based on the role that the interventionist will perform in the community (helper, advocate, protester, revolutionary) and the social level at which it will enter (individual/family, group, organization/institution, community). Furthermore, the overall conceptual perspective will be the community strength one (Berck, 1976; Rappaport, Davidson, Wilson and Mitchell, 1975). A matrix could be constructed with the role of the interventionist at the top and the level of intervention along the side. Filling each cell would force the trainer to ask such questions as: What do psychology and other social sciences know about a particular interventionist role? What is known about the populations (attitudes, norms, beliefs, etc.) of a particular level of the society? What is known about the interaction of a role and an intervention level? Finally, what can we learn about each? Any program should continually stress the use of existing information and the importance of generating new information.

An often unspoken task for the training program is to establish for the social interventionist a sense of how her or his own background and training will interact with the values, ideas, knowledge, and beliefs of the culture in which he or she has chosen to work. If social interventions are to be successful in changing people's lives in a meaningful way, then it seems reasonable for associated research to contain an interpersonal-knowledge component, i.e., a plan to obtain knowledge about how individuals and cultures interact with others, and essentially, "where they are coming from." For example, Moore (1975) has demonstrated with teen-agers that, on an individual basis, people can be taught to simulate the responses of a cross-racial counterpart on a personality questionnaire. The implications of this study are that racial stereotypes may be broken down by a process of attention and that individuals *can* learn about members of other cultures. The technique can facilitate cross-cultural learning and should be utilized in preparing social interventionists to better understand racial and ethnic minorities. As the experience of being a minority is communicated and grasped by professionals, they can more effectively match up their skills to the needs of the community.

Triandis (1976) has reported extensive work in developing a technique (cultural and assimilatory) for organizations in which inter-racial employees learn how to relate more effectively with each other. Although the actual training procedure is interesting, the development of the technique is presently more important for the purposes of this paper. From

Triandis' perspective, the key to interpersonal behavior in inter-racial groups is the subjective culture, which is defined as the norms, roles, attitudes, values, and many other concepts of individuals and cultures. The technique he employed to design the cultural assimilator is one a social intervention program can adopt for research training purposes, and for individual training in understanding of cultural differences. He established the existing differences between Blacks' and Whites' perceptions of the social environment by asking a sample of White middle class college females, White lower class high school males and Black lower class hardcore unemployed males to make 5,600 judgements of various social stimuli. This technique tends to yield rich data regarding the differences in groups and could serve as a procedure to acquaint students with members of various cultures, while providing insightful data about the culture. The actual cultural assimilator forces *observers* of cultures to begin to think more like the *actors* of the culture. A function of the training program should be to make the trainees come face to face with cultural differences and introduce them to a method to systematically identify specific differences. It is understood that not everyone can collect and utilize 5,600 judgements within the short frame of a training experience, but some paring down of stimuli and judgements would result in a manageable training tool. A trainee may apply the method to collect data on the goals and aspirations of minorities and develop social interventions that focus on their responses.

Training programs will need to concentrate on field placements where the student is first a participant observer and not a service deliverer. Rist (1970) reported his experience as an observer in an elementary school class-room, and categorized the subtle and often ignored behavior and inter-actions of children and teachers. He approached his subject (the school system) in the way that Greenfield (1973) has identified (free of precon-ceived ideas of the dimensions of the setting). Just entering a system as an observer does not, however, guarantee that etic interpretations will not be made. On the other hand, all etic interpretations are not necessarily bad, but if one can become an observer and a participant, the chances of making both (etic and emic) types of interpretations over just the etic are increased. Furthermore, observing groups, settings, communities, and cultures should confirm certain existing hypotheses, suggest new ones, and destroy old ones.

Finally, the technique of social-historical analysis should become a major data collection method for social intervention. Reppucci and Saunders (1977) has identified the need for an historical understanding of settings and institutions:

> As the field of community psychology has developed, psychologists
> have expended [sic] their applied role beyond that of individual change

agent to institutional change agent, creator of alternative settings and social policy consultant and advocate. Since the goal of such interventions is usually to change institutions of society, one ill advised change may have adverse effects for large numbers of individuals. As a result, the deficiencies of a restricted historical perspective have become more costly.

Reppucci's comments hold the same significance for communities as they do for institutions and other settings.

Because a pluralistic paradigm requires new types of knowledge generally ignored by social interventionists, new methods of obtaining that knowledge may be necessary. The social interventionists will benefit by utilizing as many forms of assessment as possible. From anthropology, such methods as participant observation and ethnography yield useful descriptive data directly important for the implication of social change (Spradley and McCurdy, 1972). Survey techniques from sociology can also provide valuable information, as can intra-psychic measures from psychology, and studies of urban planning from architecture. Research, in the cultural pluralistic paradigm should be multi-disciplinary, and, itself, be characterized by a pluralistic attitude.

It should be mentioned, however, that the interdisciplinary research may have its pitfalls. The social interventionist must carefully select and define his or her terms and concepts. Back, Bunker, and Dunnagan (1972) found that, in a discussion group examining the relationship of "science and society," those who had shared meanings of key words like "model" were able to communicate with each other and remained together, while those with different meanings became frustrated and soon left the group. The social interventionist will quite likely come across these terms and others that will need clarification when attempting to use cross-disciplinary research tools. Kelly (1970) uses a concept that could be useful for researchers in this area. He discusses empathic listening as distinctive from deliberative hearing. Deliberative hearing is an ability to hear information, analyze it, and recall it. Empathic listening, however, occurs only when a listener participates in the "spirit" or feeling of the environment of a message. Researchers should strive to develop this empathic form of listening in their dealings both with other disciplines and with the various cultures they are researching. In the language of more traditional experimental social science, it is necessary that the investigator know his or her subjects as well as possible to develop the most effective study. Otherwise, as Campbell (1964) has pointed out, when differences between subject and investigator are great, and if the extent of these differences are unknown, differences in the data are also uninterpretable.

USE OF RESOURCES

Finally, a major issue for community psychology training programs is in-house. We must reconsider training people for intervening in ethnic and racial minority communities. The problem of reconsideration is raised because many of the programs now in existence express an interventionist philosophy, but have not developed training programs unique for these communities. In addition, implicit in this intervention orientation is a set of actions that demand that the interventionists enter numerous settings in various communities, ranging from formal social institutions (schools, jails, hospitals, etc.) and social systems (education, criminal, justice, health, and government) to informal settings (neighborhoods, churches, stores, etc.). Training people to intervene in the human condition of these communities demands that program resources be managed differently. For instance, a commitment to community *work* differs from a commitment to traditional research. That is, a university calendar is designed for nine to ten months and interspersed with numerous vacation days. Consequently, all resources, but primarily time, are distributed in accordance with the school calendar. Communities, however, do not function within the same schedule as universities. They demand a great deal of time, which, when taken away from department and program responsibilities, leads to internal staff conflicts. The summer time always places any community work in jeopardy, because the personnel (students and faculty) tends to be unavailable. More directly, when inroads into a community have been made, they cannot be maintained unless continued attention is paid to them. For example, a project designed to reduce juveniles' contact with police by providing undergraduate advocates for the juvenile will create a demand when the project becomes successful. But to become successful, students and supervising faculty must be available at all times, even when the university or college is not in session. The need and demand for the project created by its success becomes a second generation problem for the training program. Again, unlike traditional research, intervening in community settings does not lend itself to easy entry and exit. Departments and training programs must be sensitive to the long-term commitment associated with community training and understand the problem of allocating and retrieving resources. This problem of allocating and retrieving resources is common to all training programs, but it is unique for community psychology because of its service aspects. Each training program must seriously examine for itself the ramifications of program training directions. Within the institution, any decision will have direct bearing on the department training program and the individuals involved. However, once program personnel recognize associated problems, they are in a better position to relate to other issues in the training program.

A closing word of caution is in order here. Social intervention is an exercise in paradox; it deals with the relative nature of human behavior. Its focus is on the creation of social systems that promote belonging and interdependence, while allowing for uniqueness. Another goal is to bring about change that creates stability. The outcomes of the efforts of a social interventionist tend more to being frustrating than glamorous. Programs have a responsibility to make this known to their students and thus be highly selective.

REFERENCES

Argyle, M. *Social interaction.* New York: Atherton Press, 1969.

Back, K.W.S., Brinker, S., and Dunnagan, C.B. Barriers to communication and measurement of semantic space. *Sociometry,* 1972, *35,* 247-356.

Baratz, S.S., and Baratz, J.C. Early childhood intervention: The social science base of institutional racism. *Harvard Educational Review,* 1970, *1,* 29-50.

Barton, A.K., Andrulis, D.P., Grove, W.P., and Aponte, J.F. A look at community psychology training programs in the seventies. *American Journal of Community Psychology,* 1976, *4,* 1-11.

Berck, P. *Building community strength: A model for conceptualizing and implementing social change.* Unpublished manuscript, University of Illinois at Urbana-Champaign, 1976.

Berkson, I.B. *Theories of Americanization.* Teacher's College of Columbia University: New York Bureau of Publications, 1920.

Campbell, D.T. Distinguishing differences in perception from failures of communication in cross-cultural studies. In P.S.C. Northrop and H.H. Livingston (eds.), *Cross-cultural understanding: Epistemology in anthropology,* New York: Harper & Row, 1964.

Clark, K., and Clark, M. Racial identification and preference in Negro children. In T.M. Newcomb and E.L. Hartley (eds.), *Readings in the social psychology of education.* New York: Holt, Rinehart, & Winston, 1947.

Gordon, M. *Assimilation in American life.* New York: Oxford University Press, 1964.

Greenfield, T.B. Organizations as social inventions: Rethinking assumptions about change. *Journal of Applied Behavioral Science,* 1973, *5,* 551-574.

Heller, K. and Monahan, J. *Psychology and Community Change.* Homewood, Illinois, Dorsey Press, 1977.

Hollingshead, A.B. and Redlich, F.C. *Social class and mental illness: A community study.* New York: Wiley 1958.

Iscoe, I., and Spielberger, C.D. *Community psychology: Perspective in training and research.* New York: Appleton-Century-Crofts, 1970.

Jones, A., and Seagull, A. Dimensions of the relationship between the black client and the white therapist: A theoretical overview. *American Psychologist,* 1977, *32,* 850-855.

Kardiner, A., and Ovesey, L. *The mark of oppression: A psychological study of the American Negro.* New York: Norton, 1951.

Kelly, C.M. Empathic listening. In Robert S. Cathcart and Larry A. Samovar (eds.), *Small group communication: A reader.* Dubuque, Iowa: William C. Brown Pub., 1970.

Kopan, A.T. Melting pot: Myth or reality? In E.G. Epps (ed.), *Cultural pluralism.* Berkeley: McCutchan Pub. Co., 1974.

Meyers, J., and Bean, L.L. *A decade later: A follow-up of social class and mental illness.* New York: Wiley, 1967.

Moore, T.L., and Baltes, P.B. Training of white adolescents to accurately simulate black adolescent personality. *Adolescence,* 1975, *38,* 231-239.

Naroll, R., Benjamin, E.C., Fohl, F.K., Fried, M.J., Hildreth, R.E., Schaefer, J.M. Creativity—a cross historical pilot survey. *Journal of Cross-Cultural Research,* 1971, *2,* 191-198.

Radzialowski, R. A view from a Polish ghetto: Some observations on the first 100 years in Detroit. *Ethnicity,* 1974, *1,* 125-150.

Rappaport, J. From Moah to Babel: Relationships between conceptions, values, analysis levels and social intervention strategies. In I. Iscoe, B. Bloom, and C.D. Spielberger (eds.), *Community psychology in transition.* New York: Hemisphere Press, 1977.

Rappaport, J., Davidson, W.S., Wilson, M.N. and Mitchell, A. Alternatives to blaming the victim or the environment: Our places to stand have not moved the earth. *American Psychologist,* 1975, *4,* 523-528.

Reiff, R. The need for a body of knowledge in community psychology. In I. Iscoe, and C.D. Spielberger (eds.), *Community psychology: Perspectives in training and research.* New York: Appelton-Century-Crofts, 1970.

Rein, M. *Social science and public policy.* New York: Penguin Books, Ltd., 1976.

Reppucci, N.D., and Saunders, J.T. History, action and change. *American Journal of Community Psychology,* 1977, *4,* 399-412.

Rist, R.C. Student social class and teacher expectations: The self-fulfilling prophecy in ghetto education. *Harvard Education Review,* 1970, *3,* 411-451.

Rogow, A.A. *The psychiatrist.* New York: G.P. Putnam & Sons, 1970.

Rosenberg, J., and Simmons, R. *Black and White self esteem: The urban school child.* Washington D.C.: American Sociological Association, 1971.

Ryan W. *Blaming the victim.* New York: Vintage Books, 1976.

Sager, C.J., Brayboy, T.L., and Waxenberg, B.R. Black patient—white therapist *American Journal of Orthopsychiatry,* 1972, *42,* 415-423.

Sarason, S.B. *The creation of settings in the future societies.* San Francisco, Jossey-Bass, 1972.

Schofield, W. *Psychotherapy: The purchase of friendship.* Englewood Cliffs, N.J.: Prentice Hall, 1964.

Srole, L. *Mental health in the metropolis: The midtown Manhattan study* (Vol. 1). New York: McGraw Hill, 1962.

Spardley, J.P., and McCurdy, D.W. *The cultural experience: Ethnography in a complex society.* Chicago: Science Research Associates, Inc., 1972.

Triandis, H.C. *The analysis of subjective culture.* New York: John Wiley and Sons, 1972.

Triandis, J.C. (ed.) *Variations in black and white perceptions of the social environment.* Urbana, Ill.: University of Illinois Press, 1976.

Trickett, E.J., and Lustman, N.M. Research, knowledge and professional growth. In I. Iscoe, B. Bloom and C. Spielberger (eds.), *Community psychology in transition.* Washington, D.C.: Hemisphere Pub. Co., 1977.

Ueda, R. The Americanization and education of Japanese-Americans—a psychodramatic and dramaturgical perspective. In E.G. Epps (ed.), *Cultural Pluralism,* Berkeley, W.: Cutchan Pub. Co., 1974.

Valentine, C.A. Deficit, difference and bicultural models of Afro-American behavior. *Harvard Educational Review,* 1971, *2,* 137-157.

Watzlawick, P., Weakland, J.H., and Fisch, R. *Change: Principles of Problem formation and problem resolution,* New York: Norton, 1974.

Wilson, M.E. The significance of communication in counseling the culturally disadvantaged. In R. Wilcox (ed.), *The psychological consequences of being a black American.* New York: Wiley, 1971.

Chapter 12

COMMUNITY MENTAL HEALTH IN A DUAL SOCIETY

Bernard M. Kramer

The purpose of this paper is to focus attention on minority relations in the context of the community mental health movement. The civil rights movement in the United States has been one of the very most significant developments of the twentieth century. Likewise, the community mental health movement has been a significant part of a larger thrust to provide human services to people in need. Both movements have shared a spiritual movement and moral concern for justice and a wish to care for our sisters and brothers. Yet their goals and programs have not brought the two movements together. Indeed, as we shall see, they may come into conflict with each other. We begin, therefore, by examining the nature of minority relations and community mental health to highlight potential points of stress, as well as harmony, between the movement to further minority progress, on the one hand, and the movement to advance the cause of mental health, on the other.

The terms, "minority relations" and "minority progress" call forth a variety of meanings and issues. Above all, however, they lead us to think about the tragic oppression of Black and other minority groups at the hand of the dominant majority of White population in the United States. Slavery was the central, decisive historic force shaping the present framework of race relations. Today's Black Americans are, after all, the descendants of yesterday's slaves. Not long after their forefathers were freed as an outcome of the Civil War, a failure of accomplishment occurred: The goal of full freedom and full equality was sidestepped and a system of segregation and discrimination was put into place as a moral equivalent of slavery.

Efforts of the Civil Rights movement in this century have yielded noteworthy, but limited, progress. In their daily existence, Blacks live in a world separate from, parallel with, and unequal to that in which Whites live (Blackwell, 1975; U.S. National Advisory Commission on Civil Disorders, 1968.). When we add to the picture other minority groups, such as Hispanic Americans, Native American Indians, and Asian Americans, we can characterize American minority relations in blunt terms—White Euro-Americans are at the top and Blacks are at the bottom.

White Euro-Americans may be thought of as a Herronvolk who reap the benefits of what is for them a highly productive democratic system (Van den Berghe, 1978); Afro-Americans and third world Americans may be thought of as pariahs excluded from full participation in the process and results of that system. Contrary to the melioristic title of this volume, we have not a pluralistic society, but a dual society.

In common usage, the term "pluralistic society" connotes that subcultural groups of differing origins have fairly equal standing as respected and contributing parts of the nation and draw accordingly on its resources. For many segments of American society, this condition indeed prevails, and the concept of pluralism is, therefore, an apt representation of reality. But no one willing to use the simplest powers of observation can fail to see that Blacks and third world minorities occupy an inferior position in the American scheme of things. In constitutional terms, they are equal. Their place of residence, however, is separate and inferior, as is their place in the political, cultural, economic, and occupational scheme of things. The prevailing relation of superordination/subordination is, therefore, best embraced by the term dual society; one segment exercises hegemony over another, based on differences in color and origin. This produces derogatory stereotypes and attitudes that correspond with and support that hegemony. These activities signal the existence not of a pluralistic society, but a dual society.

The distinction between dualism and pluralism is not merely a fine point of argument. It goes instead to the very heart of a crucial question facing American society: Can we become a truly democratic, egalitarian, indivisible nation? If the division between Black and White is permanent, then the nominal language of our constitution can never truly reflect our national condition. No amount of written law can totally undo the force of understandings that govern relations between the races. If the division is permanent, there is no hope; if not, the optimist has room. A dynamic conception of our society admits the possibility of change and permits us to consider how to move from a dual and separated national community to a pluralistic and integrated one.

Without doubt, there is a large scale national aspect to the question of how we may proceed from division to unification. The victory of the Union over the Confederacy in the American Civil War is an example of a country-wide struggle to resolve the issue. Likewise, events surrounding the Supreme Court's historic decision against racial segregation in *Brown vs. Board of Education* represent macro-level action aimed at fulfilling a national goal of equality. There is, however, also a local aspect to change and stasis. That is to say, arrangements in local communities contribute a great deal to the shape of society and the ultimate disposition of sub-groups within that society. The assertion of states rights, for example, is a sharp reminder of the fragility of federal solutions when local opposition is at work. Nullification and interposition exemplify potential avenues through which the enormous power of local veto groups may be expressed. Wittingly or unwittingly programs, at the local level may act favorably or unfavorably upon our capacity to form a respectful, pluralistic society.

One of the significant community oriented programs of our time is the set of concepts and practices spawned by the community mental health movement. That movement and its associated programs emerged from a number of trends, beginning as early as the first half of the nineteenth century and as late as the period following the second World War. Perhaps the single most important proximal factor contributing to the growth of the community mental health movement was the recognition of and revulsion against the cruel indignities heaped on patients in the nation's mental hospitals.

"Snake Pit" became part of our vocabulary of indignation. Albert Deutsch brought his angry condemnation to national attention in his land-mark book, "The Shame of the States" (Deutsch, 1948). Part of the moral outrage had to do with the sheer mistreatment of victimized human beings. In this respect, the mental health movement holds something in common with the anti-slavery and civil rights movements. Another part of the outrage, however, had to do with the hugeness of the institutions involved. State hospitals, with as many as 12,000 locked up patients, evoked images of mindless bureaucrats and vast human warehouses. Sheer size became an issue.

By the middle of the 1950's, Bockoven (1956) helped recall the moral treatment era of the 1830s and 1840s, during which emphasis was placed on small facilities in which personal attention and human sympathy prevailed as therapeutic doctrine. Drawing on experience in small units, such as the Massachusetts Mental Health Center, Greenblatt, York, and Brown (1955) hinted at the size critique in the very title of their book, "From Custodial to Therapeutic Care." In his Presidential address at the 1958 meeting of The American Psychiatric Association, Harry C. Solomon proposed that large state mental hospitals be abolished.

By this time, the open door philosophy and the availability of psycho-tropic drugs made possible a wide range of out-of-hospital, community oriented programs. Day hospitals, night hospitals, halfway houses, foster care programs, home treatments services, ex-patient clubs, and patient government were all expressions of the new approach to mental health and illness. The report of the Joint Commission on Mental Illness and Health (1961) helped galvanize Congressional passage of the Community Mental Health Centers Act of 1963. Under its terms, federal support was made available to establish, and later to staff, a national network of locally based mental health centers.

The new mental health centers were to exercise local initiative and to be small in size. These two features provide us with a starting point for thinking about the relation between the community mental health move-ment and the civil rights movement. Tensions between a pluralistic and dual society may be studied by examining the implication for minority groups of the localism and smallness implicit in current conceptions of the community mental health center.

Localism and smallness appeal to many people who yearn for a sense of community missing in modern society with its industrialism, bureau-cracy, and coldness. Individuals holding widely differing political positions share the view that human services are potentially more humane and responsive if organized, administered, and controlled at the local com-munity level, rather than at the national level, with its built-in tendency to be distant and impersonal. This article of faith flows naturally from a deep-lying distrust of the urban metropolis, where sin, vice, and corruption are thought to prevail. Central government and corporate power, in this view, are fellow travellers of the evil city. Even those who prefer to live in cities adhere to an anticentralist position, praising the virtues of local residential neighborhoods as against the over-powering "downtown." The quest for a sense of community is at once anti-urban, anti-centralist, and anti-industrial. These tendencies feed into the new ethnic revival that has blos-somed forth in the last ten to fifteen years. In turn, the new ethnicity has also fuelled the contemporary search for community.

The romantically tinged search, however, does not occur in a socio-economic vacuum. The main, decisive forces at work in contemporary society are indeed found within those very large-scale institutions and organizations that shape our lives and fates. Those factories, farms, mines, and mills producing goods that people want and use also provide the jobs and wages that people must have to live in our money-based economy. While the localist impulse plays itself out in the small details of daily life, the corporate scheme dominates the entire economy and governs the boundaries within which our lives are contained. Human services, there-fore, may be viewed simultaneously as expressions of the small scale of community existence and as results of large scale industrial society. Agencies concerned with providing human services find themselves, perforce, in the middle of the tension between these two scales of action. As facilities are built and organized to house these services, there is an inevitable tug-of-war between the idea of self-sufficient, segregated geo-ethnic units, and that of state-supported, universalistic, integrated structures.

Let us examine how this tug-of-war reveals itself in mental health centers located in urban and suburban areas. Of prime importance is the concept of relatively small residential catchment areas, for which each mental health center assumes responsibility. This concept came into recent vogue, partly because of its appeal to epidemiological sense: each geographic area provides a well defined denominator against which episodes of illness and indicators of health may be projected to gain insight into incidence and prevalence rates. Perhaps more important, however, is its potential for coordinating hitherto fragmented services into a coherent pattern for defined populations.

Since urban and suburban populations in the United Sttaes are firmly marked along class and ethnic lines, mental health centers organized on geographic lines will be significantly influenced by the class and ethnic characteristics of catchment areas they are designed to serve. This brings us to a central dilemma to which this paper is addressed, i.e., should mental health centers follow ethnic considerations in order to be responsive to distinctive needs of local populations or should they follow universalistic considerations in order to be responsive to our national concern for an integrated, unified society?

Whatever our hopes for the future may be, realities in the United States are such that racial and ethnic groups are, in the main, distributed along clearly discernible geographic lines. A reasonable estimate is that four-fifths of Black Americans live in identifiably Black neighborhoods (Clemence 1975). A similarly high percentage of Whites live in identifiably White neighborhoods. There is, to be sure, a substantial number of integrated neighborhoods (Pettigrew, 1975) along with a visible tendency of some Blacks to move into suburban areas. Despite all the obvious complexities, it seems crystal clear that Blacks and Whites reside in distinct and separate sections. For the community mental health movement, this fact is of paramount significance, because mental health centers have been and are being established along geographic lines, based on a place of residence, as opposed to place of work. To grasp the impact of this point, one need only imagine the consequences of a decision to organize mental health centers around place of work. Since Blacks and Whites are much more integrated in the work place than in places of residence, it follows that such an occupational arrangement would yield a much more integrated clientele and constituency than does the present residential arrangement.

The present mental health centers system should be labelled for what it is: a racially segregated system of facilities and clients. There are, to be sure, many exceptions and many examples of racially integrated units. The point here being made is that in its main outlines it is a segregated affair. This is a logical and straightforward outcome of the residentially based plan. Centers merely mirror the racial facts of residential life.

This state of affairs is not limited, however, to the Black-White polarity. It also exists, although to a lesser extent, with respect to Chicanos, and Asian Americans. By extension, we may speak of a grouping of Blacks and Whites and third world peoples in the United States, whose residential locations are separated from the remaining populations and whose mental health centers are correspondingly separated. Exceptions to this formulation are to be found, it should be noted, in places where these minorities are so small in number as to be ignored in psychological, as well as numerical, terms.

The racial-ethnic picture is not complete, however, without looking at another major grouping, i.e., Euro-American ethnic groups. Here one thinks of the Jewish Americans of New York City; the Polish Americans of Buffalo; the Italian Americans of San Francisco; the Irish Americans of Boston. These and other ethnic groups, mainly of European stock and mainly non-Protestant, are the raw material for the new ethnicity. No longer limited to the narrow confines of turn-of-the-century immigrant quarters, they are now to be found in urban and suburban areas. Some are concentrated in definable local sections, but many live in dispersion throughout the country.

The new ethnicity movement has in recent years come into explicit contact with the community mental health movement. This may be witnessed in such organizations as the Louis Caplan Center for Group Identity and Mental Health (Institute on Pluralism and Group Identity, 1978). Ethnic heritage is thought to be important not only for group survival and enhancement, but also for the mental health of individuals and families. The solution of emotional problems must take into account the ethnic and cultural background that gives meaning to people's lives. There are, to be sure, disagreements over the way and extent to which these factors should be considered. But the main idea is that ethnicity is a primordial orientation which should have a high priority in approaching mental health issues. Here again, as with Black and third world groups, pressure for an ethnic approach to mental health finds greatest expression in those communities and neighborhoods where substantial numbers of individuals are involved. Where numbers are low, the ethnic dimension tends to fade into the background; where numbers are great, ethnicity looms large.

In sum, then, we have three distinguishable sectors in the mental health field from the standpoint of racial-ethnic distribution: the Black and third world sector, the Euro-American ethnic sector and the White Anglo-Saxon Protestant sector. These sectors tend to display corresponding differences in the themes and emphases by which they may be characterized. Table 1 suggests a number of themes and emphases present or absent in each of these sectors.

Although some values are shared by all mental health centers, several are held. differently. The emphasis on cultural development and on the importance of sensitivity to client's cultural background is shared by the Black/Third World and the Euro-American ethnic sectors, but not by the White Anglo-Saxon Protestant sector. On the other hand, emphasis on advocacy and confrontation and on the importance of the local resident as a helper in the therapeutic process is more evident in the Black/Third World group, less so in the Euro-American ethnic group, and hardly at all in the White Anglo-Saxon Protestant group. Finally, two themes are present in the Black/Third World areas, but absent in the other two: 1) that discrimi-

Table 12-1
Themes and Emphases in Community Mental Health Centers
by Racial-Ethnic Sector

Themes and Emphases	Black/ Third World	Euro-American Ethnic	White Anglo-Saxon Protestant
Emphasis on cultural development	Yes	Yes	No
Emphasis on cultural sensitivity	Yes	Yes	No
Emphasis on Confrontation/ Advocacy	Yes	Yes/No	No
Community Resident Valued as Helper	Yes	Yes/No	No
Discrimination Seen as Important Factor	Yes	No	No
Emphasis on Community Economic Development	Yes	No	No

nation and segregation is an important contributor to emotional ill-being; and 2) that community economic development should be an important ancillary goal of the community mental health center.

From this analysis, we can see that distinctive purposes are served in the different racial-ethnic centers. From this standpoint it would seem that a meaningful value is served by the separations we have observed.

It is important to remember, however, that the opportunity for distinctive approaches occurs in the context of a society cleft along racial lines. Centers with Euro-American ethnic orientations can easily mount special approaches suitable to the particular ethnic groups involved. Though ethnically distinct, they are still part of the White Herrenvolk and, as such, still have prior access to resources of government and business. The Black/Third World centers, on the other hand, remain the pariahs of our society. Thus they experience considerable difficulties in mounting programs they consider to be uniquely suitable to their constituencies.

Since most such programs depend heavily on governmental or semi-public contributions, they must receive corresponding approval of their activities. It is true, of course, that government does not interfere in the day to day operations of these centers. Nevertheless, it seems evident, particularly in these times of economic distress, that Black/Third World centers are struggling to hold fast against outside attacks. Only the rise of political participation in the minority communities has made it possible to fend off these attacks. One wonders how long it will be possible for such centers to continue as viable agencies without giving up what they consider to be essential mental health services and approaches in the face of opposition from powerful sources of funds, which consider them to be neither essential or mental health.

In addition to the problem of continuing support, there is a more basic question concerning the validity of creating and maintaining agencies that operate to keep Black and White separate from each other. There is a tragic dimension involved that bears our most concerned attention: In our efforts to provide distinctive help along residential lines to distinctive racial-ethnic groups, we may be contributing and adding to the very segregation that has been a curse of our emotional existence. Chester Pierce (1973), for example, has identified racism as our nation's number one mental illness. Can it be that in our zeal for geography and ethnic sensitivity, we have permitted the perpetuation of segregation in yet another institutional segment of our society? Can it be that mental health professionals have been blind to the segregative impact of the catchment area concept?

These are not questions for which there are easy answers. The purpose of this paper has been to highlight the importance of analyzing the racial-ethnic dimensions of the community mental health movement. Such an analysis can proceed more effectively if we come to terms with the point, mentioned at the beginning of this paper, that we live not in a pluralistic society, made up of equally respected competing cultural groups, but in a dual society, consisting of a dominant White group exercising hegmony over Black and Third World people. If we hope to overcome this separateness, perhaps we should consider reshaping the very foundation of the community mental health center movement.

Perhaps we should shift from small-sized population units (with their almost inevitable segregative tendency) to larger-sized units which would yield greater racial mixing. Perhaps we should shift from a residential basis for mental health centers to an occupational or industrial base. Or perhaps we should begin mounting a legal challenge to segregation in the mental health sector. Perhaps we should no longer tolerate the use of public funds for what most of us would candidly recognize as a segregated system in a segregated society.

REFERENCES

Blackwell, J. E. *The black community: Diversity and unity.* New York: Dodd, Mead, 1975.

Bockoven, J. S. Moral treatment in American psychiatry. *Journal of Nervous and Mental Diseases,* 1956, *124,* 167-194, 292-321.

Clemence, T. G. Residential segregation in mid-sixties. In T. F. Pettigrew, (ed.), *Racial discrimination in the United States.* New York: Harper and Row, 1975.

Deutsch, A. *The shame of the states.* New York: Harcourt, Brace, 1948.

Greenblatt, M., York, R., and Brown, E. *From custodial to therapeutic care in mental hospitals.* New York: Russell Sage Foundation, 1955.

Institute on Pluralism and Group Identity. *The Louis Caplan Center on Group Identity and Mental Health Annual Report.* New York: Institute on Pluralism and Group Identity, 1978.

Joint Commission on Mental Illness and Health. *Action for mental health,* New York: Basic Books, 1961.

Pettigrew, T. F. Black and white attitudes towards race and housing. In T. F. Pettigrew, (ed.), *Racial discrimination in the United States.* New York: Harper and Row, 1975.

Pierce, C. M. The formation of the Black Psychiatrists of America. In C. V. Willie, B. M. Kramer, and B. S. Brown, (eds.), *Racism and mental health.* Pittsburgh: University of Pittsburgh Press, 1973.

U. S. National Advisory Commission on Civil Disorders. *Report of the national advisory commission on civil disorders,* 1968.

Van den Berghe, P. L. *Race and racism: A comparative perspective.* New York: John Wiley, 1978.

Chapter 13

PLURALISM AND COMMUNITY MENTAL HEALTH
Summary and Conclusions

Stanley Sue
Thom Moore

As explained in the introductory chapter, the purpose of this book was to bring together the research, observations, and ideas of individuals concerned with ethnicity and community mental health issues. We, of course, had more specific questions and issues in mind. For example, are the present ideas and themes of the contributors different from those expressed by other social scientists in past years? Are there significant areas of agreement or disagreement among the contributors? What kinds of implications for future research, theory, program development, or social policy can be drawn? In this final chapter, we would like to address these questions, to raise additional ones, and to draw some conclusions.

MENTAL HEALTH

One consistent theme appearing in this book is that ethnic minority groups are under particular stress and, as a result, their mental health is affected. The theme itself is not new, since social scientists have for many years documented the problems encountered by ethnic minority groups. Why does it persist? One possible explanation is that there is a continuation of past rhetoric because of the poverty of new ideas and directions. We do not believe this is the case. In many ways, the contributors to this book have offered innovative and exciting concepts, programs, and suggestions in enhancing community mental health. A more likely explanation is that the mental health of minority groups is of continuing concern in view of the slow changes that have occurred in the mental health professions and the social intervention arenas.

By presenting the testimonies of ethnic minority consumers, administrators, researchers, etc., Willie clearly indicates the wide range of unaddressed mental health needs experienced by minority groups. He captures what Chin calls the "sensibilities" or the outlooks and world view of individuals who feel alienated, concerned, or outraged over unmet human needs and expectations. These needs are very broad and deal with the quality of life. The issue of mental health should not be simply limited to the presence or absence of mental disorders. Studies into rates of psychopathology, while important in their own right, fail to capture the full meaning of mental health. Indeed, the inability to consistently demonstrate racial or ethnic differences in rates of psychopathology in this country (Dohrenwend and Dohrenwend, 1969) should not be interpreted as a refutation of the existence of stress, or of its effects on psychological well-being. Stress associated with minority groups has, perhaps, the most significant impact for the quality of one's life which involves objective circumstances (e.g., existence of discrimination, poverty, minority groups status, etc.) as well as the subjective cognitive appraisals (sensibilities, expectations, aspirations, outlooks, etc.) of one's place in society. If this is the case, more of our future efforts should be devoted to defining for empirical investigation stressors, their consequences, and the quality of life for ethnic minority groups. In making this recommendation, we are cognizant of the need to also pay attention to psychopathology and issues in institutionalization. Kramer and Zane's indication that non-Whites, in contrast to Whites, will probably show greater percentage increases in the incidence and prevalence of schizophrenia and the rate of psychiatric institutionalization demand immediate attention.

What are the kinds of mental health problems experienced by ethnic minority groups because of minority groups status? The answer to this question is, of course, complicated and must include all the disorders existing in non-minority groups, but frequently greater limits of intensity. Willie points to feelings of alienation, anger, fear, and noncontrol; and while Kramer and Zane make predictions concerning schizophrenia in non-White groups, these predictions are based upon changes in the demographic characteristics of non-White and White populations, not upon any particular stressors associated with race or ethnicity.

Another complicating factor in analyzing minority group mental health is that social scientists have traditionally adopted a deficit model view of minority groups. Given that ethnic minority groups are under particular stress and that psychological well-being (including the quality of life) is affected, several contributors believe that minority group characteristics have often been inaccurately portrayed as deficiencies. Banks feels that the self-esteem and identity among Blacks are not as negative as commonly believed. He points to methodological and conceptual limitations in past research on self-identity and racial preferences. From his perspective, Black Americans adopt healthy strategies in an often-hostile environment. It should be noted that, in contrast, Adelson implies that Blacks or other groups not given the opportunity to fully participate in society may exhibit self-hatred and negative self-esteem. Resolution of selfhood and identity, according to Adelson, will occur when parallel changes are made in society so that all groups develop control over their fates and a sense of belongingness. The positions of Banks and of Adelson with respect to self-esteem are difficult to reconcile and reflect the years of debate over the self-identity and preference of ethnic minority groups.

Snowden and Padilla also attack the deficit model of minority groups. They feel research in areas of intelligence, language skills, personality, and family structure of ethnic groups have maintained culturally biased perspectives and misunderstandings. For Snowden, one major reason for the bias is in the tendency to mistake approaches that are emics (culturally specific) rather than etics (universal). There is bias toward adopting, as etics, phenomena that are actually emics in a given society. Minority groups are often seen as deviant by the majority or mainstream group simply because they differ in characteristics or behavioral patterns. Snowden calls for more studies on the competency of ethnic groups in which emics are given full appreciation. That is, in a culturally pluralistic society, competence should be studied with full appreciation of cultural relativism.

In terms of mental health, several conclusions may be drawn. First, ethnic minority groups lack participation and control in their outcomes; consequently, they experience threat to their survival and are under stress. Second, this stress affects psychological well-being. Studies into well-being should include not only the rates and nature of psychopathology, but also the quality of life and ethnic sensibilities. Third, cultural factors must be carefully considered in ethnic mental health research. The mere fact that culturally different groups are under particular stress that affects mental health should not result in the interpretation that minority group differences are deficits. Errors in interpretation are likely when there is a single standard in society for "healthy" behaviors (i.e., an incorrect etic perspective) and there is a failure to consider adaptive and competency-based strategies that are used in response to environmental conditions. These three general conclusions have in one way or another been of concern to ethnic minority groups. They bear repeating in view of the continuing problems in studying mental health and the cogency of the arguments advanced by the contributors who offer specific appeals for reexamination of issues, research strategies, and directions. These strategies and directions will be more fully discussed in subsequent sections of this chapter.

COMMUNITY MENTAL HEALTH PROGRAMS

How can the mental health delivery system be more effective in serving culturally diverse groups? Within the traditional community mental health ideology, there are frequent appeals for increased responsiveness of community mental health centers to particular residents in catchment areas, for the services of paraprofessionals who can act as a bridge between the centers and the communities, for the hiring of ethnic specialists, for the in-service training of center staff to work with culturally diverse groups of clients, or for prevention programs. There are at least three important issues in the community mental health approach: (1) How can recommendations derived from community mental health ideology be translated into concrete, applied programs? (2) Are these programs likely to be effective? (3) If effective, what will stimulate existing community mental health facilities to adopt these programs? Let us examine the three issues.

Perhaps one of the most advanced and systematic programs to respond to a multi-ethnic community is described by Lefley and Bestman. By intensively studying the values, beliefs, and behaviors of five ethnic groups (Bahamians, Cubans, Haitians, Puerto Ricans, and Black Americans), the investigators initiated a program they believed would make psychotherapeutic services more accessible and culturally sensitive, more effective, and more prevention oriented (through early detection and intervention). The inclusion of ethnic paraprofessionals and interdisciplinary professionals on teams enabled greater collaborative efforts between the community and the program.

Attneave traces the progress of mental health services to American Indians. She provides examples of approaches that include increased American Indian input and control of programs, the use of paraprofessionals and medicine men, and more innovative services such as model dormitories and child welfare programs. The reports of Attneave and of Lefley and Bestman have common elements. The principles or assumptions in the programs are consistent with a community mental health ideology; they can be applied and developed in a systematic manner and serve as models for other programs; and the services involve community input and participation, paraprofessionals, understanding of ethnic community (i.e., the values, attitudes, and practices), and attention to strategies that are more culturally consistent with the residents of given communities. There-fore, it is highly likely that programs can be developed to serve ethnic com-munities using community mental health ideology. This ideology involves targeting clinical services, using consultation, education, and training, and employing paraprofessionals in a given cultural group or community (Goodstein and Sandler, 1978).

The question concerning the effectiveness of community mental health programs to serve ethnic communities is far more difficult to examine. Lefley and Bestman have demonstrated that their project resulted in greater access and utilization of services, low dropout rates of clients, consumer satisfactions, and low recidivism rates. We obviously need more empirical studies of outcome and more fine grained analysis of the process involved in other programs designed to respond to ethnic minority com-munities. It should be noted that the effectiveness of services is an issue that is faced by all community mental health programs, not just by those that serve ethnics. Process and outcome research is, therefore, of concern to the entire mental health profession. Similarly, the translation of community mental health ideology into practice is not unique to ethnic minority com-munities. It can be argued that the use of paraprofessionals, making services more accessible and responsive, etc., would be of benefit to all communities.

In ethnic minority communities, the development of effective services is particularly crucial, since more traditional mainstream mental health services have failed to make a significant impact. Indeed, there is ample agreement among the contributors that past mental health programs have encountered a great deal of problems in delivering effective services to ethnic minority groups. These problems have included: (1) The under-utilization of services (Lefley and Bestman; Padilla and Keefe); (2) lack of ethnic minority participation and professional personnel in the mental health fields (Attneave; Kramer and Zane; Willie); (3) little appreciation of the cultural patterns, attitudes, and beliefs of ethnic minorities in the delivery of services (Chin; Lefley and Bestman); (4) lack of bilingual staff, biased assessment procedures, and therapeutic approaches that are inade-quate matched with clients (Lefley and Bestman; Padilla; Padilla and Keefe). In many ways, the incorporation of community mental health ideology into practice stems from a dissatisfaction with the ineffectiveness of the current delivery system and from the belief that the practice can help to overcome some of the problems. Such a process of trying to find more responsive strategies in promoting mental health is interestingly similar to the community psychology movement, and which arose out of dissatisfac-tion with traditional clinical psychology approaches (Zax and Spector, 1974).

Assuming there is a need to develop and strengthen community mental health programs and other alternative forms of delivery systems, how can we go about implementing these programs? There are no magical solutions. Nevertheless, the contributors provide some direct and indirect clues. First, involvement and concern about ethnicity and community mental health must come from all Americans, not simply those members of a particularly affected ethnic group. That is, just as the contributors represent a multi-ethnic group, issues of cultural pluralism and mental health must be addressed by all Americans. Second, creation and development of mental health programs require research and knowledge about effective and ineffective approaches, about needs of the communities, and about the practicality of techniques to employ. Third, professionals, as well as lay audiences, must be educated and informed about unmet needs and problems experienced by ethnic minorities. Part of the task of the President's Commission on Mental Health was to provide some information on these needs. The Commission not only documented the plight of ethnic minorities, but also strongly asserted the necessity to take action. Finally, and, in a sense, ultimately, funding for programs must be forthcoming. Programs aimed at ethnically diverse groups, such as the one reported by Lefley and Bestman, need funding. To Kramer, programs in ethnic minority communities depend heavily upon governmental contributions. If these programs deviate too much from established policies, they run the risk of losing financial support. How can services and programs receive continued or increased levels of support and have the flexibility to be innovative? Kramer's observation, and one advocated by other contributors, is that a rise in political participation in minority communities will help to establish a stronger power base in dealing with governmental bodies. Moore, Nagata, and Whatley discuss the role of the social interventionist as one in which advocacy, community organization, and establishment of social and political linkages are important; Padilla calls upon community psychologists to use their knowledge and influence on social policies to become political allies of ethnic minority groups. Taken together, it is apparent that research, political participation, and community organization are vital in the development of responsive programs and services.

BEYOND COMMUNITY MENTAL HEALTH

In introducing the notions of political involvement, social intervention, and public policy advocacy, we are already discussing the realm of what Goodstein and Sandler (1978) and Rappaport (1977) consider community psychology, or public policy psychology. The ideas developed by the contributors, while having a strong community mental health perspective, also raise broader issues. These issues involve social change strategies, natural support systems and cultural resources, social systems analysis, and public policy. Chin presents a paradigm for analyzing and intervening in communities. Identification of causal relationship and those alterable causal factors, understanding of community dynamics, consideration of cost-effectiveness of change efforts, the ability to test, through research, the paradigm, etc., are some of the requirements for the paradigm. By tracing developments in Chinese American communities, Chin concretely illustrates how intervention strategies must consider these requirements. Implicit in his ideas is the particular difficulty in organizing *planned* social change in ethnic communities. Planned intervention is difficult to accomplish in any community. In the case of ethnic minority communities, the process is often more difficult because, as Chin indicates: (1) cultural and even international factors may impact community dynamics and choice of change strategies; (2) the sensibilities of ethnic minority groups may be quite different from those of mainstream Americans; and (3) social scientists outside of the community may not have the credibility or desire to intervene.

Community intervention strategies raise some important policy considerations. While Chin provides conceptual tools for intervention and analysis, and Padilla asserts the necessity for social change, other contributors raise a variety of potential philosophical and policy dilemmas associated with intervention.

Individual versus Institutional Rights

In treatment, prevention, and public policy, Willie notes that individual and instititutional rights often conflict. To what extent should programs be initiated for the "good of society," but against the wishes or rights of a few? Willie seems to feel that, in a democratic society, if individuals' rights are limited for the sake of others, due process and other constitutional safeguards should be followed.

Autonomy versus Homonomy

Adelson believes that two basic needs or strivings of human beings are homonomy (sense of identification and belongingness) and autonomy (freedom, self-determination, and control). In a pluralistic society, is it possible to have a sense of belongingness when different groups desire power and control? That is, competition for power and influence may divide society, so that homonomy is threatened. One way to reduce this dilemma is to inculcate in individuals a strong sense of values concerning participatory democracy and social justice, so that society can allow for increased participation and control by underrepresented groups. These groups will, of course, compete for power and influence with other groups. Nevertheless, the sense of belongingness, democratic values, and justice can be served.

Dualism versus Pluralism

Related to the previous dilemma, and one discussed earlier, is Kramer's notion that by responding to local needs and specific interests, effects such as separatism, inequities, and lack of unity may be unwittingly created. Is it possible, then, to create person-environment matches in our social change approaches that do not encourage divisiveness, separatism, and inequities in the long run? Community mental health centers, in applying the concepts of localism and catchment areas, may not only reflect, but also serve to maintain, segregation. Kramer's suggestion to explore innovative approaches, such as an occupational or industrial base, rather than a residential base for mental health facilities, should be seriously considered.

Ethnic Match versus Mismatch

Lefley and Bestman illustrate the importance of obtaining the involvement of individuals who are themselves members of those cultures or communities to which services are delivered. Presumably, ethnic matching: (1) increases the credibility and access of the interventionist in ethnic communities; and (2) facilitates the entry of an interventionist who understands the ethnic sensibilities. Is matching a necessary and sufficient condition in our social change efforts? We believe that simply being a member of a particular ethnic group is not a sufficient condition for working with that ethnic group. Credibility, understanding, and effectiveness are achieved, not ascribed on the basis of ethnicity. The question of matching as a necessary condition is more complicated. Because of the history of race relations, many individuals from minority group cultures have become suspicious of the motives and knowledge of "outsiders." Furthermore, the lack of ethnic mental health professionals (as discussed by Willie, Kramer and Zane, and Padilla and Keefe) has heightened the powerlessness and lack of control that minority group communities perceive. In the long run, if it is possible to have available sensitive and dedicated interventionists with the kind of training and characteristics described by Moore, Nagata, and Whatley, then the issue concerning ethnic matching will become less salient. Nevertheless, input, participation, and involvement of ethnic groups are essential as are the support and involvement of all persons in society.

Community Psychology versus Community Mental Health

This dilemma is very similar to those involving prevention versus psychotherapy, or changing society versus changing the individual to fit society. The underlying question is over the nature and direction of intervention efforts. Many of the contributors have presented ideas in community mental health, as noted earlier. Goodstein and Sandler (1978) believe the community mental health ideology is too traditional and conservative as an approach to human welfare and is, in fact, a hinderance to community psychology. They state that:

> Perhaps that most important distinction we have made is that between community mental health and community psychology, where we have argued that there are basic differences in philosophy, target, content, process, and knowledge base. We further insist that community psychology cannot prosper within the community mental health movement because of these basic differences, a conclusion we have not reached lightly. The role we defined for community psychology—interfacing with those social systems concerned with deviance control and socialization and support—will require creating alliances with new constituencies, developing working relationships with different disciplines, and moving away from our traditional dependency upon the mental health establishment (p. 891).

While there is no denying that community mental health and community psychology approaches often conflict and that innovative and bold approaches are needed, it is apparent that the approaches do have areas of overlap. For example, in Padilla and Keefe's research, the investigators stress the importance of having culturally-relevant mental health services and of increasing the number of Hispanic professionals. Their interest in service delivery led them not only to study utilization of mental health facilities, but also to examine Mexican American attitudes, community dynamics, social support systems, and acculturation. Lefley and Bestman demonstrate how community mental health services can be more effectively delivered to ethnic communities. In the process, organization of neighborhoods, crime prevention programs, employment services, housing projects, changes in institutional and social structures, etc., were created. Finally, although prevention is advocated, but not fully articulated, by the contributors, several chapters indicate the need to reduce stressors and to increase cultural resources. These tasks imply changes in race relations, attitudes, values, institutional structures, competency evaluations, etc.

Traditional Versus Innovative Research and Theory

A theme consistently expressed for decades among many ethnic researchers is that research and theory are biased or unable to capture the sensibility of ethnic minority group mental health, culture, or community.

While Banks, Padilla, and Snowden are highly critical of past research on ethnic minorities, none of them rejects the value of research and theory. The point of contention appears to be over the assumptions, methodology, interpretation, and bias underlying research and theory. Traditional research has often reflected the values and outlooks of a nation that has had difficulty understanding and ameliorating the situation of ethnic minorities. For example, Korchin (1980) has mentioned an interesting experience. He was the co-investigator for some research on Black competence. A paper from the study, submitted for publication, was rejected. A reviewer of the paper felt that the study should have included a White control group. Why should the study include a White control group when the interest was in Black Americans? Although inclusion of a White control group would have been interesting, studies of White Americans are not asked to include a Black control group. The uni-directional bias in research is apparent. The chapters by Banks, Padilla, and Snowden advocate changes in the way research should be conceptualized and applied. Without criticizing past research, Chin offers certain tools to analyze ethnic communties. These tools are appropriate, not only for ethnics, but also for all communities. The specific suggestions for research and theory made by the contributors are important; but perhaps a more important lesson to be learned is that good ethnic research is simply good research. Focus on ethnic research is valuable because the study of culturally different groups tests the limits and generality of psychological theories and mental health practices. If traditional assumptions and theories of mental health are valid across cultures and situations, then they constitute universals, or etic phenomena. In the absence of a culturally diverse population of study, it is difficult to know when universals have been found or when techniques and assumptions are culturally specific.

REFLECTIONS

The contributors to this book point to persistent mental health problems encountered by ethnic minorities and to the frustrations over past efforts to respond to culturally diverse groups. But, along with frustration and anger, the contributors provide a measure of *optimism* in suggesting directions for mental health programs, research, theory development, and community intervention. The challenge we face is to take action. We must arrange priorities so that attitudes, values, and policies appreciate the pluralistic nature of society. In doing so, benefits accrue, not only to ethnic minorities, but also to all Americans, in the promotion of well-being and homonomy.

As a final note, we would like to present the comments of Dr. Delores Parron, a staff member of the Presidents' Commission on Mental Health, who prepared a special statement for this volume. In outlining the charge of the Special Populations Task Panel and in drawing conclusions about what is needed, Parron's comments, it should be noted, parallel those made by the contributors to this book. Parron states that:

> Drawing conclusions and providing data about who among the minorities (as a group) are in need of mental health intervention are a complex undertaking. It was, however, the task that the President's Commission on Mental Health set before the Task Panel on Special Populations: Minorities, Women, and Physically Handicapped. The Special Populations Task Panel was established by the staff to ensure that the Commission's study of the mental health needs of the American population was truly reflective of America's culturally diverse society.
>
> Because the cultural influences of each minority group are so distinct and diverse, the Commission and its staff elected to examine issues relating to mental health of each group separately. Seven subpanels were formed under the heading Special Populations. The subpanels focused on the concerns of Asian/Pacific Americans, Black Americans, Americans of European Ethnic Origin, Hispanic Americans, American Indians, Women, and the Physically Handicapped. In choosing to collect data in this way, a bit of history was made. No other commission of this kind had ever actively sought input from the minorities through such a concerted and focused effort. Each of the subpanels utilized the opportunity afforded them by the President's Commission on Mental Health to (1) assess the state of the art of mental health service delivery, research, and personnel needs; (2) designate necessary modifications of public policy governing the mental health delivery system, research, personnel recruitment, and training to make mental health services available, accessible, and acceptable to their constituencies; and (3) suggest strategies for research, treatment, and prevention of mental disorders. The outcome of the work of the panels was 181 specific recommendations to the Commission focused on achieving a comprehensive, integrated response of the mental health system to the needs of racial and ethnic minorities. These recommendations were presented with detailed supporting documentation.
>
> The common theme of the recommendations was that each of the minority groups wanted to see public policy that was flexible enough to encompass the special needs of each of the special population groups. The bottom line for each culturally distinct group was:
>
> 1. To be an active part of the process of developing and planning services;
>
> 2. To be in control of services delivered in their communities;

3. To have services delivered by persons who share the unique perspective, value system, and beliefs of the group to be served;

4. To have access to funding that is adequate to ensure that services are provided for persons in need of them and no longer subject to erratic funding patterns which defeat the purpose of groups attempting to serve their own members.

The fact that the work of the Special Populations Task Panel did indeed have an impact on the kind of mental health system that the Commission recommended is evident in the Commission's final report to the President. But this success is only equivalent to "winning the first round." The mental health system has a long way to go in providing services for the special populations: minorities, women, and physically handicapped persons. We are still paying the price for past prejudices and unavailability/inaccessibility of services. Just as forces systematically operated to exclude minorities, there is a continuing need to systematically include minorities at every level and in all phases of the mental health system in order to keep the gains that have been made.

REFERENCES

Dohrenwend, B. P. & Dohrenwend, B. S. *Social status and psychological disorder.* New York: Wiley, 1969.

Goodstein, L., and Sandler, I. Using psychology to promote human welfare: A conceptual analysis of the role of community psychology. *American Psychologist,* 1978, *33*, 882-892.

Korchin, S. J. Clinical psychology and minority problems. *American Psychologist,* 1980 in press.

Rappaport, J. *Community psychology: Values, research, and action.* San Francisco: Holt, Rinehart & Winston, 1977.

Zax, M., and Spector, G. A. *An introduction to community psychology.* New York: Wiley & Sons, 1974.

INDEX